WALKING THE CORBETTS

VOLUME ONE: SOUTH OF THE GREAT GLEN

About the Author

Since taking early retirement from his career as a physics and sports teacher, Brian Johnson has found time for three through-hikes of the Pacific Crest Trail, a 2700-mile round-Britain walk, two hikes across the Pyrenees from the Atlantic to the Mediterranean, a hike along the Via de la Plata from Seville to Santiago and a single summer 'compleation' of the Munros (Scotland's 3000ft mountains). He has also completed a 2200-mile cycle tour of Spain and France and done multi-week canoe tours in Sweden, France, Spain and Portugal.

In his younger days, Brian's main sport was orienteering. He competed at a high level and coached both Bishop Wordsworth's School and South-West Junior Orienteering Squads. He also surveyed and drew many orienteering maps. He has walked and climbed extensively in summer and winter conditions in Britain, the Alps, the Pyrenees and California, often leading school groups.

As a fanatical sportsman and games player, Brian competed to a high level in cricket, hockey, bridge and chess. His crowning achievement was winning the 1995/96 World Amateur Chess Championships.

Other Cicerone guides by the author

Shorter Treks in the Pyrenees
The Pacific Crest Trail
The GR10 Trail
The GR11 Trail
Walking the Corbetts Vol 2 North of the Great Glen

WALKING THE CORBETTS

VOLUME ONE: SOUTH OF THE GREAT GLEN
by Brian Johnson

JUNIPER HOUSE, MURLEY MOSS,
OXENHOLME ROAD, KENDAL, CUMBRIA LA9 7RL
www.cicerone.co.uk

© Brian Johnson 2012
First edition 2012
ISBN: 978 1 85284 652 7
Reprinted 2019 (with updates)
Printed in China on behalf of Latitude Press Ltd

A catalogue record for this book is available from the British Library.
All photographs are by the author unless otherwise stated.

Route mapping by Lovell Johns www.lovelljohns.com
Contains Ordnance Survey data © Crown copyright and
database right 2012. NASA relief data courtesy of ESRI

*To my father, Howard Johnson, who died
while I was in Scotland researching this guide.*

*'Train up a child in the way he should go:
and when he is old, he will not depart from it.'
Proverbs xxii. 6*

Updates to this Guide

While every effort is made by our authors to ensure the accuracy of guidebooks as they go to print, changes can occur during the lifetime of an edition. Any updates that we know of for this guide will be on the Cicerone website (www.cicerone.co.uk/652/updates), so please check before planning your trip. We also advise that you check information about such things as transport, accommodation and shops locally. Even rights of way can be altered over time. We are always grateful for information about any discrepancies between a guidebook and the facts on the ground, sent by email to updates@cicerone.co.uk or by post to Cicerone, Juniper House, Murley Moss, Oxenholme Road, Kendal LA9 7RL.

Register your book: To sign up to receive free updates, special offers and GPX files where available, register your book at www.cicerone.co.uk.

Front cover: Beinn a' Chaolais over Loch an t-Siob on approach to Beinn an Oir (Route 10)

CONTENTS

Map key 9
Overview map 10
Preface 13

INTRODUCTION 15
What are the Corbetts? 15
Geology 17
Human history in the Highlands 19
The natural environment 22
Walking the Corbetts 26
When to go 27
The terrain 27
Weather 28
Access 29
Mountain bothies 33
Navigation 34
Safety 35
Areas in this guide 36
Using this guide 41

1 THE SOUTHERN UPLANDS 43
Route 1   Merrick 46
Route 2   Shalloch on Minnoch 49
Route 3   Corserine 52
Route 4   Cairnsmore of Carsphairn 55
Route 5   Hart Fell 58
Route 6   White Coomb 61
Route 7   Broad Law 63

2 ARRAN AND JURA 67
Route 8   Goatfell 71
Route 9   Beinn Tarsuinn, Caisteal Abhail and Cir Mhor 74
Route 10   Beinn an Oir (The Paps of Jura) 77

3 WEST OF LOCH LOMOND (ARROCHAR ALPS) 81
Route 11   Beinn Bheula 83
Route 12   Ben Donich, The Brack and Cnoc Coinnich 87
Route 13   The Cobbler 90

Route 14	Beinn Luibhean	93
Route 15	Beinn an Lochain	94
Route 16	Stob Coire Creagach (Binnein an Fhidhleir)	96
Route 17	Meall an Fhudair	98

4 EAST OF LOCH LOMOND (THE TROSSACHS) ... 101
Route 18	Beinn a' Choin	104
Route 19	Ben Ledi and Benvane	107
Route 20	Beinn Each	110
Route 21	Stob a' Choin	112
Route 22	Stob Fear-tomhais	115
Route 23	Meall an t-Seallaidh and Creag MacRanaich	118
Route 24	Meall na Fearna	121
Route 25	Creag Uchdag	124
Route 26	Auchnafree Hill	126

5 SOUTH-WEST GRAMPIANS (TYNDRUM AND DALMALLY) ... 129
Route 27	Beinn a' Bhuiridh	131
Route 28	Beinn Mhic Mhonaidh	134
Route 29	Beinn Udlaidh and Beinn Bhreac-liath	137
Route 30	Beinn Chuirn	140
Route 31	Beinn Odhar, Beinn Chaorach, Cam Chreag, Beinn nam Fuaran and Beinn a' Chaisteil	143

6 THE SOUTHERN GRAMPIANS (LOCH TAY AND GLEN LYON) ... 147
Route 32	Beinn nan Imirean	149
Route 33	Meall nan Subh	153
Route 34	Sron a' Choire Chnapanich and Meall Buidhe	154
Route 35	Beinn nan Oighreag	157
Route 36	Meall nam Maigheach	160
Route 37	Cam Chreag	161
Route 38	Beinn Dearg	164
Route 39	Creagan na Beinne	165

7 THE WESTERN GRAMPIANS (GLEN COE AND KINLOCHLEVEN) ... 169
Route 40	Creach Bheinn	171
Route 41	Fraochaidh	173
Route 42	Meall Lighiche	176
Route 43	Beinn Trilleachan	178
Route 44	Stob Dubh	181

Route 45	Beinn Maol Chaluim	184
Route 46	Beinn Mhic Chasgaig	187
Route 47	Beinn a' Chrulaiste	189
Route 48	Garbh Bheinn	191
Route 49	Mam na Gualainn	193
Route 50	Glas Bheinn	197

8 THE CENTRAL GRAMPIANS (PITLOCHRY AND LOCH RANNOCH) 199

Route 51	Leum Uilleim	201
Route 52	Meall na Meoig of Beinn Pharlagain	203
Route 53	Stob an Aonaich Mhoir	207
Route 54	Beinn a' Chuallaich	209
Route 55	Meall Tairneachan and Farragon Hill	212
Route 56	Ben Vrackie	215
Route 57	Ben Vuirich	217
Route 58	Beinn Mheadhonach	221
Route 59	Beinn Bhreac	224
Route 60	An Dun and Maol Creag an Loch (A' Chaoirnich)	227
Route 61	Meall na Leitreach	231
Route 62	Beinn Mholach	234
Route 63	The Sow of Atholl	236
Route 64	The Fara	238

9 BADENOCH (SPEAN BRIDGE TO KINGUSSIE) 241

Route 65	Sgurr Innse and Cruach Innse	243
Route 66	Beinn Iaruinn	246
Route 67	Carn Dearg (Glen Roy)	248
Route 68	Carn Dearg (N of Gleann Eachach) and Carn Dearg (S of Gleann Eachach)	251
Route 69	Carn a' Chuillinn	253
Route 70	Gairbeinn	257
Route 71	Meall na h-Aisre	260
Route 72	Carn an Fhreiceadain	262
Route 73	Meallach Mhor	265
Route 74	Leathad an Taobhain and Carn Dearg Mor	269

10 THE SOUTHERN CAIRNGORMS 273

Route 75	Mount Battock	275
Route 76	Ben Tirran	278
Route 77	Monamenach	281

Route 78	Ben Gulabin	284
Route 79	Creag nan Gabhar	287
Route 80	Morrone	290
Route 81	Sgor Mor	292
Route 82	Carn na Drochaide	294
Route 83	Creag an Dhail Bheag and Culardoch	296
Route 84	Conachcraig	299
Route 85	Morven	303

11 THE NORTHERN CAIRNGORMS 305

Route 86	Brown Cow Hill	307
Route 87	Carn Ealasaid	310
Route 88	Carn Mor	312
Route 89	Corryhabbie Hill	316
Route 90	Ben Rinnes	319
Route 91	Geal Charn	321
Route 92	Meall a' Bhuachaille	324
Route 93	Creag Mhor	326
Route 94	Geal-charn Mor	329
Route 95	Carn na Saobhaidhe	331

| **Appendix A** | Alphabetical list of the Corbetts | 335 |
| **Appendix B** | Useful information | 339 |

MAP KEY

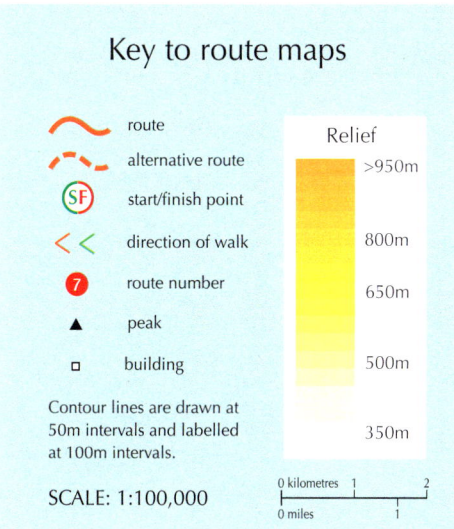

Mountain Warning

Mountain walking can be a dangerous activity carrying a risk of personal injury or death. It should be undertaken only by those with a full understanding of the risks and with the training and experience to evaluate them. While every care and effort has been taken in the preparation of this guide, the user should be aware that conditions can be highly variable and can change quickly, materially affecting the seriousness of a mountain walk. Therefore, except for any liability which cannot be excluded by law, neither Cicerone nor the author accept liability for damage of any nature (including damage to property, personal injury or death) arising directly or indirectly from the information in this book.

To call out the Mountain Rescue, ring 999 or the international emergency number 112: this will connect you via any available network. Once connected to the emergency operator, ask for the police.

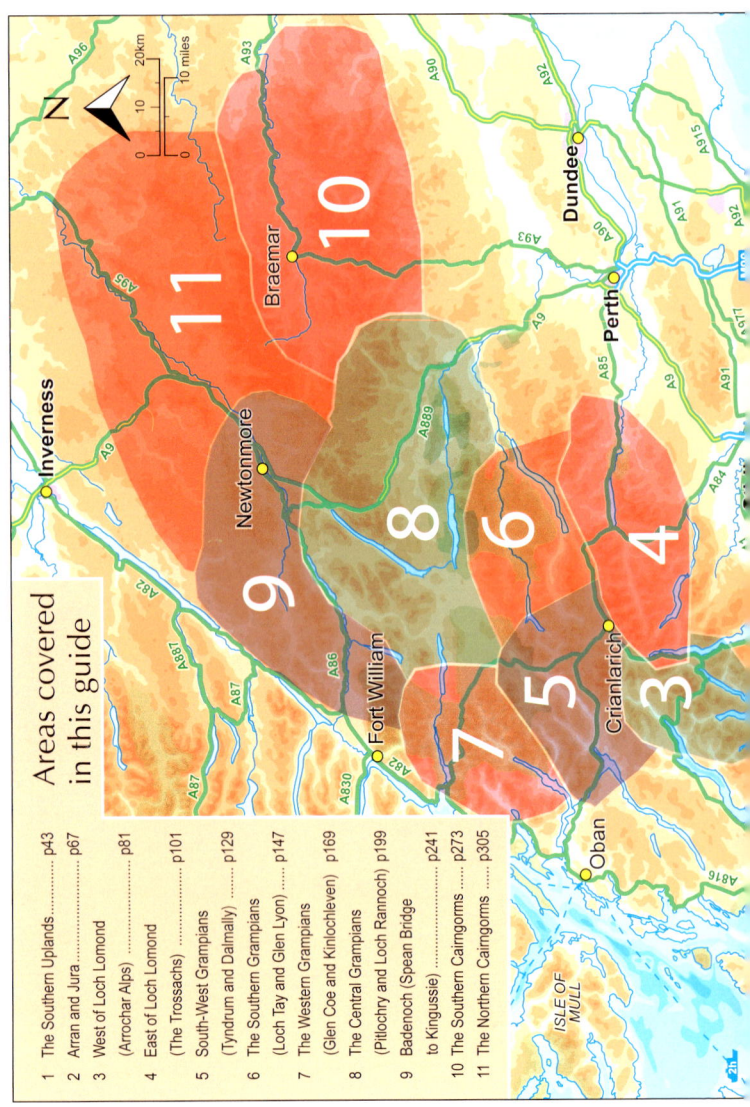

OVERVIEW MAP

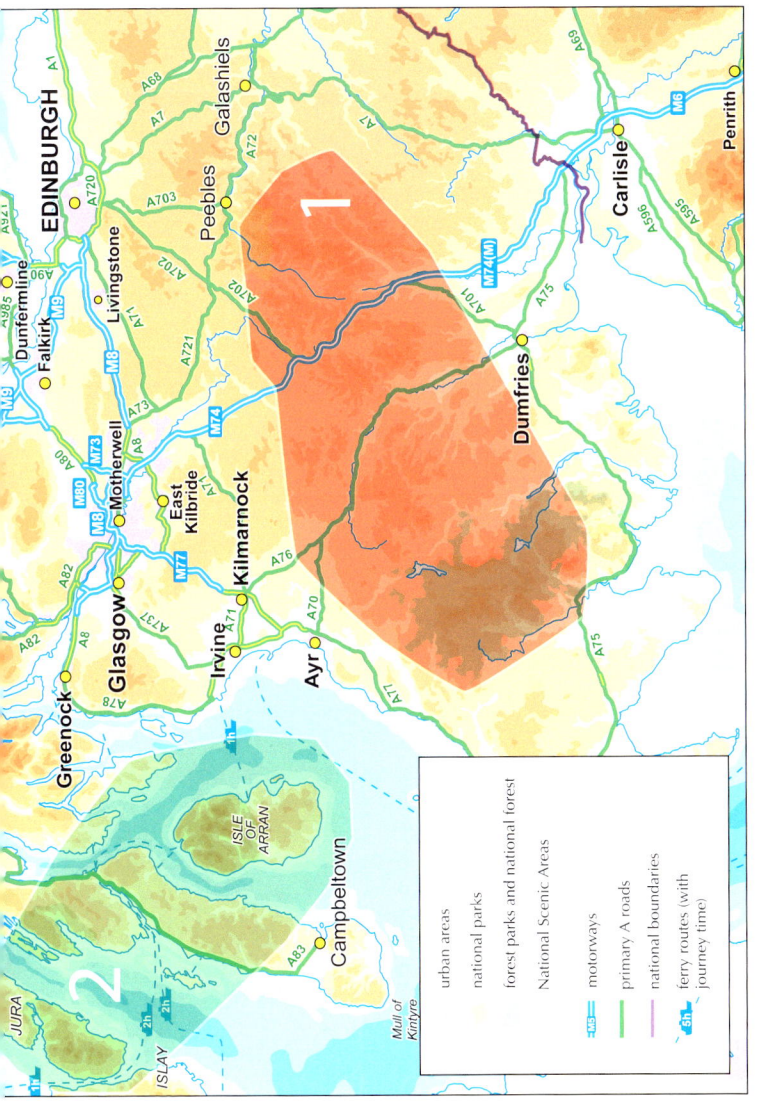

Ben Lui from the River Cononish (Route 30)

PREFACE

Those who know the Scottish Highlands won't need telling that Scotland has some of the most magnificent mountain and coastal scenery in the world. But why bother with the Corbetts when there are over 280 Munros to go at? Here are just a few compelling reasons to broaden your horizons a little.

- There are Corbetts in many areas not covered by the Munros. When I'm asked where to visit in Scotland, I always suggest heading as far north and west as possible, where rocky mountains interact with the fjord-like western seaboard to produce spectacular scenery. These are the areas where there are far more Corbetts than Munros. There are no Munros in Ardgour, Moidart or the islands of Harris, Rum, Jura or Arran, and very few in the far north.
- It is often possible to climb a Corbett when the weather is too severe to climb the Munros, and you often get better views for the simple reason that the Corbetts are frequently cloud-free when the Munros are socked in.
- The lower altitude means the walks tend to be a little shorter, which can be an advantage for those staying in hotels who want to climb a mountain between breakfast and dinner. Corbetts can also be a better proposition during the short daylight hours in winter.
- The Corbetts can offer the solitude you won't find on the Munros. Many of the Corbetts are rarely climbed and have not suffered from the human disturbance that is often seen on the Munros.
- For those walkers who have already 'compleated' the Munros, the Corbetts provide another challenge.

This guide is aimed at the walker who wants the most interesting route; but even the peak-bagger, who often just climbs the shortest route up the mountain, might have a better time on the hill if they follow the routes suggested here.

Often expecting another trudge over heather moorland, I was continually surprised by finding routes up delightful wild glens. In many ways it's the glens that make the magnificent scenery we see in Scotland, and this guide is as much about exploring the glens as it is about climbing the peaks.

Brian Johnson

Walking the Corbetts: Vol 1

Allt Coire Ghlais, Beinn a' Bhuiridh (Route 27)

INTRODUCTION

Allt Mor, Carn an Fhreiceadain (Route 72)

WHAT ARE THE CORBETTS?

Scottish Peaks over 3000ft (914.4m) became known as 'Munros' after they were listed by Sir Hugh Munro in 1891. The Scottish Mountaineering Club (SMC) published the list and 'Munro-bagging' soon became a popular sport. By 2010 over 4000 people were recorded as having 'compleated' all the Munros, although there are many more unrecorded compleatists, too.

In 1930 John Rooke Corbett, a district valuer from Bristol, became the fourth person and first Sassenach (Englishman) to compleat the Munros, but he didn't stop there. He went on to climb all Scotland's hills and mountains over 2000ft (610m) and drew up a list of mountains between 2500ft and 3000ft with a drop of at least 500ft on all sides. When Corbett died in 1949, his sister passed his list on to the SMC, who published it alongside the Munro tables.

Corbett's original list has been adjusted as the accuracy of maps has improved, and this has meant the addition of about 20 Corbetts and the deletion of others. The

Cir Mhor from Glen Rosa (Routes 8 and 9)

latest peaks to be added are Sgurr nan Ceannaichean, which was demoted from a Munro in 2009, and Cnoc Coinnich, which was promoted from a Graham in 2016. Subsidiary summits of Munros and Corbetts between 2500 and 2999ft high with a drop of at least 30m on all sides are known as Corbett Tops. Also mentioned in the route descriptions are 'Grahams', which are mountains between 2000 and 2499ft, and 'Donalds' which are hills over 2000ft in Southern Scotland.

The Corbetts are every bit as interesting as the Munros. They tend to get more spectacular as you head north and west and there is no doubt that the majority of the most exciting Corbetts are to be found to the north of the Great Glen, where isolated rocky peaks rise steeply above the sea and inland lochs, in a wild landscape of heather and bog dotted with sparkling lochs and lochans. Along the western seaboard there are few Munros, but there are spectacular Corbetts all the way from Ardgour to Cape Wrath. Climbing the Corbetts will take you to the magical islands of Arran, Jura, Mull, Rum, Skye and Harris.

Volume 1 covers the Corbetts to the south of the Great Glen, which runs from Fort William to Inverness and contains Loch Ness, probably Scotland's best-known loch. South of Glasgow and Edinburgh are the moorland hills of the Southern Uplands, where seven peaks rise to Corbett status. In the Southern Highlands the Corbetts tend to be mixed up with the Munros. There are plenty of interesting little peaks that provide spectacular views of the better-known Munros. These peaks tend to be popular because of the easy access from Edinburgh and Glasgow, and they are ideal for those wanting a relatively short hike.

In the Eastern Highlands the high plateau is dominated by the Munros of the Cairngorm Mountains, surrounded by vast areas of sprawling heather moorland containing many Corbetts. Another heather-covered plateau with a large number of Corbetts is the Monadhliath Mountains to the northwest of the Cairngorms; the Corbetts here are little visited and are ideal for walkers seeking solitude.

The South-West Highlands, an area renowned for its rock-climbing in summer and snow and ice-climbing in winter, features a magnificent mix of rocky Munros and Corbetts. This region contains the Loch Lomond and the Trossachs National Park, as well as the popular Ben Nevis and Glen Coe areas. The highlight of Volume 1 will probably be the visit to the Islands of Arran and Jura, whose spectacular rocky mountains provide fantastic walking.

Volume 2 covers the Corbetts north of the Great Glen, including the western seaboard and the islands of Mull, Rum, Skye and Harris.

GEOLOGY

Scotland's mainly metamorphic rocks are the oldest in Britain and some of the oldest in the world. Scotland is

Summit tor, Caisteal Abhail (Route 9)

WALKING THE CORBETTS: VOL 1

split into four areas by three old fault lines: the Southern Uplands Fault, the Highland Boundary Fault and the Great Glen Fault. South of the Southern Uplands Fault, the Southern Uplands is largely made up of Silurian deposits laid down 400–500 million years ago. The central lowlands, containing Glasgow and Edinburgh, is a rift valley between the Southern Uplands Fault and the Highland Boundary Fault. The Highlands are split into two by the Great Glen Fault, which runs along the Great Glen. The rocks in the Highlands are 500–3000 million years old.

Massive movements caused by continental drift produced waves of folding, such as the Moine Thrust, resulting in older rocks often lying on top of younger rocks with the contortions of the rocks readily visible in outcrops and crags. The pressure and heating involved transformed the original volcanic or sedimentary rocks into metamorphic rocks.

Around 400 million years ago the Caledonian mountains would have been as high as the Himalayas and the rocks we see today are the worn-down stumps of this mighty mountain chain. Further periods of uplift and subsequent erosion followed until about two million years ago, when Scotland was a high plateau and the drainage systems we know today would have started to develop.

The onset of a series of ice ages about one and a half million years ago shaped the land through glacial erosion, creating U-shaped valleys and the impressive corries containing the lochs and lochans that are such an important aspect of the landscape.

Erratic boulder on Beinn Pharlagain (Route 52)

The last major incursion of ice peaked about 18,000 years ago, leaving other remnant features such as the granite tors on the Cairngorm plateau.

Over the last 12,000 years the most significant geological process in the Highlands has been the deposition of peat. Peat forms when plant material in marshy areas is inhibited from decaying fully by acidic and anaerobic conditions. The peat bogs grow slowly, at the rate of about one millimetre a year.

HUMAN HISTORY IN THE HIGHLANDS

When the ice finally retreated around 10,000BC Scotland became habitable and Mesolithic hunter-gatherers moved in. Archaeologists have dated an encampment near Biggar in the Southern Uplands to 8500BC and other sites have built up a picture of a boat-building people making tools from bone, stone and antlers.

By 3000BC Neolithic farmers were forming permanent settlements and living in stone houses. Many of the standing stones and stone circles found in the Highlands and Islands date from this period. In the Bronze Age, hill forts started to appear in Scotland and by 700BC, in the Iron Age, numerous hill forts, brochs and other fortified settlements support the image of quarrelsome tribes and petty kingdoms later recorded by the Romans.

When Roman forces led by Gnaeus Julius Agricola invaded Scotland in 79AD they met fierce resistance from the local population of Picts. Despite winning a number of battles and attempting to maintain control through military outposts, the Romans eventually withdrew, concluding that the wealth of the land did not justify the extensive garrisoning requirements.

From the late 5th century the Dal Riatans began to arrive from Ireland and they took and occupied the Western Highlands. They spoke 'Scoti', from which Scotland later got its name. Scoti became known as Gaelic and became the language of the Highlands and Islands. Only a few Scots (mainly in the North-West Highlands and Hebridean Islands) now speak Gaelic, but the language is kept alive in names of the mountains and other geographical features.

In the 7th century Anglo-Saxons invaded from Northumberland and the continent, and their language, Ynglis, eventually became the predominant tongue of lowland Scotland. The Vikings arrived in the 9th century and took control of the Northern Highlands and the Western Isles.

It is not fully clear how Scotland was united into a single kingdom but by 1018 Mael Coluim II (Malcolm II) controlled all of present-day Scotland, except for the northern parts still controlled by the Vikings. When William the Conqueror invaded Scotland in 1072 Mael Coluim III submitted. Under the Norman feudal system the local aristocracy enjoyed a high degree of independence and

Rob Roy's Grave, Balquhidder (Routes 21 and 22)

the complex political situation led to many small wars for control of parts or all of Scotland.

The death of King Alexander III in 1286 and his heir Margaret in 1290 left 14 rivals for succession. To prevent civil war the Scottish magnates asked Edward I of England to arbitrate and he chose John Balliol to become King John I. In 1296 Edward invaded Scotland, deposing King John, but the following year William Wallace raised forces and defeated the English army at the Battle of Stirling Bridge. He became Guardian of Scotland for a short time before being defeated by Edward at the Battle of Falkirk. Wallace escaped but fell into English hands in 1305 and was executed for treason.

After an unsuccessful rebellion in 1306, Robert the Bruce defeated the English at the battle of Bannockburn in 1314, obtaining independence for Scotland. In 1603, following the death of the childless Queen Elizabeth I, the crown of England passed to James VI of Scotland and he took the title James I of England, uniting the two countries under his personal rule. This foreshadowed the eventual 1707 union of Scotland and England under the banner of Great Britain.

Rather ineffective rebellions took place in 1708 and 1715; then in 1745 Charles Edward Stewart, known as Bonnie Prince Charlie, defeated the English army at the Battle of Prestonpans and marched

HUMAN HISTORY IN THE HIGHLANDS

into England, reaching as far south as Derby. At that moment a decisive move would probably have captured London, but the leadership had a loss of confidence and retreated to Scotland. This gave the English time to gather an army and the rebellion was crushed at the Battle of Culloden in 1746.

The Highland Clearances

Nowadays there are very few people living and working in the Scottish glens, but walkers will see plenty of signs that the glens were once heavily populated. The 'Highland Clearances' occurred over many years.

In the aftermath of the Jacobite Risings the British Government made efforts to curb the clans, and by 1725 Highlanders were emigrating to the Americas in large numbers. The Battle of Culloden in 1746 was followed by brutal repression: the Act of Proscription required all swords to be surrendered to the Government, the wearing of tartans or kilts was prohibited and the clan system destroyed. This resulted in the end of the supportive social structures of the small agricultural communities in the Highlands and Islands.

At the same time, demand for cattle and sheep in Britain was increasing and hardy black-faced sheep were introduced to the Highlands. Many landowners or chiefs engaged Lowland or even English factors with expertise in profitable sheep farming; families who were already living at

Rainbow over a bridge on one of General Wade's military roads (Route 71)

a subsistence level were encouraged off, or forcibly removed from, the land. Other landlords wanted a supply of cheap, or virtually free, labour for developing industries such as charcoal burning for the iron industry, coal mining, herring fisheries and production of soda-ash from kelp, and families were forced off the land into new crofting townships.

Then in 1846, as in Ireland, the potato crop failed and a widespread outbreak of cholera further weakened the Highland population. In the face of starvation and death many families migrated to the Americas, Australia or the growing urban cities such as Glasgow and Edinburgh. Many young men joined the army to provide the troops needed to maintain and expand the British Empire.

What the Clearances started, the First World War almost completed: a fifth of the British men killed in the trenches were Scottish and many of these soldiers came from the Highlands.

The economy today

Whisky production is the major industry in the Highlands, accounting for £3.45 billion of exports in 2010. Food exports topped £1 billion in 2010, the largest share of this being fish and seafood, particularly Scottish salmon. The region also has a growing energy industry, with a particular focus on renewable energy.

Tourism represents another major source of income. Travellers have been admiring the grandeur of the Highlands for more than three centuries but the mid-19th century was when its reputation as a fashionable tourist destination developed, as the well-off followed the example of Queen Victoria, who spent much of her time at Balmoral Castle on Deeside.

As sheep farming became less economic, the Highland estates had to look for other sources of income and nowadays these are mainly hunting and shooting. The grouse-shooting season starts on the 'glorious 12th' of August and is followed by pheasant and rough shooting through the autumn and early winter. Deer stalking occurs in September and October for stags and November to February for hinds.

THE NATURAL ENVIRONMENT

The Caledonian Forest

Most people think of the Highlands as a natural wilderness, but it is very much a man-made environment. Frank Fraser-Darling wrote in his *West Highland Survey* in 1955 that 'The Highlands were a devastated countryside – a wet desert... Once there had been a rich natural system in the Highlands and humans had destroyed it.'

The biggest effect humankind has had on the natural history of the Highlands has been the destruction of the Caledonian Forest. This occurred mainly between AD800 and AD1100, and then from the 16th century to the

The natural environment

Red deer on Farragon Hill (Route 55)

end of the 19th century. Much of what remained was then felled in the two World Wars.

The coming of the sheep as a result of the Clearances played an important part in the transformation process: large areas of birch, willow, rowan, hazel and gorse were burnt, and overgrazing by sheep prevented any regeneration of the trees and shrubs. Moorland replaced the natural forest. Native animals and birds, which were having a difficult enough time coping with this change in their environment, were furthered decimated or exterminated by the growth of shooting for sport.

In the 19th century sheep were largely replaced by deer. The deer were just as destructive to seedlings as sheep and in the 'deer forests' the only trees surviving were likely to be over 200 years old. On other estates excessive heather burning to provide good conditions for grouse further added to the degradation of the natural environment.

After the Second World War the Government began to worry about Britain's shortage of timber and started the reforestation of the Highland glens. Unfortunately, they replanted with quick growing Canadian Sitka spruce and the European larch. These monoculture commercial plantations, apart from being scenically uninteresting, did not provide a suitable habitat for native Scottish flora or fauna.

23

Horses on Meall na Fearna (Route 24)

It is only in recent years that forestry policy has changed and a start has been made on regenerating the natural Caledonian Forests.

Wildlife

At one time Scotland was home to the lynx, brown bear, beaver, elk, wild boar, wild ox and polecat, but these animals all became extinct, mostly as a result of hunting. The last wolf was shot in 1743. Egg collectors, hunters and gamekeepers also exterminated the white-tailed eagle, red kite, goshawk and osprey. The growth of the shooting estates in the 19th century left little room in the habitat for any animals other than red deer and red grouse, and other wildlife declined in number.

However, conservation programmes in the past 50 years have helped. Birds of prey have made a comeback in the Highlands and among others you may see hen harrier, sparrowhawk, merlin, peregrine falcon, golden eagle, as well as the reintroduced osprey, red kite, white-tailed eagle and goshawk. The short-eared owl is the only owl you are likely to see in the Highlands. There are large numbers of game birds; besides red grouse you may see pheasant, black grouse and the rare capercaillie. Plump ptarmigan are to be found on the highest ridges in summer and winter. Many waders breed in the mountains, including oyster-catchers, dotterel, golden plover, snipe, woodcock and curlew, while the hooded crow and acrobatic raven are the main scavengers.

Wildfowl are not common in the Highlands but you may see grey heron, widgeon, teal, goosander and

THE NATURAL ENVIRONMENT

red-breasted merganser, as well as the rare red-throated and black-throated divers which breed on Highland lochs. Common gulls also breed on moorland here.

There are many smaller birds to be seen in the Highlands, including grey wagtail, meadow pipit, dipper, redstart, whinchat, stonechat, wheatear, ring ouzel, wood and willow warblers, goldcrest, spotted flycatcher, crested tit, siskin, redpoll, skylark, tree pipit and common crossbill. You may catch a glimpse of the Scottish crossbill, which inhabits the coniferous forests. It is Britain's only endemic bird and is one of Europe's most threatened species.

The mammals that you might be lucky enough to see include the red fox, the rare Scottish wildcat and the pine marten. There is still a population

Only in Scotland...

Highland Cattle in Glen Strae (Route 28)

of the otter-like American mink, which escaped from fur farms and was responsible for a big decline in numbers of water vole and wildfowl in Scotland. The red squirrel, which has been driven out of most parts of Britain by the introduced grey squirrel, is still thriving in the remaining Highland woodland. Mountain hare are common on the mountain ridges. The only amphibians you are likely to see are the common toad and the common frog and the only reptile is the adder.

Highland Cattle are the best known of the domesticated animals that you will encounter and semi-domesticated reindeer can be seen in the Cairngorms National Park. In addition you will see many sea birds on the islands and on the sea lochs of the Western Highlands, where you may also catch a glimpse of otters and seals.

25

Walking the Corbetts: Vol 1

WALKING THE CORBETTS

The walks in this guide were not solely designed for the peak-bagger, but also for the walker who wants an interesting day out on some of the less well-known peaks of Scotland.

Some people think the Corbetts are something to do in your declining years after you have 'compleated' the Munros. If you take this attitude you will miss out on many of the most spectacular and rewarding mountains in Scotland. It is true that as you get older you may appreciate the shorter walks offered by some of the Corbetts, but many of the Corbetts are very remote from road access and still entail a demanding hike. What is more, between many of the peaks listed as Munros, there is little drop, so you can often climb several in one day. By contrast, the requirement for a 500ft drop on all sides between listed Corbetts means that there are few occasions where Corbetts can be linked together. It is also surprising how few Corbetts can sensibly be combined with climbing a Munro.

This two-volume guide suggests about 185 day routes covering the 222 Corbetts, all walked by the author during his research. Where alternative routes are also suggested, these have not always been checked by the author. This first volume – South of the Great Glen – covers 112 Corbett summits in 95 routes.

Although this is primarily a guide for day walkers rather than backpackers, there are some areas, such

Cairnsmore of Carsphairn (Route 4)

as Knoydart, where the Corbetts are so remote that walking them in for a day will be too much for the average walker and backpacking possibilities are considered.

WHEN TO GO

You will find people walking in the Scottish Highlands throughout the year but this guidebook assumes that the Corbetts are to be tackled when they are free of snow. The mountains can be at their best in the winter, but weather and snow and ice conditions mean this won't be the time for the inexperienced walker. If you have the necessary skills and experience, winter in the Scottish Highlands can be magnificent. In the middle of winter there will be less than eight hours of daylight and climbing Corbetts could be a better option than climbing the Munros.

The spring in Scotland is often drier and sunnier than the summer and many consider April and May to be the best months for being in the Highlands. June, July and August are the warmest months, with the added advantage of the long daylight hours. The biggest problem with the Scottish Highlands in summer is the swarms of midges that can torment the walker, especially in the early morning and on still evenings. This is not too much of a problem for the day walker, but it means that this isn't the ideal time of year for backpacking and wilderness camping.

September and October are generally relatively dry and you won't have too much problem with midges. A combination of autumn storms and short daylight in November and December also means that you are likely to be on your own in the mountains.

THE TERRAIN

Many newcomers to Scotland underestimate the conditions they will encounter when walking in the Scottish mountains. The mountains in this guidebook may be under 1000m high, but you will usually be starting your walk from near sea-level and you will spend most of the time above the tree-line, which means you will get spectacular views but will be exposed to wind, rain and sun.

Hikers from Europe and the US may be accustomed to walking on well-maintained paths and trails. Climbing the Corbetts you will frequently find the only paths are sheep or deer tracks. There are good tracks in the glens, maintained by the owners of the shooting estates, but once you are above these it is only on the most popular Corbetts that you will find well-maintained paths. The going is usually relatively easy on the ridges where a combination of wind and Arctic conditions in winter keeps the vegetation down to a minimum, although on some peaks you will have to cope with peat hags or boulderfields.

WALKING THE CORBETTS: VOL 1

Heather-clad slopes and outcrop in Glen Tromie (Route 73)

There is little technical difficulty on the Corbetts south of the Great Glen, as few of these peaks are rocky enough to demand the use of hands. However, glaciation has resulted in many of these Corbetts being guarded by steep slopes, often covered with deep heather or boggy grass, which can make walking hard work.

WEATHER

The main feature of the Scottish weather is its changeability and you should be prepared for anything. Sometimes it can seem as if you get all four seasons on one day. Don't be surprised if you set out on a warm summer's day and find it cold and windy on the summit ridge.

There can be rain any month of the year, even in February when you may find it raining rather than snowing at 3000ft! In winter, snow is most likely when the wind is coming from the north-east across the North Sea, when it can be very cold. The best weather is usually associated with a high pressure building up over Scandinavia when the Scottish Mountains can be bathed in sun for days or weeks on end.

Although there may be deep snow on the Corbetts in winter, the wind will tend to blow the bulk of the snow off the peaks into the glens. Since the weather in Scotland is relatively mild for such a northerly country, the snow can melt very quickly in the glens and even on the peaks.

If there is significant snow, only those with experience of winter mountaineering should attempt the steeper peaks because of the risk of cornices above the gullies and avalanche on the slopes.

It is the wind that is the most dangerous aspect of Scottish weather. If it is windy down in the glens, it could be too windy to stand up on an exposed peak. Even in summer, with the temperature well above freezing, a combination of wind and rain can lead to hypothermia unless you are properly equipped. In winter, wind can cause spindrift in the snow, creating a whiteout, even if it isn't actually snowing. Apart from the risks of hypothermia and the difficulty of walking into a blizzard, this will also make navigation very difficult.

Mist is a feature of the weather that can cause problems for the inexperienced. If you hit a spell of cloudy weather your options can be very limited if you aren't prepared for walking in the mist. Many of the Corbetts are rarely climbed and paths haven't developed, so navigation in mist can be very demanding.

ACCESS

Scotland has a system of law based as much on common law as statute law, and trespass has never been a criminal offence in Scotland. Although in the 19th century landowners were very protective of their rights of privacy, access for walkers and climbers gradually became accepted through the 20th century and free access to

Storm over the Cairngorm Mountains (Route 81)

WALKING THE CORBETTS: VOL 1

Beinn an Lochain from Butterbridge (Route 15)

The Scottish Outdoor Access Code

The Highlands are the home of Scotland's diverse wildlife and enjoyed by the people who live and work there as well as visitors. You can exercise access rights responsibly if you:

- Respect people's privacy and peace of mind. When close to a house or garden, keep a sensible distance from the house, use a path or track if there is one and take extra care at night.

- Help land managers and others to work safely and effectively. Do not hinder land-management operations and follow advice from land managers. Respect requests for reasonable limitations on when and where you can go.

- Care for your environment. Do not disturb wildlife, leave the environment as you find it and follow a path or track if there is one.

- Keep your dog under proper control. Do not take it through fields of calves and lambs, and dispose of dog dirt.

the mountains became enshrined in the Land Reform (Scotland) Act 2003. This act gives some of the best access rights in the world and the public have access to most land (including hills, woods and pastureland) for recreation, provided they act responsibly (see box).

Deer stalking

If you're planning to walk in the Scottish hills from 1 July to 20 October, you should take reasonable steps to find out where deer stalking is taking place. As well as providing income, regular culling ensures that there is enough grazing for the herd and other animals, and that the fragile upland habitat is not damaged.

The Hillphones service provides information to enable hillwalkers and climbers to find out where red deer stalking is taking place during the stalking season, and to plan routes avoiding stalking operations. For more information go to www.snh.org.uk/hillphones.

Grouse shooting

The grouse-shooting season runs from 12 August to 10 December, with most shoots taking place during the earlier part of the season. Be alert to the possibility of shooting taking place on grouse moors and take account of advice on alternative routes. Avoid crossing land where a shoot is taking place until it is safe to do so.

Low-ground shooting

Low-ground shooting can take several forms. Pheasant and partridge shooting takes place during the autumn and winter in woods and forests, and on neighbouring land. Avoid crossing land when shooting is taking place. Avoid game bird rearing pens and keep your dog under close control or on a short lead when close to a pen.

Fishing

Access rights do not extend to fishing and the regulations are complex so you need to know the regulations before doing any fishing.

Cycling

Access rights extend to cycling. Cycling on hard surfaces, such as wide paths and tracks, causes few problems. On narrow paths, cyclists should give way to walkers and horse riders. Take care not to alarm farm animals, horses and wildlife.

If you are cycling off-path, you should avoid going onto wet, boggy or soft ground, and avoid churning up the surface. Effectively when climbing the Corbetts this means that you can use your bicycle on the estate roads and tracks to access the mountain, but the paths and off-path sections are likely to be too wet to be able to cycle without causing damage.

Wild camping

Access rights extend to wild camping. This type of camping is lightweight, done in small numbers and only for two or three nights in any one place. Avoid causing problems for local people and land managers:

do not camp in enclosed fields of crops or farm animals and keep well away from buildings, roads or historic structures. Take extra care to avoid disturbing deer stalking or grouse shooting. If you wish to camp close to a house or building, seek the owner's permission.

Leave no trace by:
- taking away all your litter
- removing all traces of your tent pitch and of any open fire
- not causing any pollution

These rights do not extend to those using motorised transport.

Lighting fires

Wherever possible, use a stove rather than an open fire. If you do wish to light an open fire, keep it small, under control and supervised. Never light an open fire during prolonged dry periods or in areas such as forests, woods, farmland or on peaty ground, or near to buildings or in cultural heritage sites where damage can be easily caused.

Human waste

If you need to urinate, do so at least 30m from open water or rivers and streams. If you need to defecate, do so as far away as possible from buildings, from open water, rivers and streams. Bury faeces in a shallow hole and replace the turf.

Dogs and dog walking

Access rights apply to people walking dogs provided that their dog is kept under proper control.

Cotton grass on Dollar Law (Route 7)

Your main responsibilities are:
- Ground-nesting birds: During the breeding season (April–July) keep your dog on a short lead or under close control in areas such as moorland, grasslands, loch shores and the seashore to avoid disturbing birds that nest on the ground.
- Farm animals: Never let your dog worry or attack farm animals. Don't take your dog into fields with young farm animals.
- Public places: Keep your dog under close control and avoid causing concern to others, especially those who fear dogs.
- Dog waste: Pick up and dispose of carefully.

Fuller details can be found at www.outdooraccess-scotland.com.

Roadside camping

There is no legal right to roadside camping from a car. At one time it was common practice and this led to pollution problems in popular areas such as Glen Coe. You will find people camping beside the road, particularly in remote glens, but you should realise that you have no right to do so. You should obey any prohibition signs and you must leave if requested to do so by the landowner. Take particular care not to cause any form of pollution.

Motorhomes are a good base if you are walking in Scotland and there is rarely any difficulty finding somewhere to park. Caravans are much less flexible and should use caravan sites. Many of the single-track roads with passing places that are still common in the Highlands are not really suitable for caravans.

Roadside camping is legal under the access laws if you are walking or cycling.

MOUNTAIN BOTHIES

The Mountain Bothies Association (MBA) is a charity that maintains about 100 bothies in Scotland. These are shelters, usually old crofts, which are unlocked and available for anyone to use. Almost all of the bothies are in remote areas and are only accessible on foot or possibly by bicycle. The MBA itself does not own any of the bothies; they are usually remote buildings that the landowner allows walkers to use.

When going to a bothy, it is important to assume that there will be no facilities. No tap, no sink, no toilets, no beds, no lights, and even if there is a fireplace, perhaps nothing to burn. Bothies may have a simple sleeping platform, but if it's busy you may find that the only place to sleep is on a stone floor. Carry out all your rubbish, as you would do if you were camping, and aim to leave the bothy tidier than you find it.

If you intend to make regular use of bothies you should join the MBA to contribute towards the costs of running the organisation. The MBA organises working parties to maintain and tidy up the bothies and they would welcome volunteers to help with this

Culsharg bothy, Merrick (Route 1)

task. For more details on using bothies, consult the MBA's excellent website: www.mountainbothies.org.uk.

NAVIGATION

The 1:100,000 maps in this guide are good for planning purposes and will give you a general idea of the route, but they don't give enough detail for accurate navigation in difficult conditions. For this reason it is essential that you carry the relevant maps.

The Ordnance Survey (OS) 1:50,000 maps, available in paper form or for GPS devices, are very good and should be all you need to follow the recommended routes. In popular areas updated OS 1:25,000 maps are available but not really necessary. Probably the best maps are the Harvey maps (mainly 1:40,000) but they don't have full coverage of the Scottish Highlands.

The contour lines on all of these maps are remarkably accurate and should be seen as your main navigational tool. Inexperienced walkers going out in good visibility should learn to relate contours to the ground so they are better prepared if they get caught out in mist.

You should always carry a good compass (those produced for orienteering by Silva and Suunto are probably the best). In good visibility it should be sufficient to use the compass to orientate the map, so that north on the map lines up with north on the ground. At present, magnetic north is near enough to grid north not to have to adjust for magnetic variation. Learn to take bearings from a map and follow them using the compass in clear conditions, before you find yourself having to navigate in mist.

The most difficult thing in navigation is knowing how far you have travelled, which can be important when navigating in mist on Scottish hills. In extreme conditions it may be necessary to pace-count to measure distance – practise this skill in good conditions, so that you are prepared.

Probably the most common navigational error is to head in the wrong direction when leaving a mountain summit. It is a good habit to always check your compass when leaving a mountain summit, even in clear conditions.

GPS

If you are experienced at using map and compass, a GPS device is not essential for navigating the Corbetts. However, even experienced mountain navigators will find it can make navigation easier in mist and the less experienced might find that using a GPS device allows them to navigate safely in poor visibility.

SAFETY

The most important thing is not how to deal with accidents, it's how to prevent them. There are three main tips for reducing your chance of a mountain accident significantly:
- Learn to navigate.
- Learn to navigate better.
- Learn to navigate even better.

Hiking family below Ben Vrackie (Route 56)

WALKING THE CORBETTS: VOL 1

Beinn a' Chaolais over Loch an t-Siob (Route 10)

It's a fact! Research done about 40 years ago suggested that poor navigation was a major contributory factor in about 90 per cent of Mountain Rescue incidents in the Scottish Highlands.

Three more tips should account for nearly all of the remaining ten per cent of accidents:

- Make sure you have good tread on your walking shoes or boots. Do not wear shoes with a worn tread.
- Use two walking poles – this greatly increases safety on steep grass slopes and during any difficult river crossings.
- Always have waterproofs, hat and gloves in your pack, whatever the weather.

Finally, if you intend to do any of these routes in winter, you should take some training in walking in snow-covered mountains. There are excellent courses at Glenmore Lodge National Outdoor Training Centre (see Appendix B for details).

AREAS IN THIS GUIDE

1 The Southern Uplands

The Southern Uplands are the range of hills between the English border to the south and the central lowlands containing Glasgow and Edinburgh to the north; and from Ballantrae on the Irish Sea north-east to Dunbar on the North Sea. The Corbetts in this section are concentrated in Galloway at the western end of the range and to the north-east of Moffat at the centre of the range.

Galloway Forest Park, the largest in Britain at 300 square miles (800km^2), contains rounded grassy mountains surrounded by boggy, rough heather and grass moorland and commercial forestry. The Moffat and Manor Hills are rounded, with broad ridges defended by steep slopes. They are predominantly grassy, with some heather, and are used extensively for sheep farming.

2 Arran and Jura

The island of Arran in the Firth of Clyde is only 30km (19 miles) long by 16km (10 miles) wide but it has a remarkable diversity of landscapes and seascapes, its beautiful coastline complemented by a rugged and mountainous interior in the north and green rolling hills and woodland to the south. The four rocky Corbetts surrounding Glen Rosa provide some of the best walking in Scotland.

Jura is a wild and inaccessible island. Its name is derived from the Viking Dyr Oe (pronounced Joora) meaning 'deer island' and today there are more than 5000 red deer, outnumbering human inhabitants by 20:1. It is worth spending time on the island rather than just visiting to climb the Corbett.

Ardgartan Forest on ascent of The Cobbler (Route 13)

3 West of Loch Lomond
(Arrochar Alps)
To the north-west of Loch Lomond, located around the head of Loch Long, Loch Fyne and Loch Goil, is a compact group of mountains known as the 'Arrochar Alps' with five Munros and seven Corbetts. These are primarily grassy hills with steep craggy slopes and narrow ridges. Around 18,000 years ago the land was covered with an ice-sheet, but the mountain peaks were left exposed; the extreme cold caused the rock to split and shatter, leaving the crags seen today on The Cobbler and other mountains surrounding Glen Croe. It is convenient to include the isolated Meall an Fhudair, at the head of Loch Lomond, in this section. These mountains are especially popular with hillwalkers, due to their proximity to Glasgow.

4 East of Loch Lomond
(The Trossachs)
The Trossachs (Na Trosaichean) is a small woodland glen lying between Loch Katrine and Loch Achray. However, the name is used generally to refer to the mountains, lochs and glens to the east of Ben Lomond, forming part of the very popular Loch Lomond and the Trossachs National Park. Despite their popularity, access to these easy grassy mountains is rather restricted by the extensive forestry in the glens, including the Queen Elizabeth Forest Park, designated in 1953 to mark the coronation of Queen Elizabeth II. The Corbetts to the east of the Trossachs are included in this section, and are heather-covered moorland plateaus.

5 South-West Grampians
(Tyndrum and Dalmally)
Most walkers visiting this area do so to climb the big Munros Ben Cruachan, Ben Lui and Beinn Dorain, which dominate the area, but the Corbetts, which are generally steep and grassy, offer some pleasant walking. There are railway stations at Crianlarich, Tyndrum, Bridge of Orchy and Dalmally on the lines from Glasgow to Mallaig and Oban, which might help those without a car climb these mountains. The West Highland Way passes through the area, parallel to the A82, and it would be possible for hikers using this trail to take time off to climb some of the Corbetts.

6 The Southern Grampians
(Loch Tay and Glen Lyon)
This section includes the Corbetts to the east of the 'Tyndrum Alps' bounded by Loch Tay and Glen Dochart to the south and Loch Rannoch and Rannoch Moor to the north. For convenience of transport Creagan na Beinne, south of Loch Tay, has been included here. The Corbetts to the east of the section are a rather undistinguished collection of moorland peaks in an area dominated by Munros, including the well-known Ben Lawers. It is the grassy Corbetts with rock outcrops at the head of Glen Lyon and Glen Lochay that provide the interest.

Boulders on Meall nan Subh (Route 33)

7 The Western Grampians (Glen Coe and Kinlochleven)

This section includes the peaks around Glen Coe, Glen Etive and Loch Leven. The Corbetts here are steep, rocky mountains and they provide some of the most exciting walking in Volume 1 of this guide. As well as being interesting mountains in their own right, these Corbetts provide fabulous views of the Munros that dominate the area.

Glen Etive might have been considered the finest glen in Scotland, if it weren't overshadowed by the splendour of neighbouring Glen Coe. During the ice ages there were massive accumulations of ice on Rannoch Moor and it was this ice, escaping to the west, that was largely responsible for sculpturing these two magnificent glens.

8 The Central Grampians (Pitlochry and Loch Rannoch)

This section consists mainly of heather-covered moorland hills on either side of the A9 north-west of Pitlochry and along the minor road which passes along the north shore of Loch Tummel and Loch Rannoch. Many of these Corbetts are remote from road access and rarely visited except by guests of the shooting estates. You might like to consider backpacking a few of the peaks in this section, as some of the routes are uncomfortably long for a day hike.

9 Badenoch (Spean Bridge to Kingussie)

This section covers the south-west half of the Monadhliath Mountains and the peaks near Kingussie to the west of the Cairngorm Mountains.

Lochan below summit crags on Meall na Meoig (Route 52)

The Monadhliath Mountains are a heather-covered moorland plateau with deeply incised glens. There is little on the hilltops themselves to maintain interest, but the approach up remote Highland glens makes these rewarding walks. The best-known glen in these mountains is Glen Roy, whose 'parallel roads' make this a 'must see' glen for geologists. The rocky peaks Sgurr Innse and Cruach Innse are the only Corbetts in the Ben Nevis mountain range.

10 The Southern Cairngorms

This section is a vast heather moor with gentle hills lying to the south-east of the main massif of the Cairngorm Mountains. The northern half is centred on Braemar in the valley of the River Dee, which rises high in the Cairngorm Mountains and runs east to its mouth at Aberdeen. The area is very popular with tourists, not only because of the magnificent scenery, but also because Balmoral Castle, summer home of the Royal Family, lies in the shadow of Lochnagar Mountain.

The remaining Corbetts are scattered up the 'Glens of Angus', which flow south to reach the sea in the Firth of Tay or at Montrose.

11 Northern Cairngorms

The central massif of the Cairngorm Mountains is dominated by big Munros, including Ben MacDui, the second highest mountain in Scotland. Stretching 50km to the north-east of these high mountains is a vast plateau of heather-covered moorland, which provides most of the Corbetts in this section. Also included are a

USING THIS GUIDE

couple of Corbetts on the edge of the Cairngorm Mountains and a couple of peaks in the north-east of the Monadhliath Mountains.

USING THIS GUIDE

Walking the Corbetts is divided into two volumes:
- Volume 1 covers the Corbetts south of the Great Glen (which runs from Fort William to Inverness) and includes the islands of Arran and Jura.
- Volume 2 covers the Corbetts north of the Great Glen and includes the islands of Mull, Rum, Skye and Harris.

Other guides to the Corbetts number and organise the Corbetts as they appear in the SMC lists. This organisation was actually designed for the Munros and is illogical for the Corbetts. There are Corbetts in many areas where there are no Munros, and in other areas adjacent Corbetts are listed in different sections of the tables. For instance, Beinn Chuirn, Beinn Bhreac-liath and Beinn Odhar are all within 5km of Tyndrum but appear in three different sections of the SMC lists.

In this guide the Corbetts have been divided into 21 sections, 11 in Volume 1 and 10 in Volume 2. Each section could be walked in a 1–2 week holiday. Corbetts have been arranged based on road access, so that it could be possible to climb the Corbetts in each section on a single trip.

Beinn an t-Sidhein over Loch Lubnaig (Route 19)

Maps to take

The 1:100,000 maps in this guide should be sufficient to give you a feel for the route, but they are not intended for detailed navigation, particularly in bad weather. You should always carry the relevant OS Landranger (1:50,000) maps suggested for the route, either as a paper copy or loaded onto a GPS device. The Harvey maps at 1:40,000 are excellent alternatives to the OS maps, but they don't cover all of Scotland.

Route descriptions

For each Corbett a single route is described. Information about distance, amount of ascent, route difficulty, time needed to complete the route, summits reached, maps required and access to the start of the route is given in the information box at the start of each description. In some cases alternative routes are also suggested, and these are marked on the route maps with an orange dashed line. The route maps are at 1:100,000 scale and based on Ordnance Survey data. Information about bases and local facilities is given in the introduction to each section.

Distances and ascents

Distances and amount of climb are quoted to the nearest kilometre (or mile) and 10m (or 100ft) of ascent.

Timings

All timings are those measured by the author's GPS device as he checked the routes. This device stops recording walking time whenever the walker stops, even for a few seconds, so the total time required to complete a walk will be considerably longer than that given in the guide. You should make an allowance for refreshments stops, taking photos and your own pace and fitness.

Grid references

All grid references are 10-figure references taken from the author's GPS device, but rounded up or down to the nearest 10m. A full grid reference with the letters indicating the grid square is given in the information box at the start, but letters are only used in the grid references in the route description if the route crosses into a different grid square. Set your GPS device to 'British Grid'.

Heights

Where spot heights are given on route maps these figures are used in the route description. All other heights were measurements from the author's GPS device quoted to the nearest 5m. GPS does not measure height as accurately as it does horizontal position and it is possible that some of these readings are as much as 10m out. For Corbetts (but not for other summits) the height is also given in feet; note that this is not the conversion of the metric height, but is the height given on the OS 1 inch:1 mile map, most of which are derived from surveys in the 1950s.

1 THE SOUTHERN UPLANDS

Water of Minnoch, Glentrool Forest (Route 2)

The Southern Uplands: Bases and facilities

Base for Routes 1–4: Newton Stewart

Newton Stewart, a small town on the A75, has good facilities for tourists.

Newton Stewart Tourist Office, Dashwood Square, Newton Stewart, DG8 6EQ Tel: 01671 402 431 www.visitsouthernscotland.co.uk

Minigaff SYHA, Newton Stewart, DG8 6PL Tel: 01671 402 211 email: minnigaff@syha.org.uk

Local facilities for Routes 1 and 2: Glen Trool

Glen Trool is on a minor road off the A714 N of Newton Stewart.

House o' Hill Hotel, Bargrennan, Newton Stewart, DG8 6RN
Tel: 01671 840 243 www.houseohill.co.uk

Glentrool Camping and Caravan Site: Camping, caravans and static caravans as well as a small shop and tourist information. Tel: 01671 840 280 www.glentroolcampingandcaravansite.co.uk

Glentrool shop and cafe: Open 10.30am–4.30pm.

Walking the Corbetts: Vol 1

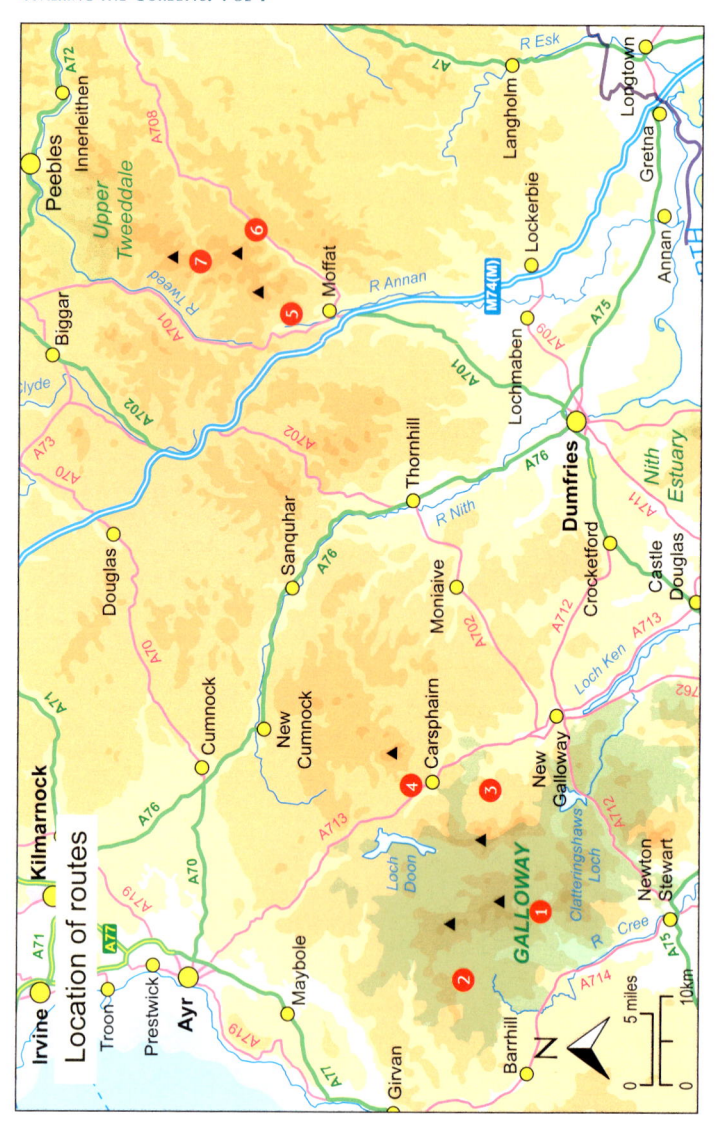

1 THE SOUTHERN UPLANDS

Local facilities for Routes 3 and 4: St. John's Town of Dalry

Dalry is on the A713 about 16 miles NW of Castle Douglas and is a small town with limited facilities. There is further accommodation at New Galloway just to the S of Dalry.

The tourist office covering the area is at Castle Douglas: Market Hill Car Park, Castle Douglas, DG7 1AE Tel: 01556 502 611

Local facilities for Route 4: Carsphairn

Carsphairn, 9 miles N of Dalry up the A713, has a small store with a tearoom: Mon–Fri: 7.00am–6.00pm, Sat: 8.00am–6.00pm, Sun: 9.00am–7.00pm. Tel: 01644 460 211

Base for Routes 5–7: Moffat

Moffat which is just off junction 15 of the A74(M) was a Victorian spa town and is now a small town with good facilities for tourists.

Moffat Tourist Office, Churchgate, Moffat, DG10 9EG Tel: 01683 220 620

Local facilities for Routes 6 and 7: St Mary's Loch

There is accommodation, camping and a cafe at the S end of St Mary's Loch on the A708, NE of White Coomb.

Glen Cafe: Sat/Sun: 10.00am–5.00pm, Mon–Fri: 10.00am–4.00pm. Tel: 07928 718 530

Tibbie Shiels Inn: reported to be permanently closed

ROUTE 1
Merrick BRANCHED FINGER

Start	Bruce's Stone car park (NX 41600 80460)
Distance	13km (8 miles)
Total ascent	960m (3100ft)
Difficulty	The ascent of Merrick is straightforward. However, the suggested descent route could test your navigation and route-finding and it finishes with a rough steep descent.
Time	4hr 30min
Summit	Merrick (843m, 2764ft)
Maps	OS Landranger 77
Access	From Newton Stewart, follow the A714 N and take the minor road up Glen Trool. At Glentrool Village follow signs right to 'Bruce's Stone' where there is a car park at the roadhead, N of Loch Trool.
Note	In bad weather it would be wise to descend by the ascent route. Details for combining Routes 1 and 2 are given under Route 2.

Merrick is the highest mountain in the Southern Uplands. The 'tourist route' follows a good footpath all the way to the summit. The suggested descent over the Rig of Loch Enoch and Buchanan Hill is rough with boggy grass and heather on rocky ridges, in a loch-studded landscape, giving a flavour of what the Galloway Hills would have been like before the forests were planted.

The stone beside the car park is known as **Bruce's Stone** and is inscribed, 'In loyal remembrance of Robert the Bruce, King of Scots, whose victory in this glen over an English force in March 1307 opened the campaign of independence which he brought to a decisive close at Bannockburn on 24 June 1314.'

Head N up a good path, above the left bank of **Buchan Burn** to Culsharg bothy (270m, 41540 82130) and

Route 1 – Merrick

continue up to a forest road. Turn right and immediately left, climbing through the forest and onto a grassy ridge. The path deteriorates as the mountain wall (610m, 41060 83580) on the SW ridge of Benyellary is approached. Follow the path along the wall to the summit of **Benyellary** (719m, 41490 83900) then follow the wall left then right. At 705m (41960 84850) the path swings right, away from the wall, to the trig point on the summit of **Merrick** (2hr, 843m, 42760 85550).

Descend ESE down a grassy slope, avoiding rocky outcrops, to the sandy beach at the W tip of **Loch Enoch** (2hr 35min, 500m, 44060 84740). Follow the wall SW to its high point and then climb to the ridge on your left and follow an indistinct path SSW along the ridge over a succession of minor summits, the **Rig of Loch Enoch**. Cross a ruined wall (450m, 43370 83340) and continue

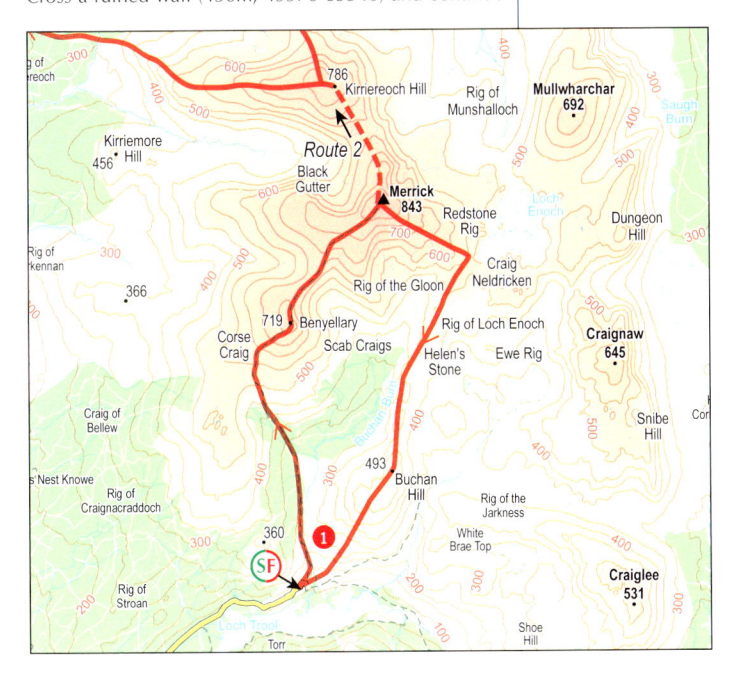

Loch Enoch to the E of Merrick

along the ridge to the summit of **Buchan Hill** (3hr 35min, 493m, 42920 81910).

Continue over the middle summit to the S summit (480m, 42470 81440). Crags prevent a descent straight down the ridge so it is best to head S then swing SW when below the upper crags. The descent is on steep rough grass with no obvious paths. There is a gate in the wall just to the left of Buchan Burn (4hr 20min, 150m, 41830 80570).

Drop down to the forest road, turn right across the bridge and follow it back to the car park (4hr 30min).

ROUTE 2
Shalloch on Minnoch

MIDDLE PLACE OF THE WILLOWS

Start	David Bell memorial car park (NX 35330 90650)
Distance	24km (15 miles)
Total ascent	980m (3200ft)
Difficulty	The route through the forest and lower slopes of the mountain is very rough and can be very boggy. Navigation between Shalloch on Minnoch and Kirriereoch Hill could be difficult in mist.
Time	6hr 30min
Summits	Shalloch on Minnoch (775m, 2528ft), Tarfessock (697m, Donald), Kirriereoch Hill (786m, Donald)
Map	OS Landranger 77
Access	From Newton Stewart, follow the A714 N and take the minor road up Glen Trool. Turn left in Glentrool village and head N until the road forks. Take the right fork and park at the car park for the Bell memorial on your left.
Note	If you can arrange transport at both ends of your walk, you could continue from Kirriereoch Hill 2km S to Merrick and then descend to Bruce's Stone in Glen Trool as described in Route 1. An alternative way to combine Routes 1 and 2 would be to continue to Merrick and then return to Kirriereoch Hill.

There is no easy approach to Shalloch on Minnoch, as it is surrounded by forestry and rough boggy grass and heather. The ridges are grassy with small rocky outcrops. The summit of Shalloch on Minnoch appears on the OS map and lists of Corbetts as being the trig point at 768m, but there is another summit which GPS measurements suggest may be about 3m higher and is shown on the accompanying route map at 775m! The recommended route continues to Kirriereoch Hill, which was listed as a Corbett until 1981, but has been deleted from the list because there is only 149m (490ft) of descent between it and Merrick.

WALKING THE CORBETTS: VOL 1

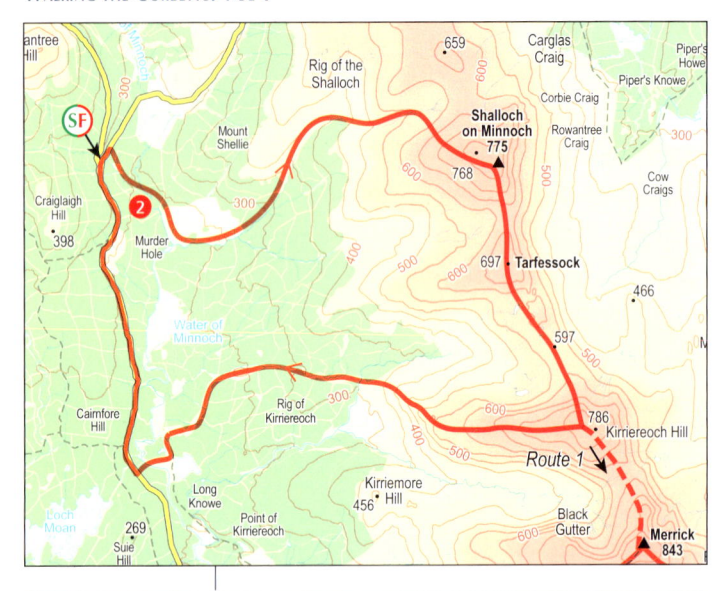

Trig point on Shalloch on Minnoch

Route 2 – Shalloch on Minnoch

The memorial at the car park commemorates **David Bell**, known as 'The Highwayman', who died in 1965. He was a cyclist, writer and environmentalist (before the term was invented?), and is also remembered in the 70-mile cycle race named after him and the book *The Highwayman* written by David Bellamy.

Head down the road a short distance NE and turn right down the first forestry road to a bridge across the **Water of Minnoch**. Cross the bridge and immediately turn right along the burn to the abandoned Shalloch on Minnoch cottage (25min, 250m, 36920 89560). Follow a faint rough path up the left bank of Shalloch Burn and continue as the path fades away. As you approach the top of the forest the burn splits and you should follow the right-hand tributary to a ruined stone shelter (1hr 15min, 410m, 38550 91220).

Continue up the burn until you reach the flat floor of a corrie (555m, 39680 91220) and head SE onto the ridge on your right and follow this to the trig point (768m, 40470 90700). This does not appear to be the highest point so head ESE to a small cairn (2hr 20min, 775m, 40760 90560), which marks the summit of **Shalloch on Minnoch**.

Follow the ridge SSE to the Nick of Carclach (628m, 40940 89880), S to **Tarfessock** (697m, 40910 89210), over a series of minor summits to a fence (590m) and then to the foot (620m, 41970 87540) of the steep rocky N ridge of **Kirriereoch Hill**. Climb the ridge to the summit. The highest point isn't the cairn on the wall that crosses the summit, nor the shelter/large cairn, but a small cairn on a flat summit (3hr 50min, 786m, 42070 86980).

Return to the ruined wall and follow it down the W ridge. When the wall veers left (580m, 40170 87050) keep straight on along the line of rusted fence posts, which soon veer right, and follow them down to a fence on the edge of the forest. Follow this fence down to a stile (4hr 45min, 320m, 38940 87670). Cross the fence to the left of the stile and go down the wide, rough, boggy ride until you reach a forest road (275m, 37650 87890). Turn

Walking the Corbetts: Vol 1

left and follow the road, ignoring twists and turns, until you reach the picnic site beside the Water of Minnoch (5hr 40min, 215m, 35910 86650).

You could end the walk here if you can organise transport. (The forest road is signed to Kirriereoch from the 'main' road.) Otherwise it is a 5km walk back to the starting point. Continue to the 'main' road, turn right and then right when the road forks (6hr 30min).

ROUTE 3

Corserine CROSS RIDGE

Start	Forrest Lodge car park (NX 55290 86240)
Distance	17km (11 miles)
Total ascent	940m (3100ft)
Difficulty	Easy terrain but with some rough, possibly boggy pasture. Navigation will be difficult in mist.
Time	4hr 25min
Summits	Corserine (814m, 2668ft), Milldown (738m, Donald), Meikle Millyea (746m, Donald)
Map	OS Landranger 77
Access	Take the A712 E from Newton Stewart to New Galloway and then the A762 N. This joins the A713, which you follow N until you see a minor road signed to Forrest Estate on your left. Follow this to the car park at the end of the road just before Forrest Lodge.
Note	If you can arrange transport, you could start at the parking place for Route 4 and traverse over the ridge from Coran of Portmark to Corserine and on to Meikle Millyea, ticking off another three or four Donalds.

Corserine, a grassy hill with broad ridges, is the highest point on the long ridge that extends from Loch Doon to Clattershaws Loch. The peaks are surrounded by the commercial forestry of the Galloway Forest Park. The suggested route climbs to the summit of Corserine then follows the ridge S over the Rhinns of Kells to Meikle Millyea.

ROUTE 3 – CORSERINE

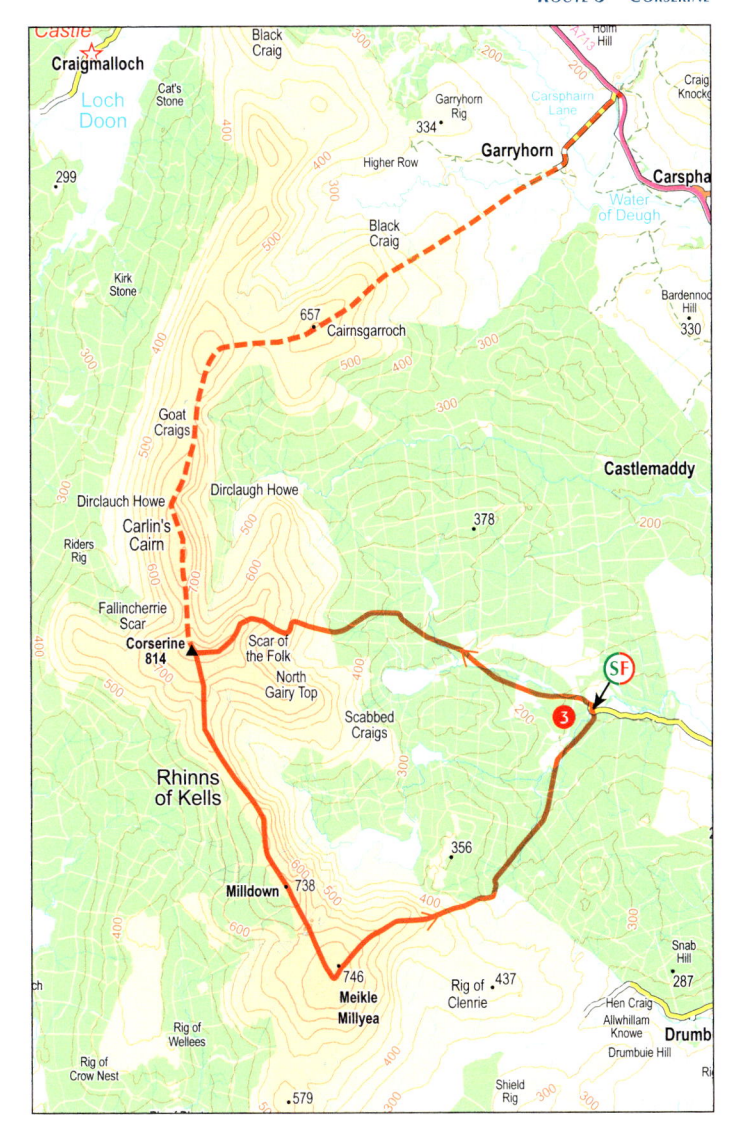

WALKING THE CORBETTS: VOL 1

It is worth heading up the entrance of Forrest Lodge to see the **figurehead** from the liner *Black Watch*, which was commandeered by the Germans when they invaded Norway in World War II. The liner was sunk in shallow water on 5 May 1945 by the Fleet Air Arm. Twenty years later the liner was salvaged for scrap and the figurehead found its way to Forrest Lodge.

Head N from the car park towards Forrest Lodge, along the red route, and turn left up the first forest road (Birger Natvig Road). Keep straight on past Fore Bush Cottage and up to a track junction (20min, 245m, 53540 86830). Fork right up Robert Watson Road and continue, ignoring signs to Loch Harrow, until you reach a left turn signed to a stile over the deer fence (335m, 52550 87440). Turn left, then fork left along a poor track before turning right across the burn up a faint path (365m, 52040 87340) to the deer fence (50min, 400m, 51780 87270). Cross the fence and follow a faint path W, which leads to a small cairn on the W ridge of Corserine (745m, 50650 87410). This path could be difficult to follow in descent. Continue up the ridge and on to the trig point at the far end of **Corserine**'s summit plateau (1hr 45min, 814m, 49790 87060).

Black Watch figurehead at Forrest Lodge

The Rhinns of Kells from Corserine

54

Descend S to a saddle (680m) and a second saddle (628m, 50290 85540) before climbing to Millfire (716m, 50830 84790), and continue along the ridge until you cross a ruined wall (695m, 50860 84270). Follow the wall that heads S along the ridge over **Milldown** (738m), down to a saddle with several small ponds (650m) and up to **Meikle Millyea**. The trig point is just to the left of the wall, just after a wall branches off left. The SW summit appears to be higher than the trig point (3hr 10min, 746m, 51840 82890).

Return to the wall junction and follow it ENE all the way down to the deer fence protecting the forest. Climb a barrier and continue between the deer fence and the wall to a stile (3hr 55min, 305m, 53890 83830). Cross the fence and head N up a rough forest ride to a forest track. Turn right along the green route, cross the Kristin Olsen Road and keep straight on down Prof Hans Heiberg Road, ignoring all turns, back to the car park (4hr 25min).

ROUTE 4

Cairnsmore of Carsphairn

BIG CAIRN-LIKE PEAK OF THE ALDER-COVERED VALLEY

Start	Bridgend Cottage near Carsphairn (NX 55730 94450)
Distance	12km (8 miles)
Total ascent	680m (2200ft)
Difficulty	Easy terrain but with some rough, possibly boggy pasture
Time	3hr 35min
Summit	Cairnsmore of Carsphairn (797m, 2614ft)
Map	OS Landranger 77
Access	Take the A712 E from Newton Stewart to New Galloway and then the A762 N. This joins the A713, which you follow N until 1 mile N of Carsphairn, There is limited parking where the A713 crosses Bow Burn at Bridgend Cottage.
Note	It would be easier to descend by the ascent route or to descend W from Dunool or Willieanna.

Walking the Corbetts: Vol 1

Cairnsmore of Carsphairn is a grassy hill with broad ridges, surrounded by steep slopes. There are magnificent views in all directions from the summit.

About 100m from the start of the walk you pass the **'Green Well of Scotland'**, now just a boggy pond. One legend suggests that a pot of gold was stolen from Lagwyne Castle and the thief threw it into the well; another tells that a man who had collected gold dust from the Gold Wells of Cairnsmore and converted it into coins, threw the coins into the well when officers of the crown came to see him. A gold coin has been found there!

A hoard of 2222 ancient coins was found at nearby Craigengillan in 1913, including Scottish pennies from the times of Alexander III, John Balliol and Robert Bruce. It is thought that they were buried in the early 14th century.

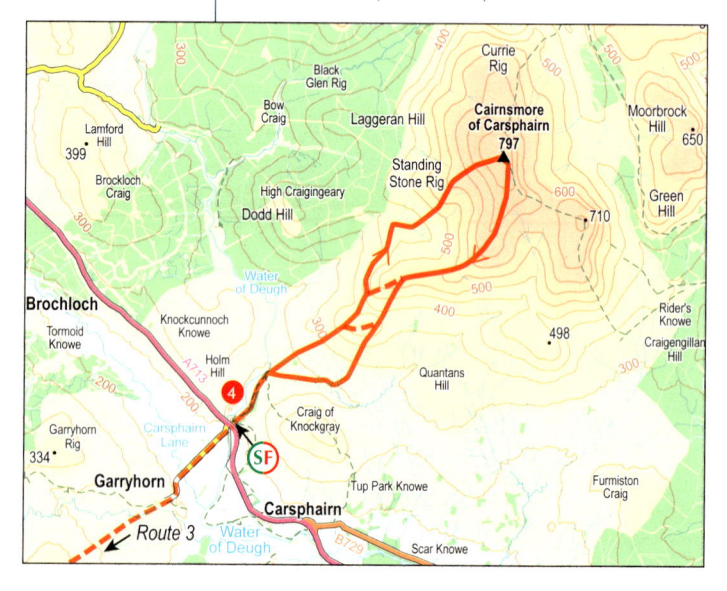

ROUTE 4 – CAIRNSMORE OF CARSPHAIRN

Take the track NE from Bridgend Cottage to the right of Bow Burn and follow it to its end where a wall joins from the left (1hr, 425m, 57850 97110). Follow the wall all the way to the trig point and summit cairn on **Cairnsmore of Carsphairn** (1hr 50min, 797m, 59450 97980).

Descend the S ridge, veering right to Black Shoulder (680m, 59270 96790) where you reach a wall end. At the time of writing there were piles of new posts suggesting that a fence will extend up the ridge from the wall end. Go down the right-hand side of the wall and follow it over Dunool (541m, 57970 96400), down to a saddle (395m) and over Willieanna (430m, 57630 95800) and down to the Benloch Burn (3hr 5min, 260m, 57230 94970). Turn right along the N bank of the burn. When you come to a barbed-wire fence you will find it easier to cross the fence on your left and follow animal tracks between the fence and the burn back to the track up Bow Burn (200m, 56170 95100). Turn left down the track back to the start (3hr 35min).

Cairnsmore of Carsphain

ROUTE 5
Hart Fell STAG HILL

Start	Old Edinburgh Road, N of Moffat (NT 07510 10330)
Distance	14km (9 miles)
Total ascent	770m (2500ft)
Difficulty	Steep but easy terrain
Time	3hr 50min
Summits	Hart Fell (808m, 2651ft), Whitehope Heights (637m, Donald)
Map	OS Landranger 78
Access	Follow the Old Edinburgh Road (now a no-through road) N from Moffat. There is limited parking just before the Auchencat Burn, 3 miles N of Moffat, and a large car park about 200m further up the road.
Note	It is possible to extend the walk over Chalk Rig Edge and Great Hill and descend into the Devil's Beef Tub. The approach up Blackhope Burn from the A708 to the SE also looks interesting on the map but the author has no knowledge of this route.

Hart Fell is a grassy hill with broad ridges, surrounded by steep slopes. There are magnificent views in all directions from the summit.

Hartfell Spa is a spring that was discovered in 1748. The 'chalybeate' water from the spring contained iron and calcium minerals, which were reputed to have health-giving properties. Regular runs were made by coach up the valley to Hartfell Spa. Recently restored, the spring is now protected by a short vaulted tunnel.

Follow a faint path, signposted to Hartfell Spa, which climbs above the left bank of the Auchencat Burn. Above the mountain wall you join a grassy track – follow this until a path forks off left to Hartfell Spa, which is further

Route 5 – Hart Fell

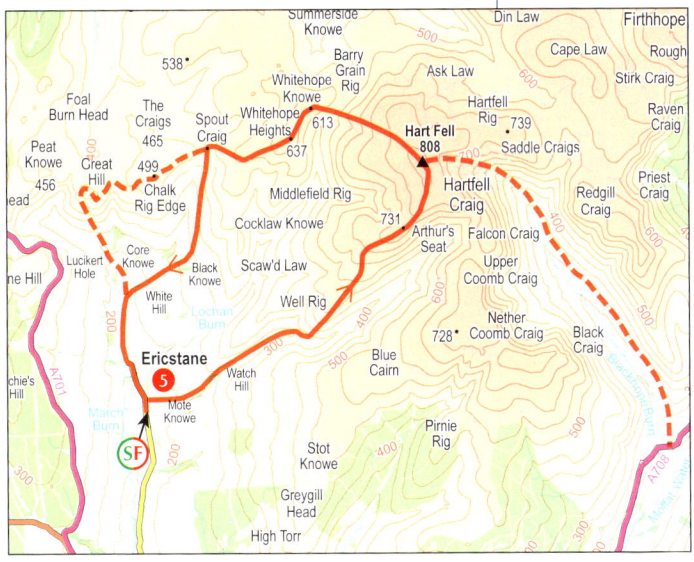

Auchencat Burn on Hart Fell

up the gully (35min, 330m, 09330 11450). Take the right fork, which descends 20m to the bottom of the gully, and then climb steeply up the grassy ridge to the right of the gully. When you reach a fence, turn left along it until you come to a gate (545m, 10160 12030). Follow the grassy track up to **Arthur's Seat** (731m, 11120 12670), continue until you reach a fence and follow this left to the trig point on the summit of **Hart Fell** (1hr 55min, 808m, 11360 13560).

Follow the fence NW, then turn left along a fence which takes you down a steep grass slope to the saddle between Hart Fell and Whitehope Knowe (530m, 10230 14360). Follow the fence as it climbs steeply to **Whitehope Knowe** and **Whitehope Heights** (2hr 35min, 637m, 09580 13900). Follow the fence that veers right, ignoring a fence going off left, and descend to a saddle with a large cairn. This cairn marks the N end of the Annandale Way, which follows the River Annan from 'Sea to Source' (2hr 55min, 445m, 08361 13838).

Turn left down this faint footpath, which descends above the left bank of the burn. When you reach a fence, go through the gate and turn right along the fence. Go through a gate and go diagonally left to the bottom left-hand corner of the field, then follow the waymarked route to the right of a small wood and down to the road by a wooden bridge (3hr 30min, 185m, 07220 11790). There is plenty of parking here and those with two cars could save themselves the 2km road walk back to the starting point (3hr 50min).

Terminal cairn for the Annandale Way

ROUTE 6
White Coomb WHITE VALLEY

Start	Grey Mare's Tail Waterfall car park (NT 18630 14500)
Distance	9km (6 miles)
Total ascent	670m (2200ft)
Difficulty	Steep but easy terrain
Time	2hr 40min
Summit	White Coomb (821m, 2695ft)
Map	OS Landranger 79
Access	Follow the A708 NW from Moffat to a large National Trust of Scotland car park at the Grey Mare's Tail Waterfall.
Note	In bad weather you may prefer to climb the mountain by the described descent route, returning the same way.

White Coomb is a rounded grassy hill on a dissected plateau with magnificent views in all directions. White Coomb is best known for the Grey Mare's Tail Waterfall, which is a tourist attraction. Look out for the herd of wild goats that frequent this mountain.

Grey Mare's Tail Waterfall drops 60m as the Tail Burn plunges down a hanging valley scoured out by glaciers during the last ice age. Sir Walter Scott fell off his horse on a visit here and wrote, 'As we were groping through the maze of bogs, the ground gave way, and down went horse and horsemen pell-mell into a slough of peaty mud and black water.'

There is an iron-age fort beside the car park, which suggests the area was inhabited over 2000 years ago.

Head 100m up Tail Burn from the car park then cross the footbridge to some display boards on the right. Follow a good path up the slopes above the E bank of the burn

WALKING THE CORBETTS: VOL 1

Walkers resting by Loch Skeen below Lochcraig Head

(ignoring the path on the W bank to the foot of the waterfall). The path returns to the burn and continues up to **Loch Skeen** (35min, 510m, 17410 15970). Now follow a rough path W then NW up the grassy ridge to the W of Loch Skeen until the path fades away at a minor summit (729m, 16400 16440). Head SW down a gentle grass slope to the top of a gully, **Donalds Cleuch Head** (16060 16270), and continue SW up a small burn until you reach a wall on a ridgeline (1hr 25min, 770m, 15380 15700).

Turn left along the wall on a grassy path to the summit of **Firthhope Rig** (800m) then turn left along a ruined

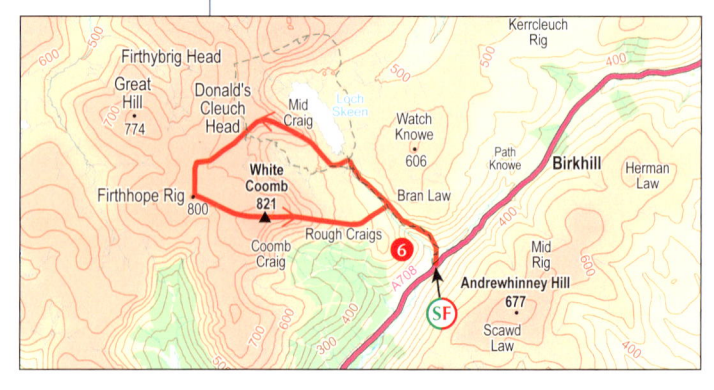

Route 7 – Broad Law

wall backed by a new fence. When the fence turns right you should go 100m diagonally right along a faint path to the small cairn on the summit of **White Coomb** (1hr 40min, 821m, 16320 15090).

Return to the ruined wall and descend steeply down a rough path to the left of the wall. The wall veers left to take you back to Tail Burn just above the waterfalls (2hr 20min, 465m, 17990 15240). Cross the burn and follow the path back to the car park (2hr 40min).

ROUTE 7

Broad Law BROAD ROUNDED HILL

Start	The Megget Stone (NT 15060 20290)
Distance	22km (14 miles)
Total ascent	920m (3000ft)
Difficulty	Easy walking with easy navigation
Time	4hr 50min
Summits	Broad Law (840m, 2754ft), Cramalt Craig (831m, Donald), Dollar Law (817m, Donald)
Map	OS Landranger 72
Access	From Moffat, follow the A701 to Tweedsmuir where you turn left along a minor road past the Talla Reservoir. The Megget Stone is an insignificant stone beside the cattle grid at the top of the road pass, where there is limited roadside parking. There is a car park at the Cramalt Monument (NT 19610 22830) beside the Megget Reservoir if you want to do the road walk first or can organise two vehicles.
Note	In bad weather, or if you want a short walk, you could descend from Broad Law by the ascent route.

This route follows the broad grassy ridge between Broad Law and Dollar Law to the NW of the Megget Reservoir. There are magnificent views in all directions. Cramalt Craig was listed as a Corbett until the metric edition of the OS map suggested the drop between it and Broad Law was only 145m (480ft).

WALKING THE CORBETTS: VOL 1

Cramalt Tower was a 15th-century stronghold, four storeys high, with its own pit prison for captured reivers and other outlaws. Border Reivers were mounted raiders from the late 13th century to the end of the 16th century. Coming from both Scottish and English families, they raided on either side of the border without regard to nationality. The tower has been moved and partially rebuilt after being flooded by the opening of the Megget Reservoir in 1983.

Follow a faint path NW up the right-hand side of a fence. This is followed all the way to the summit of **Broad Law**

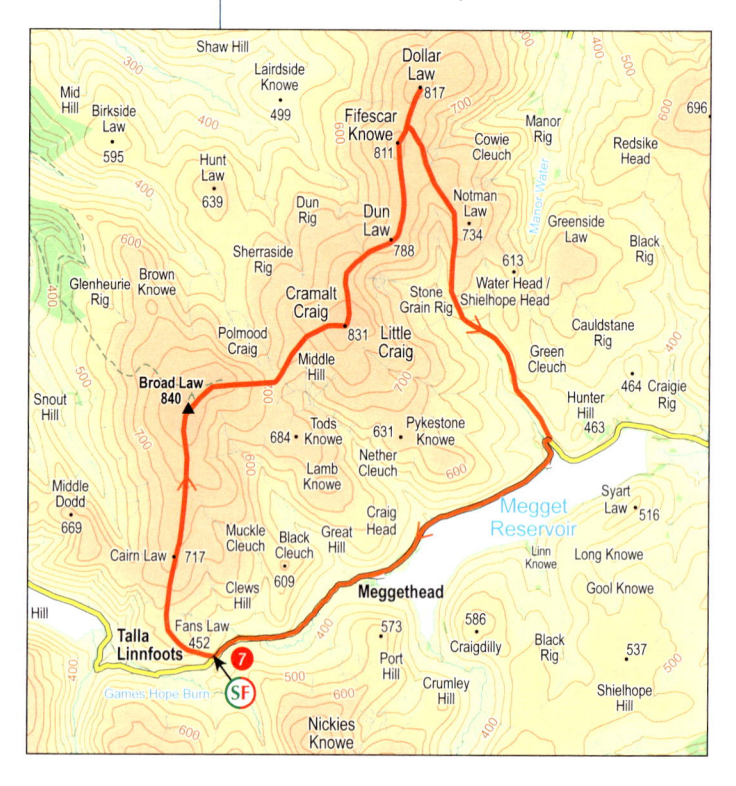

ROUTE 7 – BROAD LAW

where there is a trig point and the Talla Navigational Aid, which would look more at home in outer space than on a mountain top (1hr, 840m, 14640 23530).

Continue along the fence, cross a wall and pass a communications mast. Follow the fence down to a broad saddle (690m) and cross a new fence on the climb to **Cramalt Craig** (1hr 45min, 831m, 16850 24740). Turn left along the fence down to a saddle (755m) and up to **Dun Law** (788m, 17500 25830). Continue along the fence and when you come to a fence junction, continue along the ruined wall over **Fifescar Knowe** (811m, 17520 27080) and follow the wall to the trig point on the summit of **Dollar Law** (2hr 35min, 817m, 17820 27830).

Retrace your steps to the saddle between Dollar Law and Fifescar Knowe and take the path to the left where the wall bends right (795m, 17700 27360). In just under 1km you reach a fence corner (2hr 50min, 750m, 18050 26590). Climb the gate. Don't follow the path on the other side but head S into the valley on your right and

Craigdilly across Megget Reservoir

follow this down to the start of a hill track (660m, 18130 26080) which is followed all the way down to the reservoir (3hr 40min, 340m, 19590 23170). Unless you have organised transport back to the start you will now have to walk 6km up the road back to your starting point (4hr 50min).

2 ARRAN AND JURA

Goatfell seen from a cottage in Glen Rosa (Routes 8 and 9)

Arran and Jura: Bases and facilities

Base for Routes 8 and 9: Brodick, Arran

Brodick is a village with plenty of accommodation and good facilities for tourists.

Tourist Information Office: There is a Visitor information Office on the pier at Brodick, but advance enquiries should go to the Ayr Tourist Office, VisitScotland, Burns House, 16 Burns Statue Square, Ayr, KA7 1UT Tel: 0845 22 55 121

Glen Rosa campsite (NS 00100 37620) is an ideal base for climbing the Corbetts. It is an old-fashioned site with a wilderness feel and only limited facilities. No caravans and only car-size campervans. Tel: 01770 302 380
www.arrancamping.co.uk

Other facilities for Routes 8 and 9: Lochranza, Arran

Lochranza is not a good base for climbing the Corbetts unless you have transport, but it does have an SYHA hostel: Lochranza SYHA, Isle of Arran, KA27 8HL Tel: 01770 830 631

Base for Route 10: Craighouse, Jura

The small village of Craighouse has a shop, teahouse, hotel and the Isle of Jura Distillery. It is possible to camp at the Jura Hotel Tel: 01496 820 243 www.jurahotel.co.uk

There is no tourist office on Jura. Enquiries should go to the tourist office at Bowmore on Islay Tel: 01496 810 254

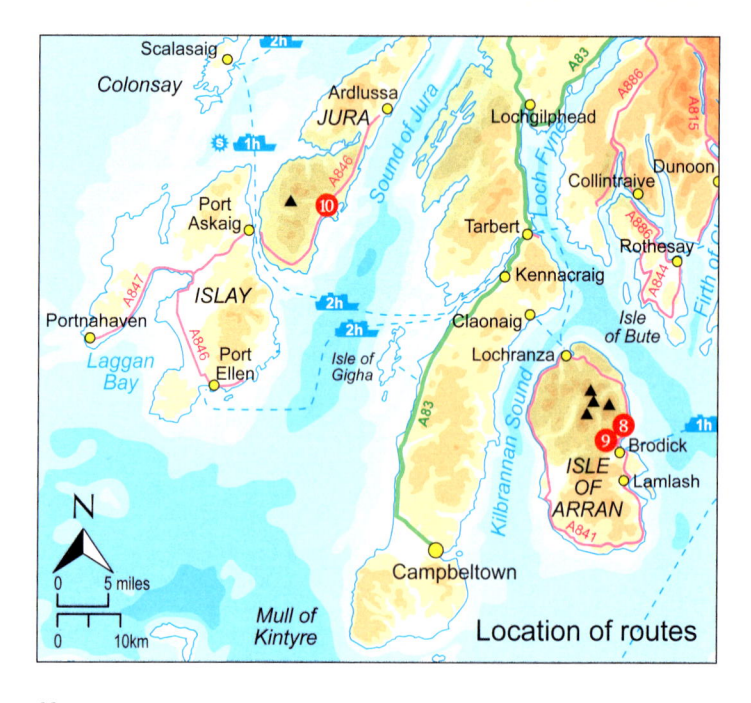

Access to Arran and Jura

Ferries to Arran

Caledonian MacBrayne operates a car ferry service from Ardrossan, on the A78 N of Ayr, to Brodick, on Arran, with 4–6 sailings/day throughout the year. Crossing time: 55min.

Calmac also runs a car ferry service from Claonaig on the Kintyre peninsular to Lochranza on the N coast of Arran, with 7–9 sailings/day from April to October. Crossing time: 30min www.calmac.co.uk

Ferries to Jura

Access to Jura is not easy and is probably best combined with a visit to Arran by taking the car ferry from Lochranza on Arran to Claonaig on Kintyre. Then cross the peninsular to Kennacraig and take the Caledonian MacBrayne car ferry to Port Askaig on the island of Islay (2–4 crossings/day). Crossing time: 2hr. ASP Ship Management Ltd runs a regular car ferry from Port Askaig on Islay to Feolin on Jura. Crossing time: 5min. If not visiting Arran you will need to take the A83 down the Kintyre peninsular to reach Kennacraig. www.calmac.co.uk; www.islayinfo.com/jura-ferry.html

It is worth considering parking at Kennacraig, Lochranza or Ardrossan and cycling to the islands. It will be cheaper than taking the car and the short driving distances on the islands make cycling a feasible proposition.

At the time of writing there is a summer (Friday–Monday) passenger ferry from Tayvallich (NR 74200 87200) on the B8025 W of Lochgilphead to Craighouse on Jura, with a crossing time of about one hour. You will need to check before depending on this ferry as funding is not guaranteed for future years. Tel: 07768 450 000 www.jurapassengerferry.com

Walking the Corbetts: Vol 1

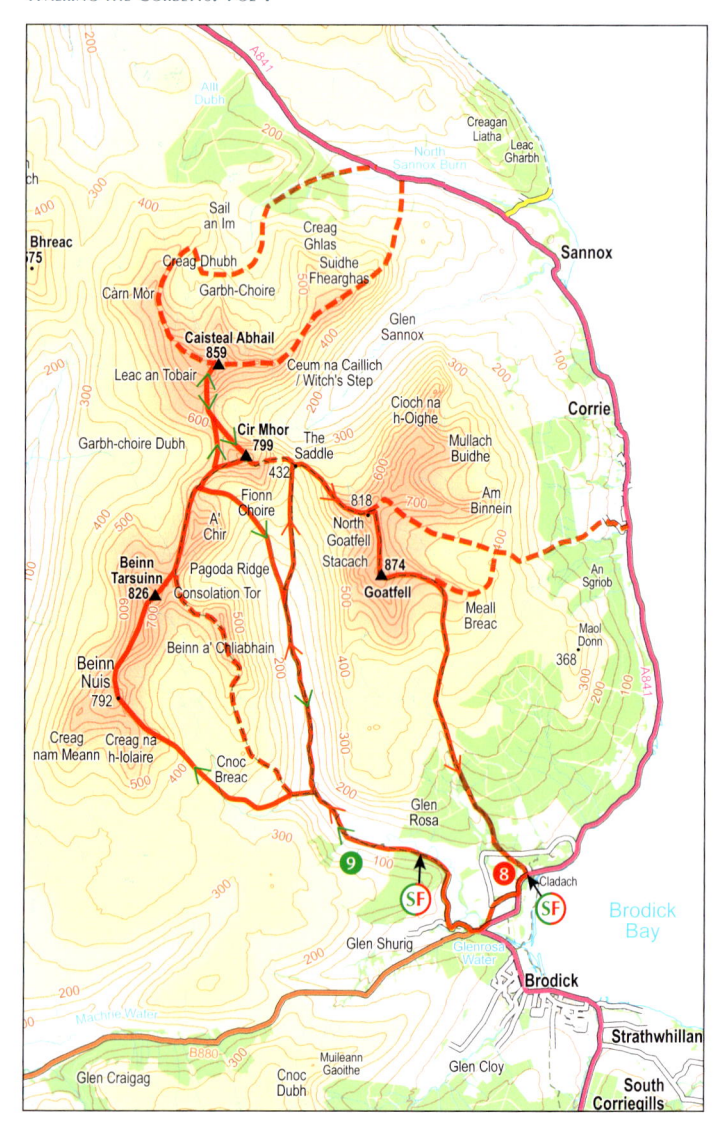

ROUTE 8
Goatfell GOAT HILL

Start	Cladach (NS 01270 37570)
Distance	17km (10 miles)
Total ascent	1000m (3300ft)
Difficulty	There is a maintained path for most of the ascent and all of the descent. The upper slopes of the NW ridge of North Goatfell require some easy but exposed scrambling on granite slabs. The difficulties on the ridge between North Goatfell and Goatfell can be avoided by following paths below the tors.
Time	5hr
Summit	Goatfell (874m, 2868ft)
Map	OS Landranger 69
Access	Head N along the A841 from Brodick to Cladach where there is a large car park (NS 01270 37570). If you are camped in Glen Rosa it would be natural to start from there and complete the road walk at the end.
Note	It would be easier to ascend and descend the 'tourist path' from Cladach. The ascent on good paths from Corrie on the east coast would also be easy, but more interesting. Routes 8 and 9 could be combined as described under Route 9.

Goatfell, the highest peak on Arran, is the SE peak on the rocky ridge surrounding Glen Rosa. It is the easiest of the Corbetts on Arran to climb as a 'tourist path' has been built up the mountain from Cladach. The approach up Glen Rosa is much more interesting.

Brodick Castle is owned by the National Trust of Scotland. It offers visitors a remarkably complete example of a stately home with excellent gardens and a country park. The castle is open to the public during the summer and the country park is open all year.

The first fortifications on the site were probably built by the Vikings, who occupied Arran until they were driven from the western seaboard of Scotland, following the Battle of Largs in 1263. Several castles were built and destroyed during the Wars of Independence and the clan battles between the Campbells and the MacLeans. It wasn't until after 1844 that the Hamilton family started construction of the major parts of the castle that can be seen today.

Follow the A841 towards Brodick and turn right along a dirt road opposite 'Arran's Cheese Shop'. At the end turn left along a tarmac road, right over the bridge, then right towards Blackwaterfoot and right up the narrow road to Glen Rosa campsite (30min, 20m, NS 00120 37610). Follow the track through the left-hand gate at the end of the campsite. The track eventually becomes a well-maintained path, which is followed all the way to **The Saddle** between Cir Mhor and North Goatfell (2hr 5min, 432m, NR 97900 43020).

Walker beside a tor on the NW ridge of North Goatfell

Turn right up the maintained path up the NW ridge of North Goatfell. Towards the top of the ridge the engineered path ends and there is some easy but exposed scrambling on granite slabs. A cairn is reached just N of the summit of North Goatfell from where there is a path NE then SE down to the Corrie Burn and Corrie. Ignoring this path, head SSE to the rocky summit of **North Goatfell** (3hr, 818m, NR 99000 42270). There are a number of granite tors on the ridge between North Goatfell and Goatfell, but these can be bypassed by taking good paths on the E face below the crags to reach the trig point and viewpoint indicator on the summit of **Goatfell** (3hr 25min, 874m, NR 99140 41530).

Follow the 'tourist path' E to a junction (625m, NR 99840 41490) on **Meall Breac** where you fork right and then veer S to cross a leat (small canal) (295m, NS 00030 39590), which was probably built to provide water for Brodick Castle. Continue down the Cnocan Burn and keep straight on as the path becomes a track in the woods. Cross a road and fork right to reach Cladach and the car park (5hr).

WALKING THE CORBETTS: VOL 1

ROUTE 9

Beinn Tarsuinn TRANSVERSE HILL,
Caisteal Abhail FORKED CASTLE
and *Cir Mhor* BIG COMB

Start	Glen Rosa campsite (NR 99670 37880)
Distance	19km (12 miles)
Total ascent	1620m (5300ft)
Difficulty	The suggested route is mainly straightforward walking on good paths, as the paths wind around the difficulties. However, there are some sections where the use of hands is required, but the scrambling is easy. This is not the place for inexperienced walkers in bad weather.
Time	7hr 55min
Summits	Beinn Tarsuinn (826m, 2706ft), Caisteal Abhail (859m, 2817ft), Cir Mhor (799m, 2618ft)
Map	OS Landranger 69
Access	Head N along the A841 from Brodick then turn left along the B880 towards Blackwaterfoot and almost immediately turn right up Glen Rosa. At the campsite you can continue another 500m along a track to a small parking area. It is not advisable to take large vehicles up Glen Rosa.
Note	The recommended route is a splendid expedition; however, many walkers will want more time to savour these magnificent mountains and might prefer to climb the mountains separately. It would also be possible to include Goatfell in a very demanding traverse by descending the E ridge of Cir Mhor to The Saddle and continuing as described in Route 8.

These three Corbetts provide the finest walking in this guidebook. The granite crags, outcrops and slabs provide dramatic mountain scenery and these popular mountains are served with a good path network. For those who want more difficult scrambling there are plenty of opportunities to take to the rock rather than follow the paths. The optional traverse of the A' Chir

ROUTE 9 – BEINN TARSUINN, CAISTEAL ABHAIL AND CIR MHOR

ridge is graded as a Grade II rock climb (moderate) with short avoidable problems at Grade III standard (Very Difficult).

For those wanting to climb these Corbetts separately the suggestion is to climb Beinn Tarsuinn by its S ridge (Beinn Nuis) and descending by the SE ridge (Beinn Chliabhain). Cir Mhor could be climbed from Glen Rosa, climbing the E ridge from The Saddle and descending as described below. Caisteal Abhail could be climbed from the North Glen Sannox car park (NR 99340 46800) on the A841 NW of Sannox, possibly climbing the NE ridge and descending the NW ridge.

Arran is very interesting geologically because the **Highland Boundary Fault** runs through the middle of the island. The Corbetts are to the N of the fault line and are part of a large granite batholith that was created by substantial volcanic activity around 60 million years ago. The granite provides good rock for the many scrambling routes on these mountains.

▶ Pass through the gate and head up **Glen Rosa**. The track becomes a well-maintained path by the time the bridge over the Garbh Allt is reached (25min, 55m, 98250 38660). Cross the bridge and turn left up the path alongside the burn. The OS map shows the path crossing the burn when it splits, but the path now stays to the N of the burn. After another 400m (330m, 96970 38740) take a path steeply down to cross the burn in a small gorge and climb out the other side. The path now leaves the burn and heads NW up the ridge to the summit of **Beinn Nuis** (2hr 20min, 792m, 95570 39910).

Follow the path easily NNE to the summit of **Beinn Tarsuinn** which has twin tops, both with rock outcrops rather than cairns marking the summit. The N top appears to be higher (3hr, 826m, 96020 41270).

Care is needed on the steep descent NE from Beinn Tarsuinn down steep grass with granite outcrops to a cairn on the saddle between Beinn Tarsuinn and A' Chir (3hr 20min, 635m, 96310 41570). There is now the option of traversing the A' Chir ridge, but this is a

See map just before Route 8.

Granite outcrop on Beinn Tarsuinn

difficult scramble/ easy rock climb (see above). Walkers will fork left along the path, which drops 100m as it traverses easily below the slabs coming down from the A' Chir ridge before climbing to a cairn on the saddle between A' Chir and Cir Mhor (3hr 55min, 590m, 96810 42850). Follow the path a little way up towards Cir Mhor then fork left at a small cairn to contour across to the saddle (624m, 96820 43590) between Cir Mhor and Caisteal Abhail. Climb the S ridge of **Caisteal Abhail**, passing a spring marked by a large cairn (700m, 96670 43860) to the S top of Caisteal Abhail (834m, 96850 44270). Don't confuse this top with the summit, which is a granite tor about 100m to the ENE. The summit tor is easiest to climb from the back (NE) (4hr 55min, 859m, 92920 44320).

Retrace your steps down the S ridge and then follow the path up the NW ridge of **Cir Mhor**, veering right to join the path up the SW ridge to reach the rocky summit (5hr 55min, 799m, 97290 43100).

Return down the SW ridge to the cairn on the saddle between Cir Mhor and A' Chir (590m, 96810 42860) and turn left down a 'staircase' which leads into **Fionn Choire**. Follow the path down to join the main path up Glen Rosa (6hr 55min, 165m 97830 41360). Head back down Glen Rosa to the campsite (7hr 55min).

ROUTE 10

Beinn an Oir (The Paps of Jura)

HILL OF GOLD

Start	Corran River (NR 54490 72060)
Distance	13km (8 miles)
Total ascent	1080m (3600ft)
Difficulty	The most difficult part of the suggested route is the ascent of Beinn Shiantaidh up boulderfield and scree. The descent of Beinn Shiantaidh and ascent of Beinn an Oir is surprisingly easy on these difficult mountains.
Time	5hr 30min
Summits	Beinn Shiantaidh (757m, Graham), Beinn an Oir (785m, 2571ft)
Map	OS Landranger 61
Access	From the ferry jetty at Feolin follow the A846 8 miles round the S of the island to Craighouse. Follow the shoreline of Small Isles Bay for a further 3 miles then, after another mile, park beside the Corran River.
Note	It would be much easier to omit Beinn Shiantaidh by heading straight for the pass between Beinn Shiantaidh and Beinn an Oir. However, the climb of Beinn Shiantaidh gives a truer taste of the roughness of the Paps of Jura than the ascent of Beinn an Oir.

WALKING THE CORBETTS: VOL 1

Beinn an Oir is the highest of the three boulder, crag and scree-covered Paps of Jura, which dominate the island of Jura. This is one of the roughest mountain ranges in Scotland and you can expect any walks in these mountains to take a lot longer than suggested by the distances involved.

If you want a real challenge try walking the route of the **Jura Fell Race**, one of the toughest races in Scotland. The race is held at the end of May each year, starting and finishing at Craighouse and covering 16 miles with 7500ft of climbing over seven mountain summits. The route goes over Dubh Bheinn, Glas Bheinn, Beinn Mhearsamail, Beinn a' Chaolais, Beinn an Oir, Beinn Shiantaidh and Corra Bheinn. You will do very well to complete this tough route in a day. The record time in the race is an amazing 3hr 7min for men and 3hr 40min for ladies.

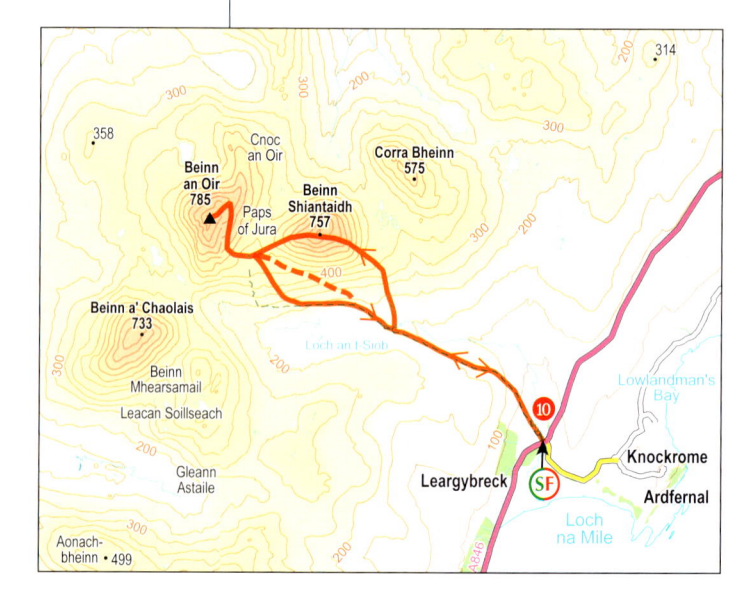

ROUTE 10 – BEINN AN OIR (THE PAPS OF JURA)

Follow the path signed 'Pap Walk' up the W bank of the Corran River. The often boggy path climbs away from the river before returning to it at the outlet of **Loch an t-Siob** (55min, 170m, 52260 73560). Cross the river on big stepping stones and climb N to the SE ridge of **Beinn Shiantaidh** (at about 345m, 52190 74390) and head up the ridge. ▶ Continue up a mixture of moss, boulderfield and scree to the summit cairn (2hr 15min, 757m, 51360 74770).

Head down the W ridge. There is a path that you should locate and follow as it takes you easily through the crags and gives a descent that is mainly on grass to arrive at the broad pass between Beinn Shiantaidh and Beinn an Oir (2hr 50min, 450m, 50630 74620). Head WSW to the obvious path, which soon turns N up a ramp on the E face of Beinn an Oir. When the path fades away by a ruined shelter (630m, 50130 74960) head NW up the slope towards a prominent crag on the ridge, which is reached by another ruined shelter (750m, 49940 75060). Turn left along the easy ridge to the trig point, surrounded

Beinn Shiantaidh from Beinn an Oir

At about 450m a path comes up from the right, but there isn't much point in following it left as it just fades away on the S face of the mountain.

by a sheltering wall, on the summit of **Beinn an Oir** (3hr 35min, 785m, 49830 74960).

Return to the pass between Beinn Shiantaidh and Beinn an Oir and then head SE down easy grass slopes to reach a faint path (at about 250m, 50800 73820). Turn left back to the outlet of Loch an t-Siob (4hr 40min), cross the burn and follow the path back to the parking place (5hr 30min).

3 WEST OF LOCH LOMOND (ARROCHAR ALPS)

Loch Long (Route 13)

West of Loch Lomond (Arrochar Alps): Bases and facilities

Base for Routes 11–17: Arrochar and Ardgartan

Arrochar is on the A83 at the head of Loch Long just W of Loch Lomond, and Ardgartan is a couple of miles W of Arrochar on the NW shore of Loch Long.

Arrochar is a small village with a couple of shops and plenty of accommodation and eating/drinking places for tourists.

Ardgartan Visitor Centre and Tourist Office: Open April–October, 10.00am–5.00pm Tel: 01301 702 432

Ardgartan campsite: Camping, caravans, cabins, cafe and small shop. Tel: 01301 702 293 www.forestholidays.co.uk

Local facilities for Route 11: Lochgoilhead

Lochgoilhead is at the head of Loch Goil at the S end of the B828, which leaves the A83 at the Rest and be Thankful Pass.

Argyll Holidays run the Lochgoilhead Hotel and the Drimsyne Estate Hotel and Holiday Village, with all facilities open to non-residents: Hotel, static

caravans, cabins and a small but well-stocked shop. Tel: 01301 703 344
www.argyllholidays.com

Local facilities for Route 17: Ardlui and Inverarnan

Ardlui is on the A82 at the N end of Loch Lomond. Ardlui Holiday Home Park includes Ardlui Hotel, static caravans, cabins and space for touring caravans and camping, as well as a small shop. Tel: 01301 704 243 www.ardlui.com

Inverarnan, just N of Ardlui, has the Drovers Inn and Lodge.
Tel: 01301 704 234 www.thedroversinn.co.uk

Beinglas Farm campsite, which is 500m N of Inverarnan, also has self-catering accommodation, a bar, restaurant and a small shop.
Tel: 01301 704 281 www.beinglascampsite.co.uk.

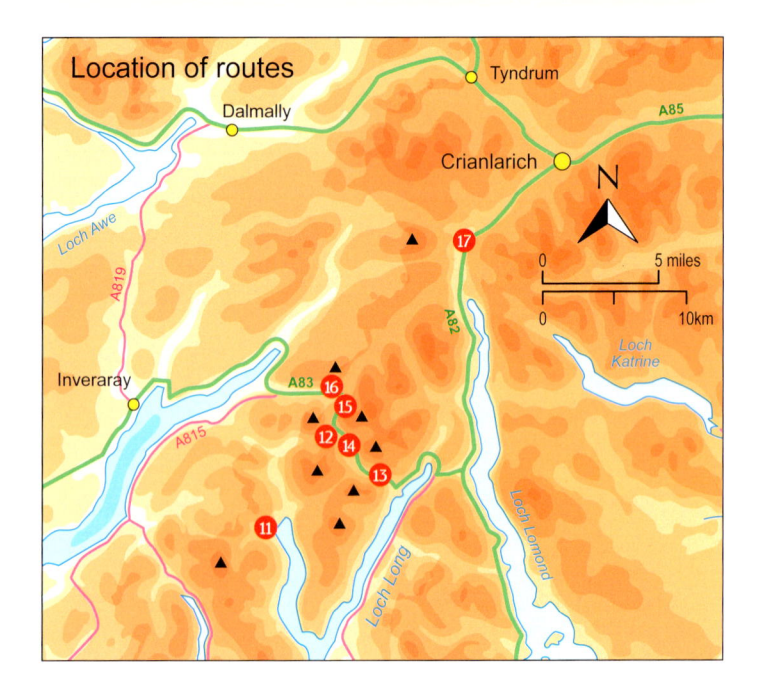

ROUTE 11
Beinn Bheula HILL OF THE FORD

Start	Lettermay, Lochgoilhead (NN 18810 00190)
Distance	13km (8 miles)
Total ascent	880m (2900ft)
Difficulty	There is rough going on the lower mountain. Navigation is demanding on the ridges and route-finding would be very difficult in mist.
Time	3hr 40min
Summit	Beinn Bheula (779m, 2557ft)
Map	OS Landranger 56
Access	Follow the A83 W from Arrochar and the B828 SW from the Rest and be Thankful Pass to Lochgoilhead. Take the minor road down the W side of Loch Goil. There is very limited parking at the unsigned dirt road to Lettermay, just before the school sign.
Note	It would be easier to ascend Beinn Bheula from Invernoaden on the A815 to the W, but this route isn't very interesting.

Beinn Bheula is a steep grassy hill well protected by crags and forestry plantations. The W side of the mountain is more gentle and easier to climb but is much less interesting. The forestry is not well mapped on the OS map and routes given in some other guides are no longer viable.

Beinn Bheula is associated with the Ian Fleming character, **James Bond**. Bond was based on Sir Fitzroy Maclean, the legendary soldier who lived at Strachur at the W foot of the mountain. The mountains above Lochgoilhead were used for the scene in the 1963 film *From Russia with Love* in which Bond (played by Sean Connery) eliminated two villains in a helicopter by firing gunshots at them.

WALKING THE CORBETTS: VOL 1

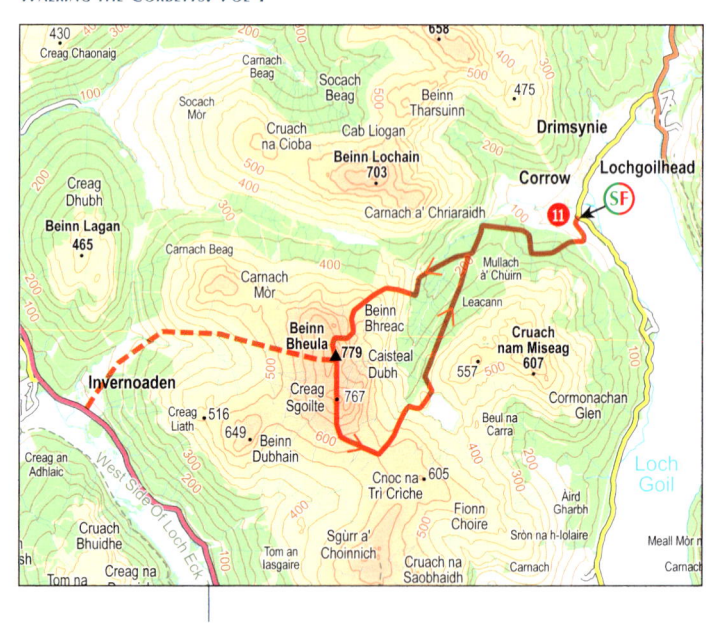

Beinn Bheula from Creag Sgoilte

Follow the road past the cottages at Lettermay, turning left and right onto the forest road through Lettermay Forest. Fork left at the first fork (the old route up the N side of Lettermay Burn is no longer passable) and right at the second fork down a new forest road (25min, 205m, NS 17460 99650), which may not be marked on OS maps. After crossing Lettermay Burn, turn left up a grassy ride, marked by a white post (180m, NS 16980 99550). This ride soon veers right and takes you above the forest. Turn left along a faint path at a waterfall and continue up a grassy ramp when the path fades away. When you reach a fence, cross it and turn right along it to the crest of the ridge (55min, 358m, NS 16370 99240).

Climb the ridge, avoiding the small crags, to a saddle (585m, NS 15690 98820). Rather than heading directly up the crags, you should follow a grassy ramp to the left and cut up a grassy gully to the right and then left along the easy summit ridge to the trig point on **Beinn Bheula** (1hr 55min, 779m, NS 15480 98320).

Descend SSW to a saddle (740m, NS 15420 97970) and veer left to the N summit of **Creag Sgoilte** (767m, NS 15550 97720). ▶ Drop down to the saddle between the two summits and descend SSW down steep grass, then swing back left below the crags, looking out for the remains of a crashed aircraft, to a fence on a broad saddle (2hr 30min, 552m, NS 16080 97120). Turn left down the fence and when you reach the top of the forest cross the burn (370m, NS 16480 97680) and turn right along the top of the forest until you reach a burn (2hr 55min, 395m, NS 16780 97920). Turn left down a faint, rough, often boggy path down the left bank of the burn, then cross the burn and turn right when you reach a forest ride. Follow this down to a forest road (255m, NS 17130 99120) which takes you back to the start (3hr 40min).

Do not attempt to descend the crags on the SE face of Creag Sgoilte.

Walking the Corbetts: Vol 1

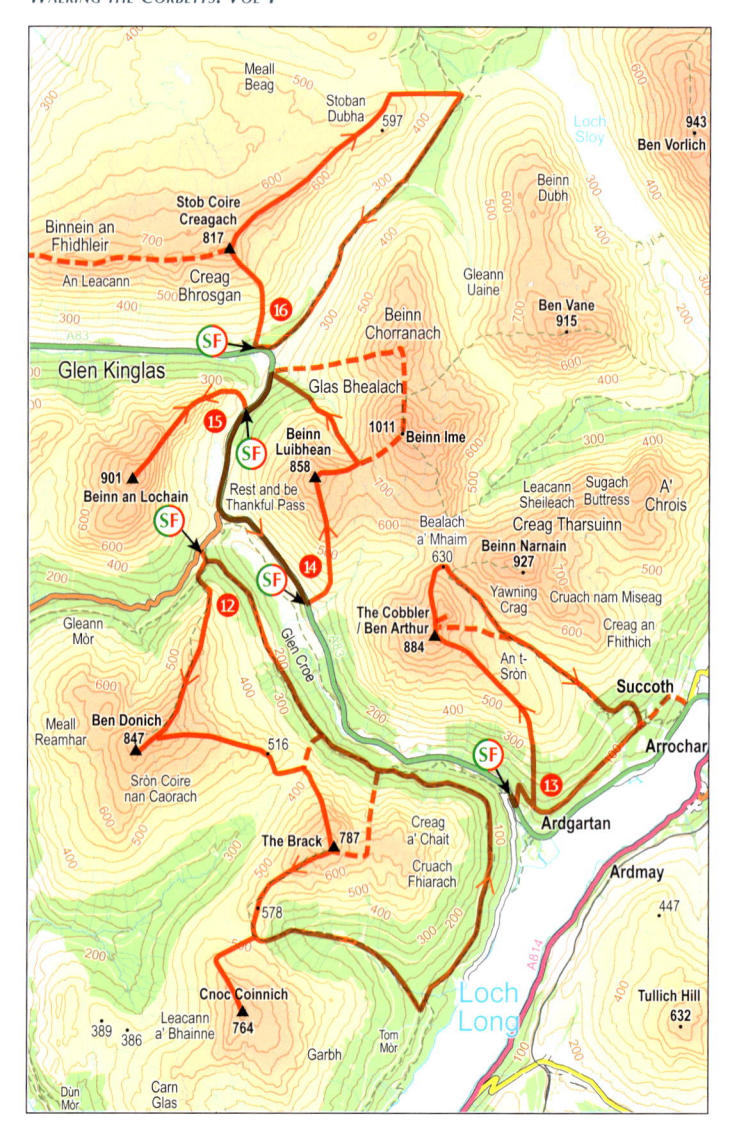

ROUTE 12

Ben Donich BROWN HILL, *The Brack* SPECKLED HILL *and Cnoc Coinnich* MOSSY KNOLL

Start	SW of Rest and be Thankful Pass (NN 22790 06960)
Distance	24km (15 miles)
Total ascent	1650m (5400ft)
Difficulty	The ascent of Ben Donich is on a path and is easy apart from a simple scramble on a small rockstep. The ridges to The Brack and Cnoc Coinnich and the descent from The Brack will test your route-finding ability through a multitude of crags, and could be difficult in mist.
Time	8hr 15min
Summits	Ben Donich (847m, 2774ft), The Brack (787m, 2580ft), Cnoc Coinnich (764m, 2505ft)
Map	OS Landranger 56
Access	Follow the A83 W from Arrochar to the Rest and be Thankful Pass and turn left along the B828 Lochgoilhead road. After 500m there is a forestry road with a car park on your left.
Note	See below for suggestions if you want to climb these Corbetts separately. Cnoc Coinnich was only promoted from Graham status to Corbett status in 2016, well after the research for this guide was done. It has been added to the original Route 12 but some of data and route description has been added without checking the route.

Ben Donich and The Brack are grassy mountains with extensive crags, especially on the NE flanks of The Brack. Access points are rather limited because of the forest surrounding these hills. The route up the NE ridge of Ben Donich is a popular climb.

If you want an up-and-down ascent of Ben Donich you should climb up the NE ridge as for the main route and come down the same way. The shortest way to climb The Brack is to start at the Ardgartan Visitor Centre (26940 03670) and follow the Cat Crag loop. At the first hill access point (25260 03990) pick up a faint path which climbs steeply through the crags protecting the E ridge, then descend the grassy N ridge to Bealach Dubh-lic and follow the white posts down to the second access point (24120 04780) and return to Creagdhu.

WALKING THE CORBETTS: VOL 1

'Rest-and-be-Thankful' are the words that were engraved on a **stone** near the junction of the A83 and the B828, placed there in 1753 by the soldiers who built the original military road. The original stone fell into ruin and was replaced by a commemorative stone at the same site. The climb out of Glen Croe is so long and steep at the end that it was traditional to rest at the top, and be thankful that you had got to the highest point.

Head S up the forestry road into Gleann Mor Forest and take the second left turn up a track, signed to Ben Donich, which ends just above the forest (385m, 22870 06410). Follow the clear path up the ridge. Apart from one small rockstep, the path takes you easily to the trig point on the summit of **Ben Donich** (1hr 45min, 847m, 21840 04300).

Retrace your steps about 300m (820m, 22060 04420) and head E down the ridge, being very careful towards the bottom as there are big crags to be bypassed, probably on their right. Reach a broad saddle with a

Crags on Ben Donich

Route 12 – Ben Donich and The Brack

fence (2hr 40min, 384m, 24130 04080). Climb easily up the steep, grassy N ridge to the trig point on the summit of **The Brack** (3hr 45min, 787m, 24570 03060).

Turn right, heading WSW down the grassy ridge, avoiding a succession of small crags, to a lochan (560m, 23750 02540). Continue over a minor summit (578m) and down to a fence on another broad saddle (4hr 20min, 505m, 23450 01970).

Head roughly SW, veering SSE up the ridge to the summit of Cnoc Coinnich (5hr 20min, 764m, 22346 00772). Retrace your steps to the broad col between The Brack and Cnoc Coinnich (5hr 50min). Cross the fence and follow it down to a stile (445m, 23660 01780) at the edge of the forest. Follow a good path, crossing the Coilessan Burn and veering right down to a forestry road (335m, 24020 01940). Follow this, forking right then crossing the burn to join a cycle route (which is followed back to the starting point). Turn left at a T-junction to a tarmac road, which is followed until the Cat Crag Road forks off left (5hr 5min, 80m, 26180 01330).

If you have arranged transport the tarmac road will take you to Ardgartan, otherwise fork left. When the forestry road switchbacks, follow a path straight up the hillside then turn right along a path which takes you back to a forestry road. Fork left (a right-hand turn would take you down to Ardgartan Visitor Centre) and pass two footpaths which provide access to the steep N slopes of The Brack. Continue until you reach a gate with a communication mast (300m, 22810 06770) and turn right back to the start point (8hr 15min).

ROUTE 13
The Cobbler (Ben Arthur)

Start	Ardgartan Visitor Centre and Tourist Office (NN 26970 03670)
Distance	13km (8 miles)
Total ascent	960m (3100ft)
Difficulty	The route follows footpaths and is relatively easy, with just a few rocksteps on the ascent. The summit is an intimidating rock pinnacle, which requires easy, but very exposed scrambling and could be dangerous in winter conditions.
Time	3hr 50min
Summit	The Cobbler (884m, 2891ft)
Map	OS Landranger 56
Access	From Arrochar, head W along the A83 and park at the Ardgartan Visitor Centre and Tourist Office at the foot of Glen Croe.
Note	Most walkers climb the 'tourist route' that starts at the N end of Loch Long where there is a large car park (29430 04860). From here there is the option of climbing the suggested descent route or taking the direct route to the big cairn just S of the N summit. The Cobbler can also be approached from the A83 about 4km up Glen Croe. This is the shortest route but misses most of the scenic attraction of the peak. The Cobbler could easily be combined with an ascent of the Munros Beinn Narnain (to the E) or Ben Ime (to the N).

The Cobbler is understandably one of the most popular mountains in Scotland, with its three rocky peaks giving the mountain an impressive appearance. The name arose because the summit features are supposed to look like a shoemaker bending over his last. The proper name for the mountain is Ben Arthur which is the English translation of the original Gaelic name 'Beinn Artair'.

ROUTE 13 – THE COBBLER

The SE top of The Cobbler

The **'Arrochar Alps'** became popular in the 1930s during Scotland's industrial depression, when unemployed workers from the shipyards and factories of Glasgow made their way to the rugged mountain peaks at the head of Loch Long. In those days, The Cobbler was a training ground for Scottish climbers, who stayed up there for days at a time, often bivouacking at the Narnain Boulders.

▶ Walk 100m down the A83 and turn sharp left up a cycleway/footpath (part of the Cowal Way) and switchback through the forest until you reach a rough path on the left marked by a white post (15min, 75m, 27370 03530). Turn left up the path, cross a forest road (170m, 27440 03850) and continue to the top of the forest (295m). Follow the

See map just before Route 12.

Passing through the hole is known as 'threading the needle'.

Eagle carving at Ardgartan Visitor Centre

path easily up the grassy ridge to a saddle (595m, 26770 05300). The path now climbs more steeply. It is possible to lose the path through a boulderfield, but you can regain the path by keeping to the left of the big buttresses of the SE peak of the mountain. You suddenly arrive at the foot of the pinnacle that is the highest summit of **The Cobbler** (1hr 55min, 884m, 25960 05820).

The summit appears impossible to climb but it is actually an easy scramble in dry, non-windy conditions. From the N side climb through the hole on the right, which is known as 'Argyll's Eyeglass'. ◄ Then climb the sloping ledge on the S side before climbing easily up the E end of the pinnacle. Climb down from the summit, then follow the eroded path going diagonally down the path to the N. You reach a path on the left (820m, 26050 05970), marked by a small cairn. This is the recommended descent route; but first head N to a big cairn, which marks the top of an alternative descent route, and continue to the N summit (870m, 26160 06020). Return to the descent route and turn sharp right down it. This path takes you round the crags on the N ridge and then down to **Bealach a' Mhaim** (2hr 25min, 630m, 26140 06580).

Turn right down the 'tourist route' to a path junction (530m, 26870 05880) with the steep path that descends from the cairn on the summit ridge. Continue down, past the Narnain Boulders (two huge boulders) and down into the forest. The path now switchbacks down to a communication mast on a forestry road (3hr 20min, 100m, 28900 04650). Turn right (or turn left and right to reach **Arrochar**) and then fork left at a junction and continue back to the **Ardgartan** Visitor Centre (3hr 50min).

ROUTE 14

Beinn Luibhean

HILL OF THE LITTLE PLANT

Start	Glen Croe (NN 24170 06220)
Distance	9km (5 miles)
Total ascent	790m (2600ft)
Difficulty	The route is relatively easy but care would be needed with route-finding on the ridges in mist because of the many small crags that need to be avoided.
Time	3hr 20min
Summit	Beinn Luibhean (858m, 2811ft)
Map	OS Landranger 56
Access	Park at a lay-by on the right on the A83 as you head up Glen Croe on the A83 N of Arrochar. There are several lay-bys and you should choose the one with a stile, just before where the forestry to the E of the road ends.
Note	If you want an up-and-down route you would be better using the descent route. The traverse of Beinn Luibhean, Ben Ime and Beinn Chorranach from Butterbridge is a worthwhile option for a longer walk.

Beinn Luibhean is a steep grassy peak with a multitude of small crags on the summit ridges. It is a satellite peak to the Munro Ben Ime, with which it would normally be climbed. There is only 190m of descent from Beinn Luibhean to Ben Ime so it only just meets the requirements to count as a Corbett.

In the summer, **cattle and goats** were brought here to graze and while the men remained below on the crofts, the women and children spent their time herding the cattle and making butter and cheese, staying in shielings. The remains of their stone huts are still visible. The tradition is remembered in names such as Beinn Ime (Gaelic for 'butter mountain'), which towers over the glen, and in Butterbridge itself.

See map just before Route 12.

◀ Climb the stile and follow a faint path, which soon disappears, up the lower slopes of the mountain onto the S ridge (340m, 24500 06450) of **Beinn Luibhean**. Follow this ridge N to the summit (1hr 30min, 858m, 24290 07910).

Descend the E ridge, taking care to avoid the small crags, down to the broad saddle of Bealach a' Mhargaidh (680m, 24940 07930). Turn left to pick up the path down the left bank of the unnamed burn that flows down to join Kinglas Water. The path brings you out on the A83 by a ruined cottage just above Kinglas Water (2hr 30min, 195m, 23710 09430).

If you can arrange transport there is a lay-by just S along the A83 (23650 09180) or at Butterbridge (23460 09570) across Kinglas Water. Otherwise you will need to walk left for 4km along the A83 back to your starting point, taking care as the A83 is a fast road (3hr 20min).

ROUTE 15

Beinn an Lochain

HILL OF THE LITTLE LOCH

Start	North of Loch Restil (NN 23390 08820)
Distance	5km (3 miles)
Total ascent	720m (2400ft)
Difficulty	There is a rough path, with occasional small rocksteps, which makes the ascent relatively easy.
Time	2hr 30min
Summit	Beinn an Lochain (901m, 2992ft)
Map	OS Landranger 56
Access	Head up the A83 from Arrochar and park in one of the lay-bys about 0.5km N of the N end of Loch Restil, N of the Rest and be Thankful Pass.
Note	It would be possible to climb Beinn an Lochain from the Rest and be Thankful Pass, but this is uncomfortably steep and not to be recommended.

Route 15 – Beinn an Lochain

Beinn an Lochain is a steep grassy hill, the main features being the crags on the E flanks of the mountain and the impressive crags to the N of the summit. The best route up the mountain is the NE ridge, which is steep and narrow in places and would be difficult if there wasn't a path leading the walker through a succession of crags on the ridge. The ridge should be approached from Bealach an Easain Duibh, as the lower slopes of the ridge are protected by forestry above Butterbridge.

Beinn an Lochain appeared in earlier **Munro tables** at 3021ft but was demoted to a Corbett in the 1981 list when more accurate measurements were made. It may have lost its Munro status, but it is still a magnificent little mountain which is popular with walkers.

▶ Cross the burn and follow the path onto the NE ridge of **Beinn an Lochain**. Follow this path which crosses a small col (620m, 22380 08600) before climbing steeply to the cairn on the summit (1hr 20min, 901m, 21870 07970).

The S top appears to be about the same height as the N top but is about 1m lower. Return by the same route (2hr 30min).

See map just before Route 12.

NE ridge of Beinn an Lochain

ROUTE 16

Stob Coire Creagach (Binnein an Fhidhleir)

PEAK OF THE ROCKY CORRIE

Start	Butterbridge (NN 23460 09570)
Distance	11km (7 miles)
Total ascent	670m (2200ft)
Difficulty	The route from Glen Kinglas is up a steep grassy slope protected by bands of crags. Route-finding could be very difficult in mist, especially in descent.
Time	3hr 5min
Summit	Stob Coire Creagach (817m, 2680ft)
Map	OS Landranger 56
Access	Follow the A83 W from Arrochar to Butterbridge on the A83 in Glen Kinglas. Just after the road crosses Kinglas Water there is a large parking area.
Note	A traverse of the ridge from Loch Fyne at the W end of Glen Kinglas, over Binnein an Fhidhleir to Stob Coire Creagach and then along the NE ridge as described below would be a good expedition, especially if you could arrange transport to avoid a walk back along the A83.

This Corbett is not named on the OS map. It appears on some lists as Binnein an Fhidhleir, but that is in fact a subsidiary summit about 1.5km W of the Corbett. The corrie to the E of the summit is called Coire Creagach and it has been proposed that the Corbett should be called Stob Coire Creagach. The ridge rises steeply above Glen Kinglas and the S approaches to the summit are guarded by bands of crags.

Every autumn, cattle were driven from the W to the markets and fairs in the S along a **drove road** over the Rest and be Thankful Pass. After the Jacobite rebellion of 1745 the redcoats (English army) built a military road from Dumbarton on the River Clyde to Inveraray on Loch Fyne, following the course of the

ROUTE 16 – STOB COIRE CREAGACH

current A83 down Glen Kinglas, crossing Kinglas Water on the bridge, known as Butterbridge, that can be seen beside the car park.

▶ From the car park walk about 100m along the road to the E and climb steeply N up the right-hand side of the fence to a stile over a deer fence (310m, 23490 09920). Head slightly right, towards the obvious grassy gully through the lower crags (400m, 23570 10180). At the top of the gully veer left up the ridge to the foot of a grassy gully (620m, 23300 10690), which will take you through the second band of crags. There are more ways up the upper band of crags but they are probably slightly easier to breach a little to the left. Continue to the summit of **Stob Coire Creagach** (1hr, 817m, 23070 10910).

Head easily down the grassy NE ridge, which gradually broadens, until a rough off-road vehicle track reaches the ridge (670m, 24020 11720). You can either follow this track or continue along the ridge until three power lines cross the ridge (505m, 25440 12980). Turn right along the power lines and follow them down to the estate road in **Glen Kinglas** (2hr 15min, 325m, 26290 12870). Turn right and follow the road back to the A83 (3hr 5min).

See map just before Route 12.

Butterbridge over Kinglas Water

ROUTE 17
Meall an Fhudair
ROUNDED HILL OF THE GUNPOWDER

Start	Glenfalloch Farm (NN 31900 19670)
Distance	14km (9 miles)
Total ascent	860m (2800ft)
Difficulty	There are no footpaths on the approaches to Meall an Fhudair and the going is rough and boggy in places. Although a path is beginning to develop along the summit ridge, it is intermittent and navigation would be very demanding in misty conditions.
Time	4hr 40min
Summit	Meall an Fhudair (764m, 2508ft)
Map	OS Landranger 56
Access	From Arrochar head E along the A83 then N up the A82 along the banks of Loch Lomond. At the end of the loch continue N until 1.2km N of Inverarnan, where there is very limited parking opposite Glenfalloch Farm.

Meall an Fhudair is the W peak on the broad ridge that that stretches from Troisgeach. The ridge has a multitude of rocky knolls as well as many small lochans, which makes it an attractive walk. There are fine views, with Ben Lomond, Ben Lui and the Ben More range dominating.

The 95-mile **West Highland Way**, Scotland's most popular long-distance footpath, joins Milngavie on the outskirts of Glasgow to Fort William, following the E shore of Loch Lomond and continuing up Glen Falloch. The West Highland Way is detailed in the Cicerone guide by Terry Marsh.

Follow the hydroelectric road W up the lower slopes of Troisgeach to a T-junction just after passing under the power lines (230m, 30920 19580). Turn left and follow

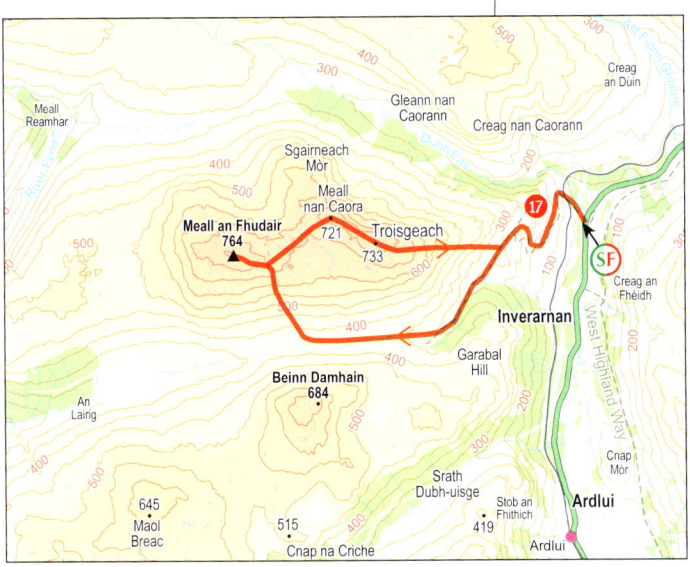

ROUTE 17 – MEALL AN FHUDAIR

Lochan on the W ridge of Meall an Fhudair

99

the track which ends in Lairig Arnan at a small catchment dam for the hydroelectric scheme (1hr, 330m, 29680 18150). Follow the burn up rough, often boggy grassland to a large lochan at the pass (380m, 28040 18060). Climb NNW up the hillside, avoiding small rock outcrops, veering W to the summit of **Meall an Fhudair** (2hr 35min, 764m, 27080 19230).

Head E then ENE to a broad saddle with a lot of lochans and then on to **Meall nan Caora** (721m, 28380 19750) and follow the knobbly ridge SSE to **Troisgeach** (3hr 20min, 733m, 29030 19390). Head down the E ridge, avoiding any crags. Care will be needed on the final descent to the hydroelectric road which is down steep rough grass with bracken and with large crags to be bypassed. On reaching the track, head to the track junction under the power lines and descend back to the A82 (4hr 35min).

4 EAST OF LOCH LOMOND (THE TROSSACHS)

Burn on Auchnafree Hill (Route 26)

East of Loch Lomond (The Trossachs): Bases and facilities

Base for Routes 18–23: Callander

Callander is on the A84 NW of Stirling and is a town with good facilities for tourists.

Tourist office: Rob Roy and Trossachs Visitor Centre, Ancaster Square, Callander, FK17 8ED Tel: 08707 200 628 www.incallander.co.uk

Local facilities for Route 18: Aberfoyle, Inversnaid and Stronachlachar

Aberfoyle, a small town on the A81 N of Glasgow, has very good facilities for tourists.

Aberfoyle Tourist Information, Trossachs Discovery Centre, Aberfoyle, FK8 3UQ Tel: 08452 255 121 www.aberfoyle.co.uk

Inversnaid, on the banks of Loch Lomond, and Stronachlachar, beside Loch Katrine, are NW of Aberfoyle at the end of the B829.

Inversnaid Hotel: Inversnaid Hotel runs a seasonal ferry from Inveruglas on the W bank of Loch Lomond to Inversnaid. Tel: 01877 386 223 www.lochsandglens.com

Inversnaid Bunkhouse has accommodation, meals, bar and camping. Tel: 01877 386 249 www.inversnaid.com

Inversnaid Lodge, now a hotel, overlooks Loch Lomond and was originally built in 1790 as the Duke of Montrose's hunting lodge. Tel: 01877 386 254

Stronachlachar Lodge Tel: 0141 955 0772 www.stronachlacharlodge.co.uk

There is also a tearoom at Stronachlachar.

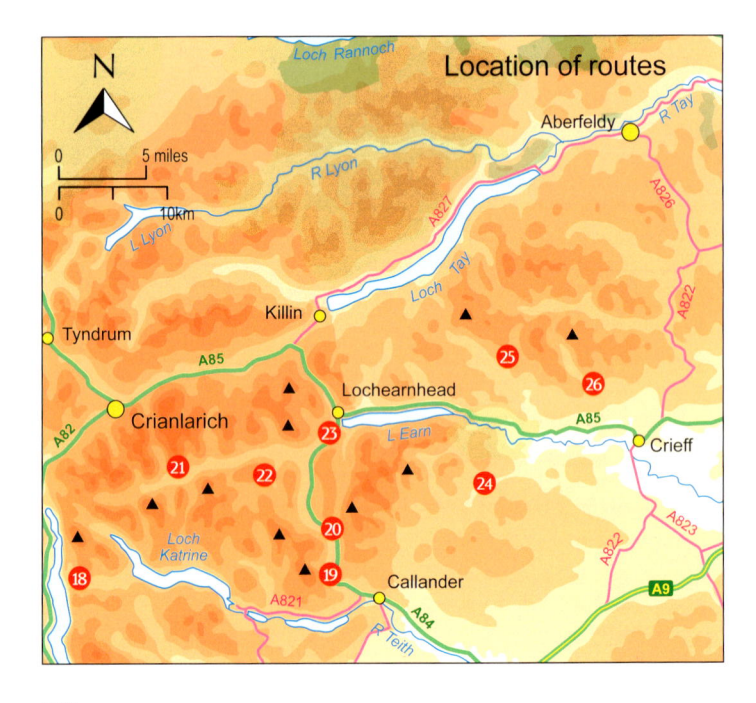

4 East of Loch Lomond (The Trossachs)

Local facilities for Routes 20–23: Strathyre, Balquhidder and Lochearnhead

Strathyre, Balquhidder and Lochearnhead are further N up the A84 from Callander.

Strathyre Forest Cabins on the W shore of Loch Lubnaig has luxury cabins. The reception has a small amount of supplies and a coffee shop. Tel: 0845 130 8223 www.forestholidays.co.uk

Strathyre has three hotels as well as the Immervoulin Caravan and Camping Park, which has a small store. Tel: 01877 384 285 https://immervoulinpark.co.uk

Balquhidder has the Balquhidder Braes Holiday Park
(Tel: 01567 830 293 www.balquhidderbraes.co.uk) for camping, caravans and chalets with a small shop.

Lochearnhead is a small village with two hotels, several B&Bs, a small store and cafes.

Base for Routes 24–26: Crieff

Crieff, on the A85 W of Perth, is a town with good facilities for tourists.

Tourist Information Centre, High Street, PH7 3HU Tel: 01764 652 578 www.perthshire-scotland.co.uk

Local facilities for Routes 24–26: Comrie Croft

Comrie Croft on the A85 W of Crieff before you reach the village of Comrie is a hostel with camping. Tel: 01764 670 140 www.comriecroft.com

WALKING THE CORBETTS: VOL 1

ROUTE 18
Beinn a' Choin HILL OF THE DOG

Start	RSPB Inversnaid Nature Reserve (NN 34870 09670)
Distance	10km (6 miles)
Total ascent	720m (2400ft)
Difficulty	The lower slopes of the mountain are rough and care will be needed with route-finding on the ascent in mist.
Time	3hr 50min
Summit	Beinn a' Choin (770m, 2524ft)
Map	OS Landranger 56
Access	From Callander take the A81, then A821 to Aberfoyle, then the B829 to Stronachlachar and turn left along the N shore of Loch Arklet and towards Inversnaid. Park at the Garrison car park, at the RSPB Inversnaid Nature Reserve about 1km E of Inversnaid.
Note	In bad weather the easiest option would be to climb the suggested descent route, as the fence will solve any navigation problems. It would be possible to start at Corriearklet Farm, halfway along Loch Arklet, and climb Maol Mor, then Beinn a' Choin, descending over Stob an Fhainne. The nearest parking to the farm is by Loch Arklet dam.

Beinn a' Choin is N of the very popular Ben Lomond to the E of Loch Lomond. It is a grassy peak with plenty of crags to add interest to any walk.

There would be a lot to be said for climbing Beinn a' Choin while doing the peaks in Section 3 by using the passenger ferry across Loch Lomond from Inveruglas to Inversnaid Hotel.

Inversnaid Garrison was one of four barracks built in 1718 by the Government in an attempt to control the Scottish Highlands. This was the time of Rob Roy MacGregor, clan chief, dispossessed landowner, cattle trader and rustler, who was born in Glen Gyle to the NE of Beinn a' Choin. Rob Roy was romanticised as a highland hero by Sir Walter

Route 18 – Beinn a' Choin

Scott in 1817, and again in 1995 when he was portrayed as a 'Robin Hood' figure in the film *Rob Roy*.

Follow the farm track from the car park to 'Garrison sheep fank' (sheepfold) and continue up a grassy track that is returning to nature. Cross a bridge (250m, 34560 11260) and continue along the faint track to a small burn (50min, 355m, 34420 12390). You could find a route directly through the crags to the summit of Beinn a' Choin from here, but it is easier to continue about 200m to a gully with a small burn, climb the gully and, at the top, continue to reach a bigger burn by an old stone shelter. Follow the burn uphill, initially above the right bank then left bank and then back to right bank before reaching a ruined wall. Follow this wall to the summit of **Beinn a' Choin** (1hr 55min, 770m, 35430 13020).

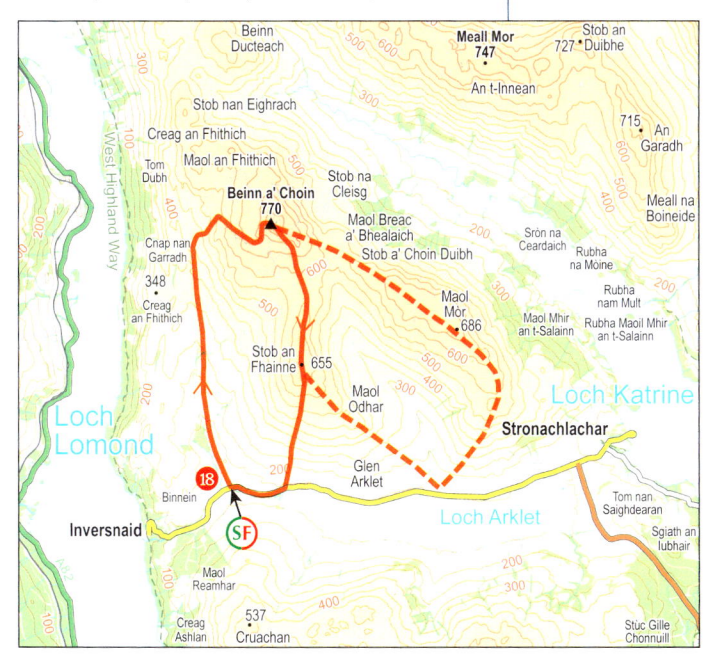

Ben Vane and Ben Vorlich from Beinn a' Choin

Head a few metres E to a fence and follow it right, taking care to avoid crags. In bad weather follow this fence all the way to the summit of **Stob an Fhainne**, but in clear conditions swing left to follow the ridge to the summit (2hr 50min, 655m, 35860 11090). Descend steeply down to the left of the fence, avoiding small crags, to the road just W of **Loch Arklet** dam (155m, 35540 09480). Turn right along the road 900m back to the car park (3hr 50min).

ROUTE 19

Ben Ledi GENTLE SLOPED HILL and Benvane WHITE HILL

Start	Strathyre Forest Cabins (NN 58710 09130)
Distance	23km (15 miles)
Total ascent	1220m (4000ft)
Difficulty	The going is straightforward until the summit of Benvane, then it's a little rough and care is needed with route-finding on the descent to Loch Lubnaig.
Time	6hr 25min
Summits	Ben Ledi (879m, 2883ft), Benvane (821m, 2685ft)
Map	OS Landranger 57
Access	Take the A84 N from Callander until the sign to Strathyre Forest Cabins on the left S of Loch Lubnaig. Turn left across the bridge and immediately left to parking spaces.
Note	If you don't want to combine these two Corbetts, the easiest option is to climb and descend Ben Ledi by the recommended ascent route and to climb Benvane from Ballimore Farm, the starting point for Route 22. If transport could be arranged, the traverse from Ballimore Farm to the S end of Loch Lubnaig over Benvane and Ben Ledi would be a fine traverse.

Ben Ledi is one of the most popular Corbetts, with a 'tourist path' to the summit. It is joined to Benvane by a long grassy ridge with a few small peat hags. Forestry on the slopes above Loch Lubnaig restricts access to the mountain ridge.

The **railway** reached Callander in 1858, and the Callander and Oban Railway Company was formed in 1864 with the objective of linking Callander to Oban on the west coast. The single-track line eventually reached Oban in 1880. The railway was never economic, but managed to survive until 1965 when it was closed by a landslide in Glen Ogle just before it was due to close because of the

WALKING THE CORBETTS: VOL 1

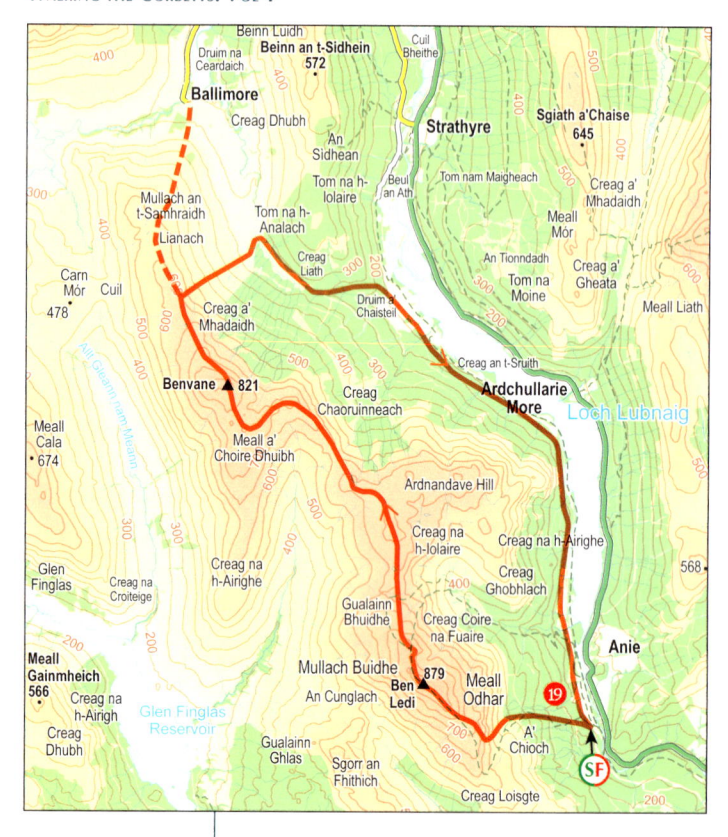

'Beeching axe'. The section along the W shore of Loch Lubnaig is now part of the National Cycle Network's 'Route 7'.

Return to the end of the bridge and follow the well-engineered path (blue waymarks) up the hillside. Cross a forest road (245m) to a stile (435m) at the top of the forest. The 'tourist path' now becomes a mountain path, which is followed easily to the summit of **Ben Ledi** where there

ROUTE 19 – BEN LEDI AND BENVANE

is a memorial cross just before the trig point is reached (1hr 35min, 879m, 56240 09770).

Head down the N ridge. Navigation along the ridge ahead is made easy by the old fence line, which is followed all the way to Benvane. Pass Lochan nan Corp (655m) and a couple of minor tops to reach a low point (606m) before following the fence posts up **Benvane**. The fence posts pass about 100m W of the summit, so you need to veer right to reach the cairn on the summit (3hr 40min, 821m, 53520 13720).

Return to the fence line and follow it NNW to pick up a better fence. Follow this NNW until the ridge levels a little (4hr, 610m, 52810 14770). Head ENE down the steep grass slopes to where a burn leaves the forest (4hr 30min, 275m, 53970 15630). Cross the burn and turn right, crossing the deer fence, and continue to a gate at the far left end of the long clearing (54630 15040). Pass through the gate onto a grassy track. Turn right at the forest road and left at the next junction. Follow the main track as it switchbacks right and left, and then turn left at the bottom to a junction with National Cycle Netwok Route 7 (5hr, 150m, 55690 15200). Turn right down the well-waymarked cycle track and follow it for 7km past Strathyre Forest Cabins and back to the car park (6hr 25min).

Benvane seen across Loch Lubnaig

ROUTE 20
Beinn Each HORSE HILL

Start	Ardchullarie More Lodge, Loch Lubnaig (NN 58310 13700)
Distance	7km (4 miles)
Total ascent	680m (2200ft)
Difficulty	Easy
Time	2hr 30min
Summit	Beinn Each (813m, 2660ft)
Map	OS Landranger 57
Access	Take the A84 N from Callander and park in the lay-by on the right where Loch Lubnaig bends to the NW near Ardchullarie More Lodge
Note	For a full day's walk continue from the summit of Beinn Each NE to Stuc a' Chroin and Ben Vorlich. From here head NW to Ben Our, W into Glen Ample before turning S up the glen to return to the starting point.

Beinn Each on the S edge of the Highlands is a subsidiary summit on the SW ridge of the much better known Munro Ben Vorlich, with which it would often be combined. This heather and grass peak is hidden from Loch Lubnaig by subsidiary ridges. The described route is very short and would be suitable for an evening walk after a late arrival in the Highlands or a morning walk before a long drive S.

Beinn Each did not appear as a Corbett until 1984 when study of the OS 25,000 map suggested that there might be a 500ft drop to Bealach nan Cabar. The OS 1:50,000 map suggests the drop to be about 154m (505ft), which indicates that more accurate measurements are required to be certain that Ben Each is actually a Corbett.

Every May, the **Stuc a' Chroin Race** ascends Beinn Each from Strathyre and continues to the summit of Stuc a Chroin, before returning to Strathyre. Despite the 1500m of climb involved, the record time for the 22km fell race is just under two hours.

ROUTE 20 – BEINN EACH

Approaching Beinn Each by its SW ridge

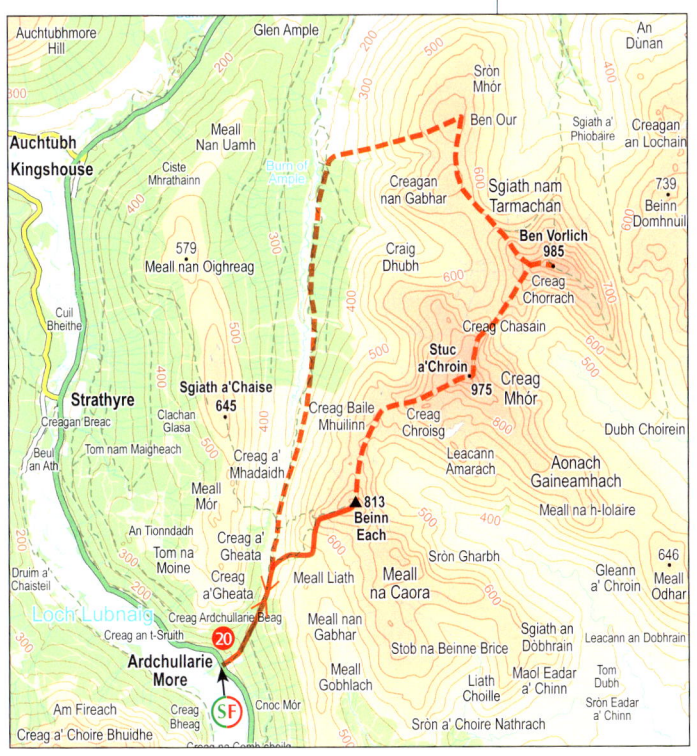

Take the paved drive towards the lodge and follow the signed footpath to the left. When the forest is reached the path veers left, crosses a burn and then climbs to a forest road, which is followed to the left. Pass through a gate at a deer fence at the top of the forest and continue along the track to a pass where there is a signpost to Beinn Each (30min, 340m, 58980 15050). Turn right up a small but clear path, which takes you to the summit of **Beinn Each** (1hr 30min, 813m, 60160 15800).

Return by the same route (2hr 30min).

ROUTE 21

Stob a' Choin PEAK OF THE DOG

Start	Inverlochlarig Farm (NN 44580 18460)
Distance	11 km (7 miles)
Total ascent	880 m (2900ft)
Difficulty	The route is steep and tough. It is not recommended for inexperienced walkers in bad weather.
Time	4hr 15min
Summit	Stob a' Choin (869m, 2839ft)
Map	OS Landranger 56
Access	Take the A84 N from Callander and take the turn to Balquhidder at the Kings House Hotel. Follow this minor road to a parking area and picnic site at the head of the public road E of Inverlochlarig Farm.
Note	The ascent route may be uncomfortably steep to descend so it is not recommended to do the route in the reverse direction.

Stob a' Choin is a steep, rough grassy hill, well protected by crags, with knobbly ridges. Older maps and guides may show the 865m N top as the main summit, but the S top is actually about 4m higher.

The **first church** in Balquhidder, the Eaglais Beag or 'Little Church' was built in 1250. A stone in

Route 21 – Stob a' Choin

the kirkyard records how, in 1558, the MacGregors of Glen Dochart attacked the MacLarens and murdered 18 MacLaren families before settling on their land in Balquhidder Glen. At the time, the MacGregors largely evaded responsibility for what would today be called an act of genocide. But when they killed several hundred members of Clan Colquhoun in 1603 the entire Clan MacGregor was outlawed by James VI. It became a capital offence even to carry the name MacGregor. In 1631 the Eaglais Beag was replaced by what is now called the 'Old Church', whose ruins still stand in the kirkyard. In 1734 Rob Roy MacGregor was buried beside the 'Old Church', where his grave is now a tourist attraction.

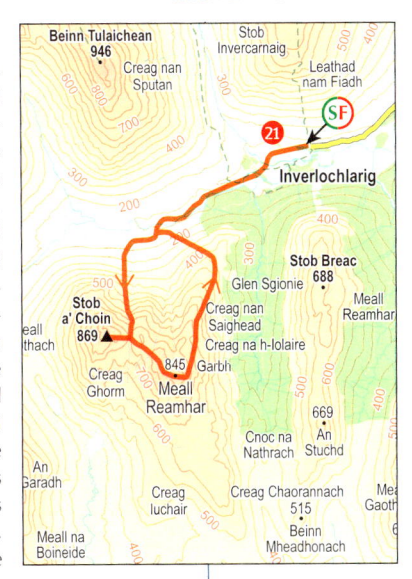

Head up the right-hand farm track, past Inverlochlarig Farm (which sells venison) and continue along the N bank of the River Larig to a footbridge (30min, 150m, 42730 17470). Cross the bridge and the fence and then turn right along the fence through rough pasture to some sheepfolds (42200 17280). Follow a fence uphill towards a wooded gully. Cross the burn just below the gully and continue up its right-hand side, bypassing the upper crags on the right, to Bealach Coire an Laoigh (1hr 40min, 745m, 42070 15960). Turn right along the old intermittent fence line to the S top of **Stob a' Choin**, which is marked by a small cairn on a rock outcrop (1hr 55min, 869m, 41730 15970).

The lower N top is less than 100m to the N and gives better views along the River Larig and down to Loch Voil. Return to Bealach Coire an Laoigh and follow the fence

113

Gully on Stob a' Choin

line E then SE up **Meall Reamhar** to a high point (845m), Continue along the fence line, turning left and left again on the next ridge (840m, 42720 15400). Descend the fence line NNE, taking care to avoid a few crags, until a deer fence crosses the ridge (430m). Follow this fence left and edge away from it after crossing another fence to descend down to the footbridge over the River Larig (3hr 45min, 150m, 42370 17470). Return to the car park by the same route (4hr 15min).

ROUTE 22
Stob Fear-tomhais SURVEYOR'S PEAK

Start	Ballimore Farm, Glen Buckie (NN 52940 17480)
Distance	14km (9 miles)
Total ascent	680m (2200ft)
Difficulty	A relatively easy route, despite being mainly over pathless rough pasture. Care would be needed with navigation in mist.
Time	4hr 20min
Summit	Stob Fear-tomhais (771m, 2513ft)
Map	OS Landranger 57
Access	Take the A84 N from Callander and take the turn to Balquhidder at the Kings House Hotel. At Balquhidder take the minor road S up Glen Buckie to Ballimore. There is adequate parking at the head of the public road by Ballimore Farm.
Note	It would be easy to complete the round of the head of Gleann Dubh by climbing the peaks to the S of the glen.

Stob Fear-tomhais, to the S of Loch Voil, isn't named on the OS maps, but the name 'Surveyor's Peak' is used locally because of the trig point on the summit. It is well protected by forestry on its steep N slopes, so is best approached from its gentler E flank. It is also referred to as Beinn Stacach from a feature SE of the summit called Bealach Stacach, which appears on the OS 1:25,000 map.

How did peaks get the **names** used on the OS map? An English surveyor came along and asked a local shepherd for the name of the peak. The shepherd may well have been illiterate and the surveyor may well have recorded the name inaccurately. As the surveyor was unlikely to speak Gaelic the local may have given the surveyor an English translation which was later translated back into Gaelic. In this case the surveyor probably got the wrong idea and then the Gaelicisation of the name 'Surveyor's Peak'

Allt a' Ghlinne Dhuibh

Route 22 – Stob Fear-tomhais

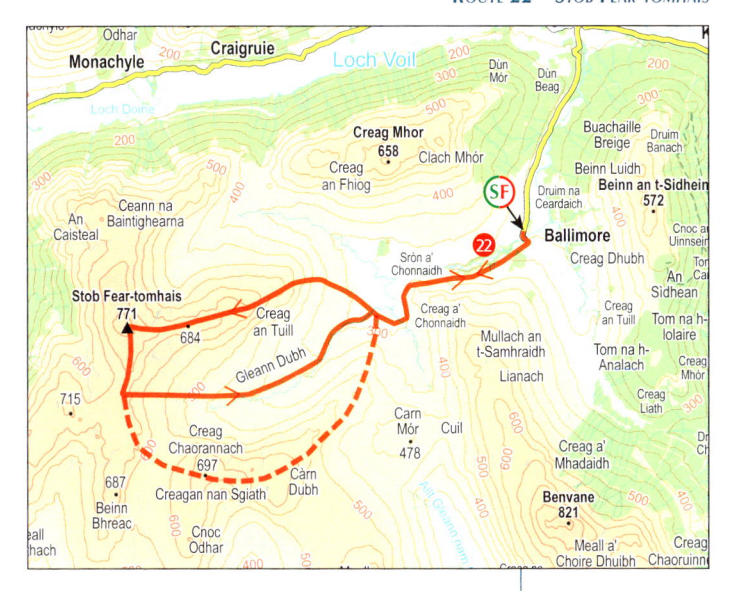

led to the name Stob Fear-tomhais and a new peak name had been invented.

Cross the bridge over the Calair Burn and immediately turn right up a sometimes boggy and unclear footpath signed to Brig o' Turk. When this path swings S you will see a bridge ahead over the Allt a' Ghlinne Dhuibh. Make your way to this bridge (45min, 285m, 50820 16460). Cross the bridge and head NW up rough pasture onto the broad E ridge of **Stob Fear-tomhais**. Follow this ridge, veering right towards the trig point on the summit (2hr 30min, 771m, 47440 16310).

Head S, following a broken fence until the ridge levels out (2hr 45min, 685m, 47390 15540). Head SE down into **Gleann Dubh** and follow the Allt a' Ghlinne Dhuibh all the way down to the bridge (3hr 40min) and return to the car park by the same route (4hr 20min).

ROUTE 23

Meall an t-Seallaidh ROUNDED HILL OF THE SIGHT
and *Creag MacRanaich* MACRANAICH'S CRAG

Start	Carstran Woodland (NN 58330 22180)
Distance	15km (10 miles)
Total ascent	1070m (3500ft)
Difficulty	The suggested route is steep and rough in places and is not recommended for the inexperienced walker in bad weather. As there are few paths, navigation would be difficult in mist.
Time	5hr 30min
Summits	Meall an t-Seallaidh (852m, 2794ft), Creag MacRanaich (809m, 2600ft)
Map	OS Landranger 51
Access	Follow the A84 N from Callander and about 1 mile after the Kings House Hotel there is a sign for Edinchip Estate on the left. There is limited parking 100m further on, in a gateway to Carstran Woodland on the right.
Note	The route could be extended by finishing over Meall Reamhar. It is easier to climb these two peaks separately: Meall an t-Seallaidh is easy if you just descend by the ascent route; the simplest route up Creag MacRanaich will be from the NW up Gleann Dubh.

Meall an t-Seallaidh and Creag MacRanaich, to the W of Loch Earn, are guarded by impressive crags facing Glen Kendrum. Creag MacRanaich has two tops, which the author measures at the same height. You should visit both tops to be sure of climbing the Corbett.

Lochearnhead has a long history. The first evidence comes from Mesolithic arrowheads found in Glen Ogle. A burial chamber at Edinchip and cup-marked stones in what is known locally as the Druid Field suggest a settled population is in evidence in the Neolithic period. There are two crannogs (man-made islands) visible on Loch Earn, probably dating

ROUTE 23 – MEALL AN T-SEALLAIDH AND CREAG MACRANAICH

from the Bronze Age. Loch Earn was on the frontier between the land of the Picts and Dalriada, the kingdom of the incoming Scots from Ireland, and it is believed that the name Earn comes from Eireann, in other words 'the loch of the Irish'.

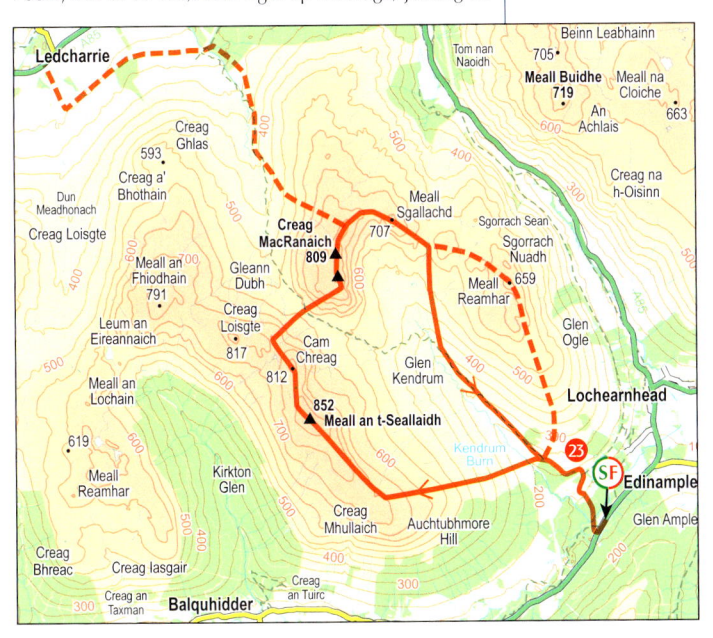

Return to Edinchip Estate road and follow it (ignoring the cycle track) to a junction. Turn right (signed Glen Kendrum) and then left (signed) along the edge of a field and left again just before the disused railway and onto the railway bridge (15min, 190m, 57890 22640). Cross the bridge and follow the farm track up Glen Kendrum as far as the top of the forestry (230m). Leave the track here and head down to **Kendrum Burn**, which is crossed on boulders. Follow a small burn up the hillside and continue, bearing slightly left, to reach the ridge (at about 700m, 55100 22400). Turn right up the ridge, joining an old fence line coming in from the left. Follow the fence to the trig point on the summit of **Meall an t-Seallaidh** (2hr 30min, 852m, 54220 23400). The trig point is about 1m higher than the twin top to the W.

Follow the fence line to **Cam Chreag** (812m) and continue along it as it veers steeply down to the NW to avoid big crags. Turn right at the small pass (740m, 53830 24310) and drop steeply down rough ground to the track that separates Cam Chreag from Creag MacRanaich (3hr 5min, 595m, 54150 24820). Keep straight on up the steep grass slopes, avoiding the crags, and along the summit plateau to the S top of **Creag MacRanaich** (3hr 40min, 809m, 54590 25300).

This is the same height as the N top, which is a rocky knoll about 250m further N (3hr 45min, 809m, 54570 25560). Continue NNE over a minor top (780m) and follow the knobbly ridge as it swings right to **Meall Sgallachd** (707m, 55390 25970). Descend SE, avoiding crags, to a small pass (570m, 55850 25690) and then descend S into **Glen Kendrum** and down to where the track crosses Kendrum Burn (4hr 45min, 375m, 55880 24440). Follow the track down Glen Kendrum and back into the forest before retracing your steps back to the parking area (5hr 30min).

Outcrop on the S ridge of Meall an t-Seallaidh

ROUTE 24
Meall na Fearna
ROUNDED HILL OF THE ALDERS

Start	Glenartney Church (NN 71100 16090)
Distance	22km (14 miles)
Total ascent	800m (2600ft)
Difficulty	Fairly easy, but there is pathless rough pasture. Care will be needed with navigation if descending in mist.
Time	5hr 50min
Summit	Meall na Fearna (809m, 2500ft)
Maps	OS Landranger 51 and 57
Access	From Crieff head W on the A85 to Comrie then head S along the B827 and then right along the minor road to Glen Artney. There is a large car park at Glenartney Church about 2km before the roadhead. There is no further parking up the glen or at the roadhead.
Note	The shortest approach is from Ardvorlich on Loch Earn to the N, but this route lacks interest.

Meall na Fearna appeared on sheet 54 of the OS 1 inch:1 mile map as a ring contour at 2500ft (762m) but now appears on OS 1:50,000 map at 809m! Meall na Fearna is a subsidiary peak on the E ridge of Ben Vorlich. The hill itself isn't particularly interesting, but the recommended route takes you up the spectacular Srath a' Ghlinne glen to approach the summit from the N.

Glen Artney was part of the ancient royal deer forest of Strathearn, which supplied venison to the sovereigns of Scotland. The glen was immortalised in Sir Walter Scott's epic poem *The Lady of the Lake*.

Head 2km up the road to the roadhead, pass through the gate and bear right up the main track, then fork left and right up Srath a' Ghlinne and follow the track until it crosses the burn (1hr 25min, 295m, 67190 19350). Stay left of the burn and follow it upstream through a spectacular glen,

WALKING THE CORBETTS: VOL 1

gradually veering left as it swings round the crags guarding the NE face of Meall na Fearna. When the burn fades away continue SE to the ridge (at about 685m, 65680 18800) and turn right up the ridge to the summit cairn on **Meall na Fearna** (3hr 30min, 809m, 65090 18690).

Head S from the summit to pick up a burn descending SW through rough pasture. This joins a burn coming down from Ben Vorlich. Cross the burn and turn left down to an old ruin (4hr 10min, 430m, 64530 16700). Cross to the left-hand side of the **Allt an Dubh Choirein** burn and follow a rough path to a footbridge high over the burn. The track shown on the OS map isn't readily

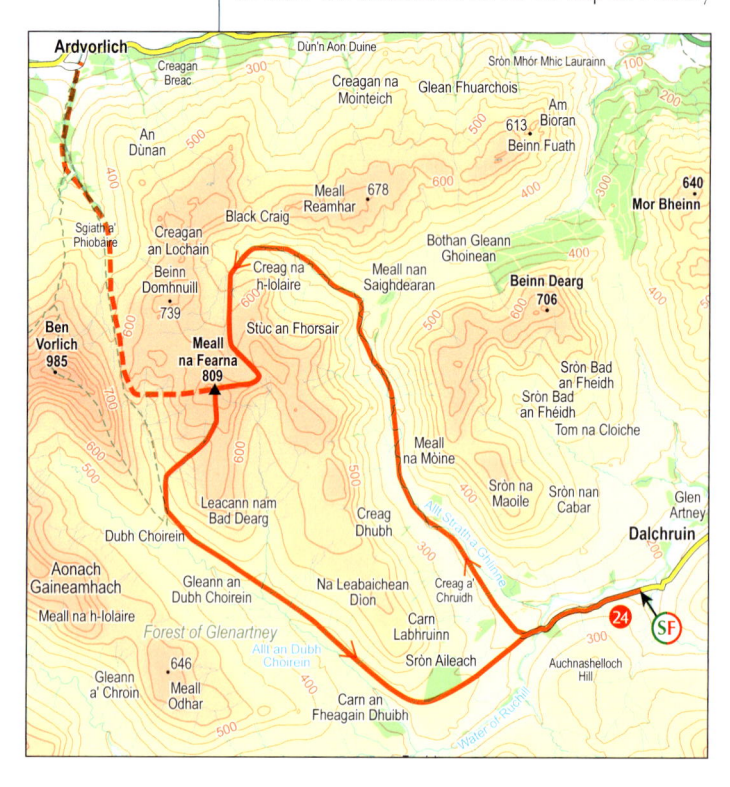

There is little sign of the path shown on the OS maps.

visible here so it's easiest to continue downstream until the track joins from the left. Follow the track down, ignoring a track off to the right. The track eventually veers left and climbs before dropping down to the roadhead in **Glen Artney**. Follow the road back to the car park (5hr 50min).

Allt Srath a' Ghlinne

Walking the Corbetts: Vol 1

ROUTE 25
Creag Uchdag CRAG OF THE HOLLOWS

Start	Invergeldie (NN 74300 27270)
Distance	14km (9 miles)
Total ascent	750m (2500ft)
Difficulty	Generally easy underfoot, but care would be needed with navigation in mist
Time	3hr 45min
Summit	Creag Uchdag (879m, 2887ft)
Map	OS Landranger 51
Access	Take the A85 W from Crieff and then take the minor road from the W end of Comrie, N into Glen Lednock. There is plenty of parking at Invergeldie.
Note	Creag Uchdag is often climbed from Ardeonaig to the NW or Ardtalnaig to the N on Loch Tay. Possibly the best route would be to park at Ardtalnaig as for Route 39 and take the track to Dunan and follow the River Almond to its source on Creag Uchdag. It would be possible to combine Creag Uchdag with Creagan na Beinne (Route 39) but this would be a very long walk.

Creag Uchdag is the highest point on an area of rough pasture and moorland to the N of Loch Lednock Reservoir.

An Dun, Glen Lednock

124

Route 25 – Creag Uchdag

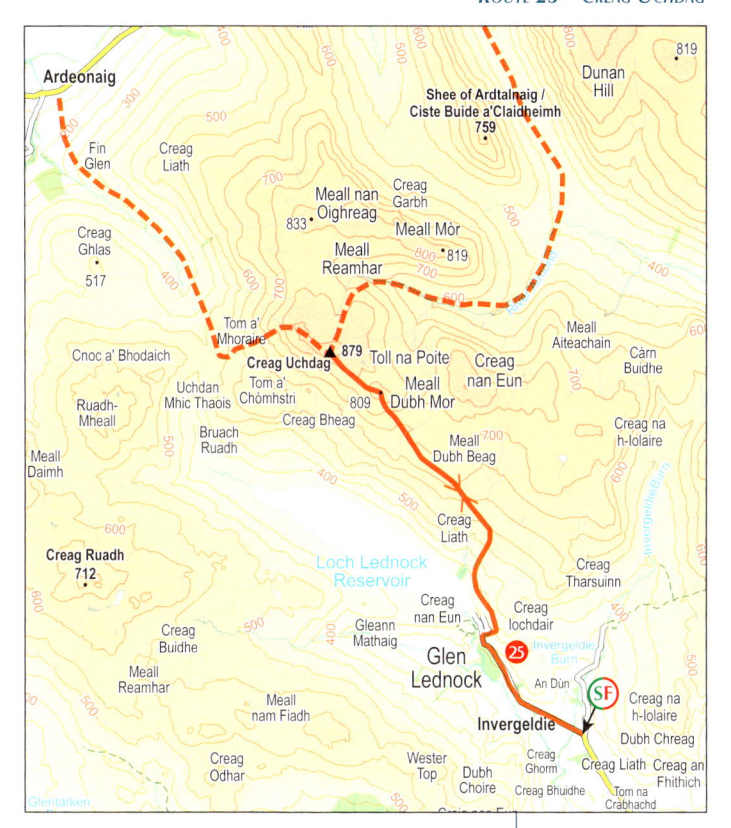

As you drive up Glen Lednock you will see the impressive 72ft obelisk, the **Melville Monument**, built on the peak of Dunmore in 1811. It commemorates the first Lord Melville, Henry Dundas, who was the First Lord to the Admiralty under William Pitt the Younger during the Napoleonic Wars.

Fork left and continue on the road up **Glen Lednock**. After 700m you reach a locked gate where there is very

125

limited parking. Go through the gate, forking right and right again, before forking right up a track just before the dam. Fork right again, steeply uphill, just before a wood and climb until you fork left to a gate (1hr, 545m, 72950 30000). Cross the gate and a burn and follow a faint grass track, which eventually fades away at a burn (685m, 71830 31090). Continue across peat hags and then climb rough pasture to the summit of **Meall Dubh Mor** (809m) then follow the broad ridge NW to the trig point on the summit of **Creag Uchdag** (2hr 15min, 879m, 70830 32310).

Return by the same route (3hr 45min).

ROUTE 26
Auchnafree Hill
HILL OF THE DEER FOREST

Start	Loch Turret (NN 82110 26440)
Distance	14km (9 miles)
Total ascent	670m (2200ft)
Difficulty	Most of this route is on a good hill track making easy walking. In mist it could be difficult to locate the summit cairn on the summit plateau.
Time	3hr 40min
Summit	Auchnafree Hill (789m, 2565ft)
Map	OS Landranger 52
Access	Follow the signs for Loch Turret from the A85 just NW of Crieff. The private Scottish Water road to the reservoir is open to the public and there is a large car park just below the dam.
Note	Auchnafree Hill could be climbed from Auchnafree in Glen Almond to the N, but this glen is closed to cars so you would need to walk or cycle up from Newton Bridge on the A822. A magnificent walk would be to complete the round of the head of Glen Turret by continuing from Auchnafree Hill to the Munro Ben Chonzie and descending its SE ridge.

ROUTE 26 – AUCHNAFREE HILL

Auchnafree Hill is a rounded, heather-clad hill to the W of the impressive Glen Turret. The hill is on the S edge of the Highlands with good views to the lowlands to the S. Although the summit plateau lacks interest, the approaches to the mountain and the descent of Glen Turret make this an attractive route.

At the foot of Glen Turret is the **Famous Grouse distillery**. Established in 1775, this is the oldest distillery in Scotland and as well as producing world-renowned brands of whisky provides good facilities for the tourist, including restaurant, shop, tours and whisky tasting. Tel: 01764 656 565
www.thefamousgrouse.com

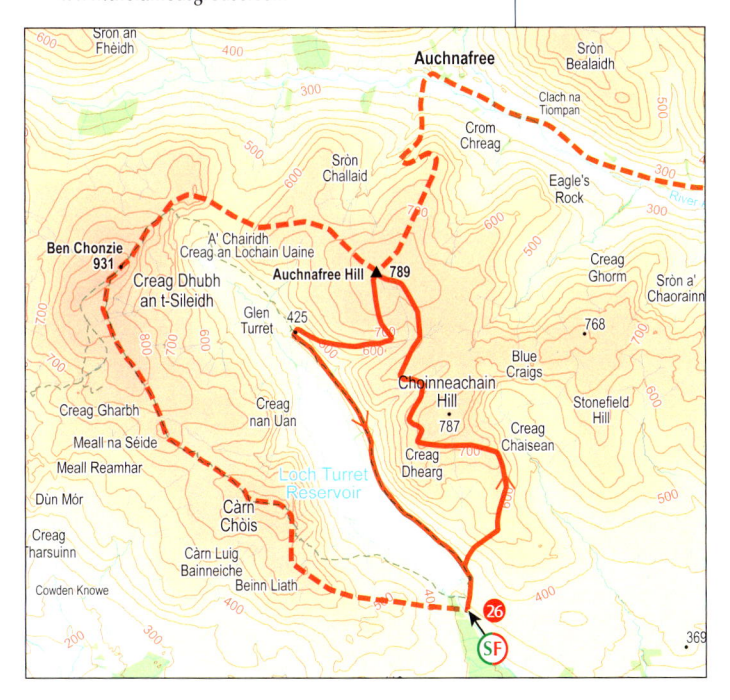

Cairn on Choinneachain Hill

Take the paved track to the right-hand end of the dam and head about 100m along the track beside **Loch Turret** until you reach a faint path to the right (82110 26810). Follow this path, which becomes little more than a sheep track and may be difficult to follow, up the heather-covered hillside until you reach a good track along the ridge (40min, 580m, 82560 27350). Turn left along the track. You will pass a big cairn (770m) as you skirt the summit of **Choinneachain Hill** and continue along the track, descending to cross a burn (675m, 81600 29350). The track now crosses a ridge, Ton Eich, and another burn before reaching a burn that descends from the summit of **Auchnafree Hill** (1hr 50min, 690m, 81300 30700). Leave the track here and follow this burn N, veering NW as you reach the summit plateau. The summit is marked by a small cairn (2hr 10min, 789m, 80860 30810) with a larger cairn about 50m to the W of the summit.

Note the mounds of moraine left behind when the glacier that used to fill the glen retreated.

Head S (the direct route SW is rather steep) until you regain the track and turn right to reach a track junction in **Glen Turret** (2hr 40min, 425m, 79690 30040). ◄ Turn left along this track down to Loch Turret and back to the dam and car park (3hr 40min).

5 SOUTH-WEST GRAMPIANS (TYNDRUM AND DALMALLY)

Beinn Dorain from the slopes of Beinn Odhar (Route 31)

South-West Grampians: Bases and facilities

Base for Routes 27–31: Tyndrum

Tyndrum is a small but very popular tourist village with hotels, B&B, bunkhouse and campsite, shop and cafe.

Tourist Information Office, Main Street, Tyndrum, Perthshire, FK20 8RY Tel: 08452 255 121 www.undiscoveredscotland.co.uk/tyndrum/tyndrum/index.html

Pine Trees Leisure Park is a camping and caravan site with hiker huts and luxury log cabins. Tel: 01838 400 349 www.pinetreescaravanpark.co.uk

Local facilities for Routes 27 and 28: Dalmally

Dalmally is a village with one big hotel, some B&Bs and a store.

The Dalmally Hotel Tel: 01838 200 393

Walking the Corbetts: Vol 1

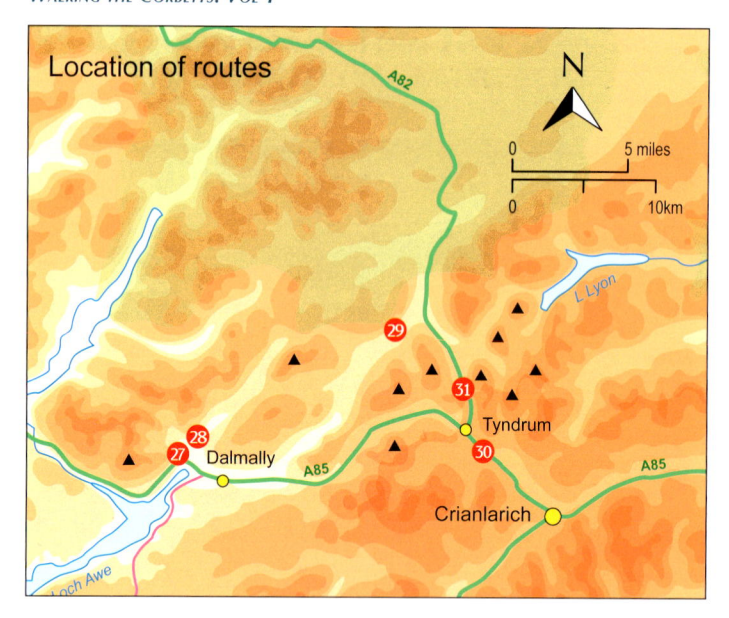

Location of routes

Other facilities for Routes 29–31: Bridge of Orchy and Crianlarich

The Bridge of Orchy Hotel has a bunkhouse as well as normal hotel facilities. Tel: 01838 400 208 www.bridgeoforchy.co.uk

Crianlarich has a store, restaurant, hotels and a youth hostel.

Crianlarich Hotel Tel: 01838 300 272 www.crianlarich-hotel.co.uk

Crianlarich SYHA, Station Road, Crianlarich, FK20 8QN Tel: 01838 300 260

Strathfillan Wigwams between Crianlarich and Tyndrum also has a limited shop and snack bar. Tel: 01838 400 251
www.wigwamholidays.com/strathfillan

ROUTE 27

Beinn a' Bhuiridh HILL OF ROARING OF STAGS

Start	Head of Loch Awe (NN 13260 28380)
Distance	11km (7 miles)
Total ascent	900m (3000ft)
Difficulty	The final slopes of the Coire Ghlais are steep and there is some boulderfield on the steep ascent to the summit of Beinn a' Bhuiridh. Care will be needed if descending in mist. The route is not recommended for inexperienced walkers in bad weather.
Time	3hr 50min
Summit	Beinn a' Bhuiridh (897m, 2941ft)
Map	OS Landranger 50
Access	From Tyndrum take the A85 past Dalmally to the head of Loch Awe. Turn up the B8077 signed to Stronmilchan and there is limited parking by the junction.
Note	If you have time and energy you should climb Beinn a' Bhuiridh as part of a traverse of the Munros Ben Cruachan and Stob Diamh from the Falls of Cruachan.

Beinn a' Bhuiridh is a fine mountain with many big crags. It is the SE peak of the magnificent ridge, including Ben Cruachan, which surrounds the Cruachan Reservoir. The recommended route takes in the wild Coire Ghlais and the knobbly E ridge with a multitude of small crags and erratic boulders.

Cruachan power station, opened by the Queen on 15 October 1965, was the first reversible pump storage hydroelectric system to be built in the world. The scheme uses cheap electricity, at night, to pump water from Loch Awe up to Cruachan Reservoir. In times of peak electricity demand the water flows back to Loch Awe generating electricity in the power station buried deep under Ben Cruachan. You could take a guided tour of the power station.

WALKING THE CORBETTS: VOL 1

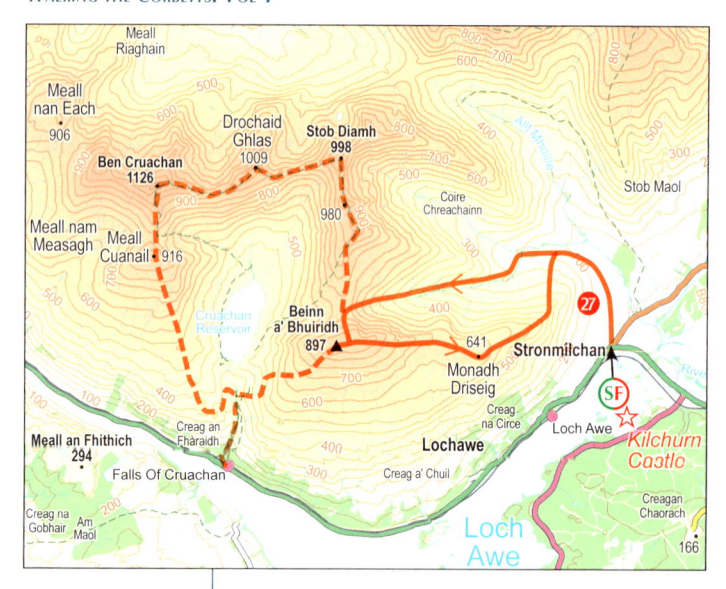

At the time of writing, work was underway on renovating the hydroelectric works on the lower parts of this route. Tracks were being created or 'improved' and the place was a bit of a mess. Hopefully, by the time you read this they will have finished and restoration of the damage will be well underway, but it could mean some of the route description is no longer accurate. There is in fact a lot of hydroelectric work being done in the glens, as much of the infrastructure dates from before World War II and the aim of the Scottish Government is to make Scotland 100% reliant on renewable energy for electricity generation.

Follow the newly 'improved' track, ignoring tracks off to the right, until a bridge over the Allt Coire Ghlais is reached (30min, 155m, 12020 29530). Head up the burn. The slope becomes rather steep towards the top of the corrie and here you will probably find it easier to

ROUTE 27 – BEINN A' BHUIRIDH

the right of the burn. Continue up until the pass between Beinn a' Bhuiridh and Stob Garbh is reached (1hr 40min, 725m, 09580 28850). Head roughly S up the final slope over grass and boulderfields, avoiding small crags to arrive at the middle top (885m, 09670 28480). Turn right along a faint path to the summit cairn on the highest top of **Beinn a' Bhuiridh**, at the W end of this knobbly ridge (2hr 10min, 897m, 09430 28360).

Retrace your steps along the faint path that leads to the E top. Now descend the largely pathless E ridge to a pass with peat hags (625m, 11000 28300) and continue on to the trig point on **Monadh Driseig** (2hr 50min, 641m, 11320 28150), which is on the S edge of the summit plateau, not on the highest point. Head ENE down the ridge and then (at about 450m, 12260 28660) head just right of N, avoiding the crags and dropping down left of old quarry and mine workings to reach the access track (130m, 12520 29590). Turn right back to the parking area (3hr 50min).

Beinn a' Bhuiridh

WALKING THE CORBETTS: VOL 1

ROUTE 28

Beinn Mhic Mhonaidh

HILL OF THE SON OF THE MOOR

Start	Glen Strae (NN 14550 29450)
Distance	24km (15 miles)
Total ascent	940m (3100ft)
Difficulty	The recommended route takes the gentlest route up and down the mountain, but there is some rough pasture on the ascent and rough heather on the descent. The River Strae could be difficult or unpleasant to cross if it is running high, but the route can be amended to avoid the river crossing, as described in the route description. Care will be needed if descending in mist.
Time	7hr
Summit	Beinn Mhic Mhonaidh (796m, 2602ft)
Map	OS Landranger 50
Access	Head W from Tyndrum along the A85 and turn right at Dalmally along the B8077 signed to Stronmilchan. There is limited parking at the gateway just after crossing the River Strae.
Note	The shortest approach is through the forest from Glen Orchy to the SW, but this route misses the essence of this mountain.

Beinn Mhic Mhonaidh is an impressive whale-backed mountain at the head of Glen Strae, with magnificent views in all directions.

Kilchurn Castle, at the head of Loch Awe, was built in about 1450 by Sir Colin Campbell, first Lord of Glenorchy, and it started life as a five-storey tower house with a courtyard defended by an outer wall. Further buildings went up during the 1500s and 1600s, and in 1690 the castle was converted into a barracks capable of holding 200 troops. Kilchurn was on a small island, scarcely larger than the

ROUTE 28 – BEINN MHIC MHONAIDH

castle itself, until the water level of the loch was lowered by clearance of the loch's outflow in 1817. In 1760 the castle was badly damaged by lightning and was completely abandoned. It is now in the care of Historic Scotland.

Follow the track up **Glen Strae**, forking right at the first junction and passing a superb swimming hole after 2.2km. Fork left at a plantation and continue until the second meander in the river after the end of the woodland (1hr, 105m, 17290 32850). If the water level is too high to cross the river you should continue until a new bridge (18680 34030) and then cut back to the right of

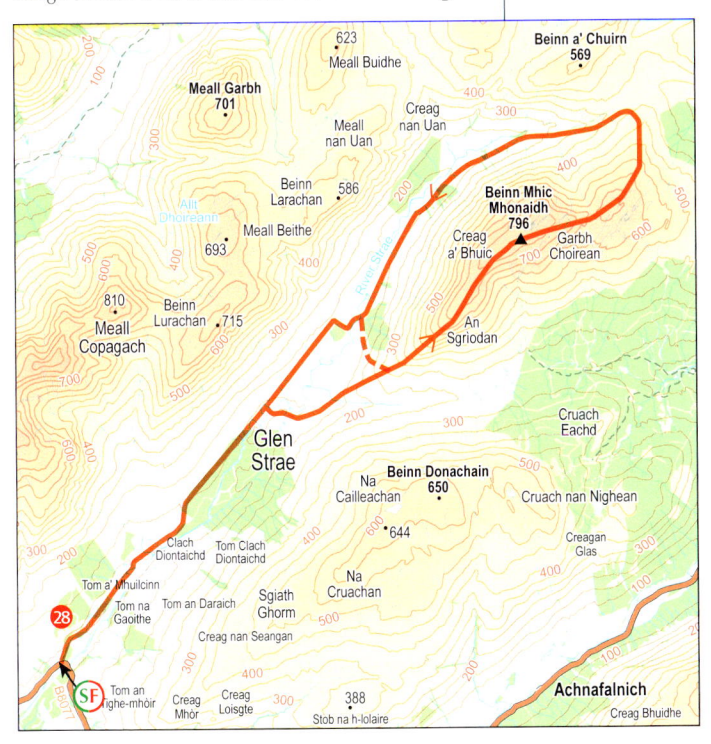

Beinn Mhic Mhonaidh seen from Glen Strae

the plantation to the SW ridge of Beinn Mhic Mhonaidh. Otherwise ford the river at some shallows and follow the river past the ruins of Inbhir-nan-giubhas and cross the Allt nan Giuthas burn (at about 18250 32950). Head up the SW ridge of **Beinn Mhic Mhonaidh** to a cairn on the SW top (736m, 20070 34200) and continue easily along the broad summit ridge to the summit cairn. This is not actually the highest point, as the twin top about 30m SE is about 2m higher (3hr 20min, 796m, 20830 35020).

Follow the ridge ENE past a lochan, taking care to avoid some small crags as you descend to a pass and on to Top 679 (22190 35510). Pick up an old fence line and follow it down the N ridge to the pass between Beinn Mhic Mhonaidh and Beinn a' Chuirn (4hr 15min, 380m, 22320 36790). Follow the **River Strae** left from its source. Stay high enough above the left bank to cross a burn above a small gorge by a sheepfold (21300 36360). The terrain is a little rough, but animal tracks are starting to develop into paths in places. Eventually pick up a track on a grassy flat beside the river (5hr 10min, 150m, 19760 35770).

Follow this track to a new bridge across the River Strae (18680 34030) and then back to the parking area (7hr).

ROUTE 29

Beinn Udlaidh GLOOMY HILL
and Beinn Bhreac-liath SPECKLED GREY HILL

Start	Glen Orchy (NN 27780 36740)
Distance	12km (7 miles)
Total ascent	940m (3100ft)
Difficulty	The approach through the forest is a little rough, but the going on the mountain is easy. Care will be needed with navigation in mist, particularly on the descent from Beinn Udlaidh whose broad curving ridge has a few crags that need bypassing.
Time	4hr 10min
Summits	Beinn Udlaidh (840m, 2759ft), Beinn Bhreac-liath (802m, 2633ft)
Map	OS Landranger 50
Access	Take the A82 N from Tyndrum and turn left down the B8074 into Glen Orchy. After 3km park in a gateway to the forest, just after the small cottage at Invergaunan.

Beinn Udlaidh and Beinn Bhreac-liath are steep grassy mountains squeezed in between Glen Lochy and Glen Orchy. Access is limited by the forestry that surrounds them.

Coire Daimh, a gloomy corrie to the W of Beinn Udlaidh, has a rim of low, damp cliffs, which are of little interest to the rock climber. However, after a long winter freeze the dripping cliffs produce fantastic icefalls, which provide some of the best ice-climbing in Scotland.

Go through the gate and follow the edge of the woodland up the W bank of the cascading Allt Ghamhnain. There are some animal tracks that ease the way through the rough terrain. Continue to the fence corner just after the end of the woodland (35min, 255m, 28720 35180). Cross

WALKING THE CORBETTS: VOL 1

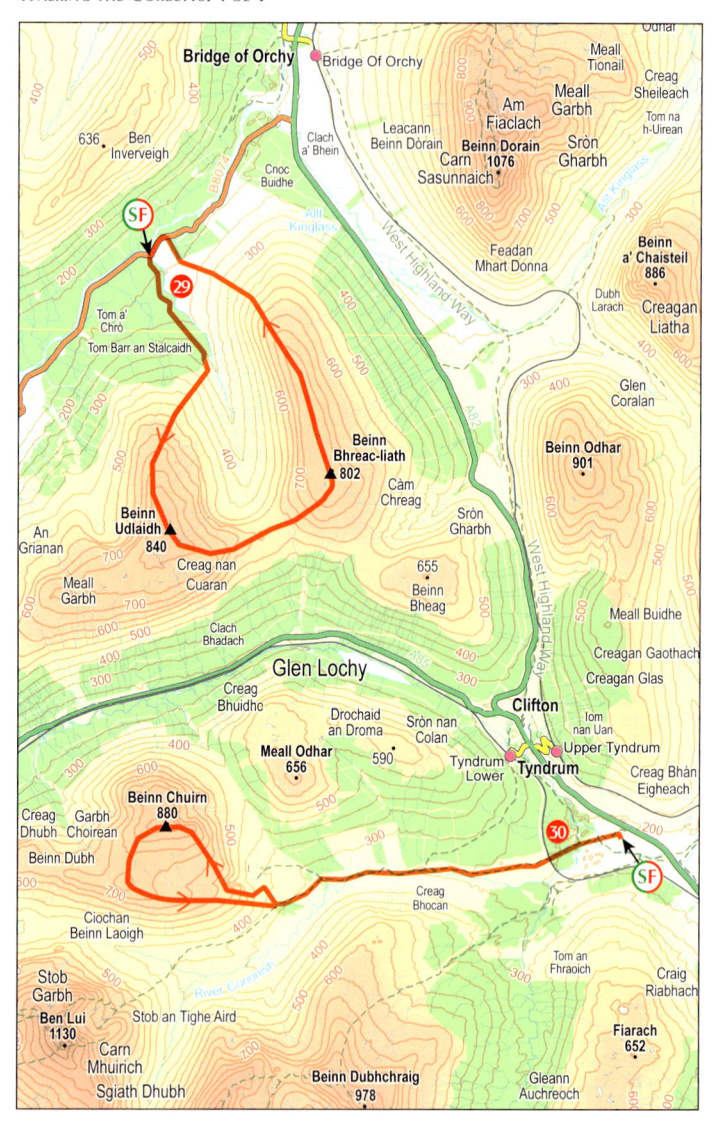

Route 29 – Beinn Udlaidh and Beinn Bhreac-liath

Allt Ghamhnain on Beinn Udlaidh

the fence and head WSW to pick up a line of quartzite-veined outcrops, which are followed easily onto the N ridge of **Beinn Udlaidh**. Continue to the well-built cairn surrounded by debris from a communications mast at the recognised summit (28030 33260). However, the author does not believe this is actually the highest point and he is fairly confident that a quartzite outcrop about 150m further S is about 1–2m higher (2hr, 840m, 28060 33120).

In mist you should pay careful attention, as the natural line of the ridge could take you over the crags of Creag nan Cuaran. Descend S, gradually veering to ENE to find the breaks through the small crags above the pass and descend to the pass (2hr 25min, 587m, 29420 33050). It is best to swing a bit right on the ascent of **Beinn Bhreac-liath** to give a gentler gradient, avoiding crags. Reach the small cairn on the Beinn Bhreac-liath at the S end of the long summit plateau (3hr, 802m, 30280 33910). Head NNW along the plateau and continue down the ridge. It is best to get well down the ridge before swinging WNW to the corner of the wood near Invergaunan. Follow the edge of the wood down to the road (28040 37010) and turn left back to the parking area (4hr 10min).

ROUTE 30
Beinn Chuirn CAIRN HILL

Start	Dalrigh (NN 34380 29110)
Distance	16km (10 miles)
Total ascent	810m (2700ft)
Difficulty	Easy going on a pathless, grassy hill
Time	4hr 20min
Summit	Beinn Chuirn (880m, 2878ft)
Map	OS Landranger 50
Access	Park at a large car park at Dalrigh on the A82 about 2km SE of Tyndrum.

Beinn Chuirn is a fine looking mountain as seen from Glen Cononish, but it is dwarfed by the grandeur of its neighbour, Ben Lui. There are big crags on the NE face of Beinn Chuirn, but the other crags on the OS maps are largely figments of the mapper's imagination.

Nearby is **Cononish Gold Mine**. In 1984 a gold bearing quartz vein was discovered on the SE slopes of Beinn Chuirn just above Cononish Farm at Eas Anie. The gold occurs as minute particles inside Pyrite and Galena in the quartz vein. It is believed that there are a million tonnes of ore present on the site, which could produce 5 tonnes of gold and about 25 tonnes of silver. In the 1990s a 1300m tunnel was driven into the hillside; however, the falling price of gold meant that such a small deposit was uneconomic at the time. Scotgold Resources from Australia have purchased the mineral exploration concession but their application to start gold production is meeting resistance from the planning authorities because of the environmental damage the mining would cause.

ROUTE 30 – BEINN CHUIRN

▶ Head back towards the A82, then turn left, signed 'to Old Church'. Follow signs to Ben Lui NNR, passing to the right of Dalrigh House, then forking right and keeping straight on when the West Highland Way goes off to the right. Keep straight on under the railway and follow the good track to Cononish Farm. Pass through the farm, ignoring the right turn to Cononish Gold Mine, and continue until a gate through a fence by a plantation (1hr 5min, 335m, 29490 28110). Follow the fence up to a gate then head up the hillside, aiming for a grassy ramp to the left of the main crags. Veer right (NW) above the crags, crossing the Eas Anie burn (at about 590m, 28780 28430) and continue up the ridge, veering left at the top to a dilapidated cairn on the summit of **Beinn Chuirn** (880m, 2hr 25min, 28030 29230).

Head WSW, then SSW, following an old fence line to Top 773 (27470 28450). Descend the E ridge, veering right lower down to stay clear of the crags, aiming for the gate (3hr 15min, 335m, 29490 28110). Follow the track back to the car park (4hr 20min).

See map in Route 29.

The SE ridge of Beinn Chuirn

WALKING THE CORBETTS: VOL 1

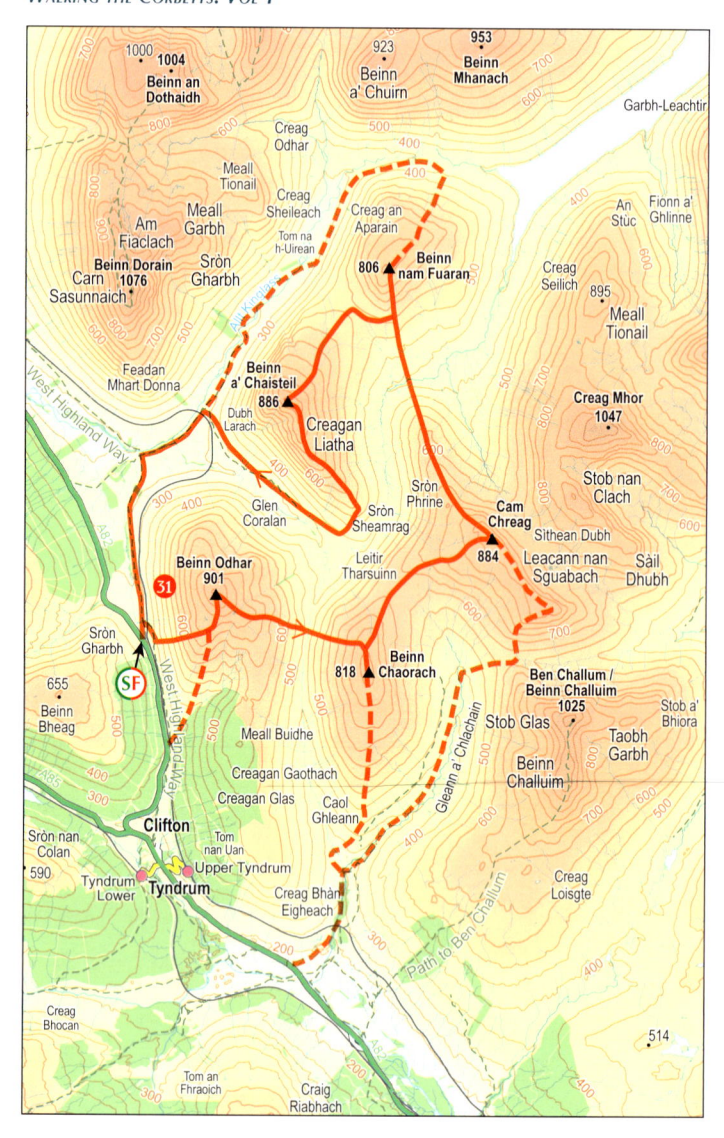

ROUTE 31

Beinn Odhar DUN-COLOURED HILL, *Beinn Chaorach*
SHEEP HILL, *Cam Chreag* CROOKED CRAG, *Beinn nam Fuaran*
HILL OF THE WELL and *Beinn a' Chaisteil* HILL OF THE CASTLE

Start	A82 N of Tyndrum (NN 32840 33120)
Distance	23km (14 miles)
Total ascent	2060m (6800ft)
Difficulty	The terrain is easy underfoot, but there are some uncomfortably steep grassy slopes, which could become dangerous in adverse weather conditions.
Time	9hr 35min
Summits	Beinn Odhar (901m, 2948ft), Beinn Chaorach (818m, 2685ft), Cam Chreag (884m, 2823ft), Beinn nam Fuaran (806m, 2632ft), Beinn a' Chaisteil (886m, 2897ft)
Map	OS Landranger 50
Access	Take the A82 N from Tyndrum and park at the high point of the pass.
Note	The traverse of all five Corbetts in one day is a tough expedition and will be too much for many walkers. You might like to break it up into three walks, as described below. The suggested alternatives also have the advantage of reducing the number of descents down steep grassy slopes.

This is a group of five steep-sided grassy Corbetts to the NE of Tyndrum. Curiously they are immediately S of a similar group of five steep-sided grassy Munros, including the prominent Beinn Dorain. The traverse of all five peaks in one day is a tough undertaking.

The Battle of Dalrigh was fought just S of Tyndrum in the summer of 1306 between the army of King Robert I (Robert the Bruce) of Scotland and the MacDougalls of Argyll, allies of the English. Bruce's army, reeling westwards after defeat by the English at the Battle of Methven, was intercepted and all but destroyed. Bruce himself narrowly escaped capture.

WALKING THE CORBETTS: VOL 1

Lochan on Beinn Odhar

Head N down the track signed 'Public footpath to Glen Lyon by Auch Glen'. After 350m turn sharp right under the railway along the West Highland Way. Follow it S until above the parking area and then head straight up the uncomfortably steep hillside until the gradient eases on the S ridge of **Beinn Odhar**. Follow the ridge to the large summit cairn (1hr 30min, 901m, 33740 33870).

Descend steeply SE then ESE to the pass (444m, 35040 33280) and climb steeply ESE to the trig point on the summit of **Beinn Chaorach** (3hr 10min, 818m, 35890 32810).

You might have picked up a curious line of very short posts, part of an old electric fence system, on the way up Beinn Chaorach. This fence line can be followed down the N ridge to a pass (638m, 36200 34010) and part way up Cam Chreag. When these posts head off N, continue ENE to the summit cairn on the craggy **Cam Chreag** (4hr 15min, 884m, 37550 34660). There are numerous tops on Cam Chreag, some appearing higher than the actual summit, but the author is confident that they are all at least 2m lower. ◀

If you have time it is worth wandering along to the SE top of Cam Chreag.

Route 31 – Beinn Odhar to Beinn a' Chaisteil via Cam Chreag

Head NW, taking care to stay left of the steep crags on the NE face of Cam Chreag and follow the ridge as it veers NNW down to a junction of the Allt a' Mhaim and Abhain Ghlas (395m, 36270 36610). Head up the right bank of the Allt a' Mhaim and veer up the steep S ridge to the summit cairn on **Beinn nam Fuaran** (6hr 15min, 806m, 36110 38180).

The direct descent towards Beinn a' Chaisteil goes over crumbling crags and the fence line to the right is uncomfortably steep, and could be dangerous when wet; instead, retrace your steps down the S ridge until level with the pass between Beinn nam Fuaran and Beinn a' Chaisteil and contour across to the pass (546m, 35670 37660). Follow the fence easily to the small summit cairn on **Beinn a' Chaisteil** (7hr 40min, 886m, 34720 36400).

Follow the fence down the SE ridge (direct descents to Auch Glen are dangerously steep with big crags). When the fence veers left continue down the ridge until it steepens (at about 35680 35030) when you can head SW, veering W to pick up the track up **Glen Coralan**, which

Beinn nam Fuaran seen from Beinn a' Chaisteil

has recently been improved and lengthened (8hr 20min, 340m, 35150 34750). Turn right along the track to reach Auch Glen under the railway viaduct where you turn left to reach the West Highland Way (9hr, 200m, 32710 35710). Turn left up the track back to the parking area (9hr 35min).

Alternative three-walk ascent of five Corbetts
- Climb Beinn Odhar by its SW ridge from the point where the West Highland Way crosses the railway, 1 mile (1.8km) N of Tyndrum.
- Starting from the A82 about 2.5km SE of Tyndrum, climb Beinn Chaorach by its S ridge, traverse to Cam Chreag and descend via Bealach Ghlas Leathaid and Gleann a' Chlachain.
- From Auch Glen and Glen Coralan, climb the SE ridge of Beinn a' Chaisteil, traverse to Beinn nam Fuaran, descend NE and return down the Auch Glen.

6 THE SOUTHERN GRAMPIANS (LOCH TAY AND GLEN LYON)

Glen Lochay

The Southern Grampians: Bases and facilities

Base for Routes 32–39: Killin

Killin is a small town with good facilities for tourists.

Killin Tourist Office, Breadalbane Folklore Centre, Falls of Dochart, Killin
Tel: 01567 820 254 www.visitscotland.com

Local facilities for Routes 33–38: Bridge of Balgie

Glen Lyon Teahouse is also a small store.

Ben Lawers Bunkhouse, Milton Eonan, Bridge of Balgie, Glenlyon,
PH15 2PT Tel: 01887 866 318

Walking the Corbetts: Vol 1

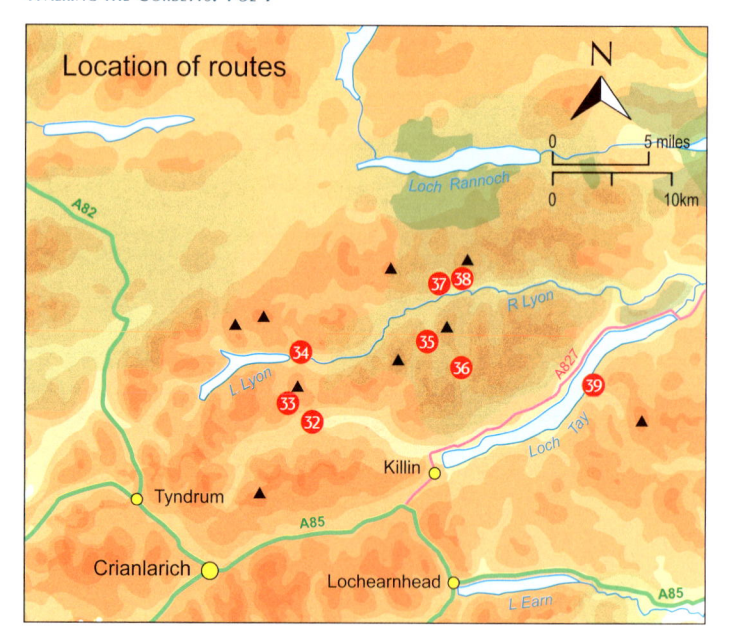

ROUTE 32

Beinn nan Imirean

HILL OF THE RIDGE

Start	Kenknock, Glen Lochay (NN 46650 36430)
Distance	21km (13 miles)
Total ascent	780m (2600ft)
Difficulty	Easy, apart from a descent down a steep grass slope
Time	5hr 25min
Summit	Beinn nan Imirean (849m, 2769ft)
Map	OS Landranger 51
Access	From Killin take the road up Glen Lochay where there is limited parking at the roadhead. There is a car park (NN 47690 36840) 1km before you get to the roadhead, with a notice: 'No parking beyond this point, please'.
Note	It would be possible to combine Beinn nan Imirean with a traverse of Meall Glas and possibly other Munros on the S side of Glen Lochay. The shortest route up Beinn nan Imirean is from Glen Dochart to the S, but this ascent would involve much heather and peat hags and miss the splendour of Glen Lochay.

Beinn nan Imirean is an outlier of the Munro Meall Glas on the ridge between Glen Dochart and Glen Lochay. The grassy peak isn't particularly interesting in itself, but the recommended route gives a magnificent walk up the dramatic Glen Lochay.

Moirlanich Longhouse, on the Glen Lochay Road (S branch) 1 mile NW of Killin, has been restored by the National Trust for Scotland. It is an outstanding example of a traditional cruck frame cottage and byre, dating from the mid-19th century. The cottage has been furnished according to archaeological evidence and displays a rare collection of the working and 'Sunday best' clothes found in the longhouse,

WALKING THE CORBETTS: VOL 1

and an exhibition interprets the history and restoration of the building. (Open 2.00–5.00pm Wednesdays and Sundays, in summer)

Follow the good track up **Glen Lochay**, ignoring right and left turns. The track goes much further than is shown on some of the older maps and you should follow it as the glen turns S and continue until a rough track heads up the hillside to the pass between Meall Glas and Beinn nan Imirean (1hr 30min, 310m, 41380 32870). Turn left, crossing the River Lochay on boulders, and follow the

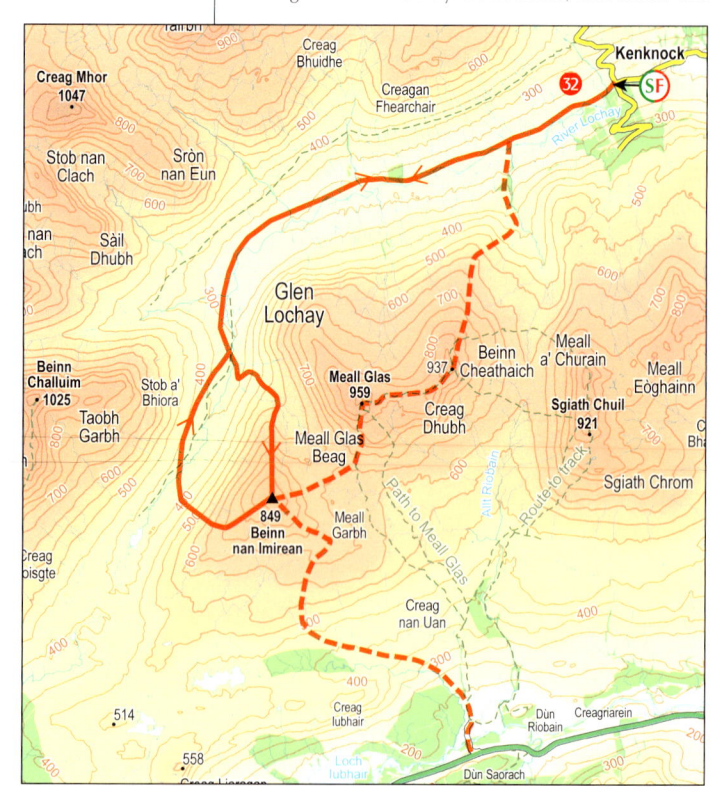

ROUTE 32 – BEINN NAN IMIREAN

track until its end (2hr 5min, 560m, 42110 32300). Head SSW to the N ridge and climb it easily to the summit of **Beinn nan Imirean**, which is marked by a small cairn on a rock outcrop (2hr 55min, 849m, 41930 30950).

It is easiest to descend by the ascent route, but for variety (in good weather) head SW then W down a steep grass slope to the River Lochay (3hr 30min, 370m, 40700 31250). Cross the river on boulders, climb to the track, turn right and follow it all the way back to the parking area (5hr 25min).

Beinn nan Imirean seen from Glen Lochay

Walking the Corbetts: Vol 1

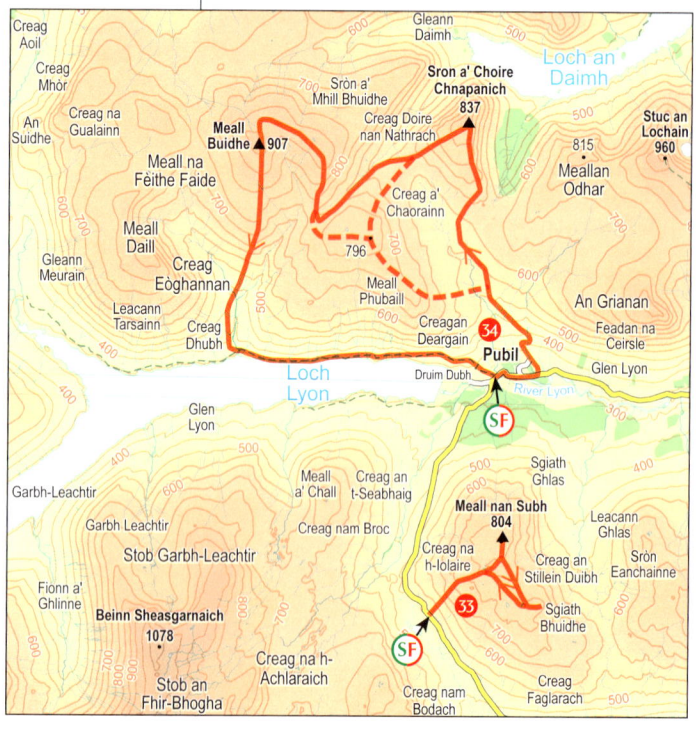

Cairn on SE summit of Meall nan Subh

ROUTE 33

Meall nan Subh

ROUNDED HILL OF THE RASPBERRY

Start	Lochan Learg nan Lunn (NN 45040 38820)
Distance	5km (3 miles)
Total ascent	350m (1200ft)
Difficulty	The initial climb and final descent is steep. Care would be needed with navigation in mist to locate the summit and to ensure a safe descent.
Time	1hr 45min
Summit	Meall nan Subh (804m, 2638ft)
Map	OS Landranger 51
Access	From Killin drive up Glen Lochay to Kenknock then take the hydroelectric road towards Glen Lyon. This is a private gated road but (at the time of writing) the gates are not locked and cars are permitted to use the road. The OS map still only shows this as a hill track but it is actually a steep, single-track tarmac road reaching a height of over 500m. It is unlikely to be passable in winter conditions. Take care as there are many large potholes. Park by the gate at the high point of the road.

Meall nan Subh is a mountain with character and despite its size it is possibly the best Corbett in Section 6. There are many small crags on the ascent and the knobbly summit plateau has many tops.

In 1700 **Pubil**, just N of Meall nan Subh, was the home of Angus Macanleister, the seventh chief of the Fletcher Clan. Much of the land he would have farmed is now drowned as a result of the dam at Lubreoch, which more than doubled the size of Loch Lyon.

Follow the fence uphill until past the power lines, then veer slightly left to avoid the large crags. Continue ENE onto **Meall nan Subh**'s summit plateau (at about 735m,

Walking the Corbetts: Vol 1

45660 39310) and head roughly NE to the summit cairn on the highest top (50min, 804m, 46080 39740).

You could return by same route, but you might as well head S then SE to the SE summit, which has an impressive cairn (760m, 1hr 10min, 46630 38900). Head NW back to the top of the ascent route (45660 39310) and descend WSW back to the parking area (1hr 45min).

ROUTE 34

Sron a' Choire Chnapanich NOSE OF THE LUMPY CORRIE
and Meall Buidhe ROUNDED YELLOW HILL

Start	Pubil, Glen Lyon (NN45940 41880)
Distance	17km (10 miles)
Total ascent	1040m (3300ft)
Difficulty	There are no paths on these hills, but the going is mainly on easy rough pasture. There is one area of peat hags and a steep descent down a grassy ridge.
Time	4hr 55min
Summits	Sron a' Choire Chnapanich (837m, 2250ft contour), Meall Buidhe (907m, 2976ft)
Map	OS Landranger 51
Access	From Killin drive up Glen Lochay to Kenknock then take the hydroelectric road to Glen Lyon (see Route 33). There is roadside parking where the hydroelectric road joins the public road in Glen Lyon.
Note	It would be possible to climb Peak 796 en route from Sron a' Choire Chnapanich to Meall Buidhe, or to return over this peak to descend to Allt Phubuill.

Sron a' Choire Chnapanich and Meall Buidhe are grassy hills between Loch Lyon and Loch an Daimh. These are two good Corbetts in an area dominated by Munros. On the OS 1in map Sron a' Choire Chnapanich was an unnamed peak with a 2250ft contour, compared with 837m (which is equivalent to 2746ft) on the latest OS 1:50,000 map.

Route 34 – Sron a' Choire Chnapanich and Meall Buidhe

The water stored in Loch Lyon is released into the River Lyon through a turbine at the base of the massive **Lubreoch Dam**. Two miles downstream the river is arrested by a smaller dam at Stronuich. At this point water from Loch Daimh to the N is also received via a tunnel bored for several miles through the hills. Most of the water collected at the Stronuich Dam is diverted into another tunnel through the hills to a power station in the Glen Lochay, to the S, before discharging into Loch Tay.

▶ Go E along the road to **Pubil**. The track marked on the OS map through Pubil is fenced off and does not allow access to the hillside. Continue down the road to a gated driveway (46540 41950), turn left up this track and fork right just before the house, then follow the track to a water catchment dam on the Allt Phubuill (40min, 510m, 45770 42990). Carry on easily up the burn. At some point (about 570m, 45260 43930) head NE towards the S ridge of **Sron a' Choire Chnapanich**, reached at about 695m, and pick up an old fence line which is followed to the summit. When the fence turns left go a short distance

See map just before Route 33.

Sron a' Choire Chnapanich seen from Allt Phubuill

155

diagonally right to the small summit cairn (1hr 40min, 837m, 45610 45300).

Return to the fence and follow it SW down to a pass covered in peat hags (2hr, 615m, 44770 44690). It is possible to climb Peak 796, but the recommendation is to head W down to the Feith Thalain (44290 44670) and head up this burn until it fades away (at about 690m, 43680 44140). Head NW and pick up an old fence line which is followed up the ridge, turning left and left again onto **Meall Buidhe**. The fence does not go to the summit, so turn left at the high point to a dilapidated cairn: this cairn is probably on the highest point rather than the better cairn on a lower point on the plateau (3hr 20min, 907m, 42700 44960).

Descend the S ridge. Towards the bottom veer right to cross the Eos Eoghannan (450m, 42360 43040) and avoid the gullies on Eas nan Aighean to your left. Stay fairly high as you descend so you can cross an unmapped burn (42350 43040) above an awkward gully and reach the good track along **Loch Lyon** (4hr 10min, 370m, 42410 42240). Turn left. It is now 4km back to the parking area (4hr 55min).

ROUTE 35
Beinn nan Oighreag
HILL OF THE CLOUDBERRIES

Start	Allt Bail a' Mhuilinn (NN 57190 43830)
Distance	9km (6 miles)
Total ascent	630m (2100ft)
Difficulty	The ascent is easy, but the suggested descent route starts down pathless grassy slopes, heather and peat hags before descending the Allt Breisleich. There are landslips into this burn and you will have to judge whether to find a way along the burn or follow animal tracks high above the water.
Time	3hr 15min
Summit	Beinn nan Oighreag (909m, 2978ft)
Map	OS Landranger 51
Access	From Killin go E along the A827 and turn left along the minor road W of Ben Lawers. A little before the forestry on the descent from the pass you will see a footbridge over the Allt Bail a' Mhuilinn. There is limited parking in a lay-by near the bridge. There is a car park and picnic area about 900m further down the glen.
Note	The inexperienced might prefer to descend by the ascent route. You could approach the mountain from Glen Lochay to the S.

Beinn nan Oighreag is a big hill filling the gap between the Munros Meall Ghaordaidh and Meall nan Tarmachan. Older maps show the middle top as the high point, but the S top is actually about 2m higher. Take care in mist because the N top has the most impressive cairn and could easily be assumed to be the summit.

It is much more difficult to measure **altitude** than many people realise. The author's GPS measurements suggest that the S top of Beinn nan Oighreag is about 5m higher than is shown on the OS map. In fact it was suggested in the 1930s that Beinn nan Oighreag could be a Munro. However, you should

Walking the Corbetts: Vol 1

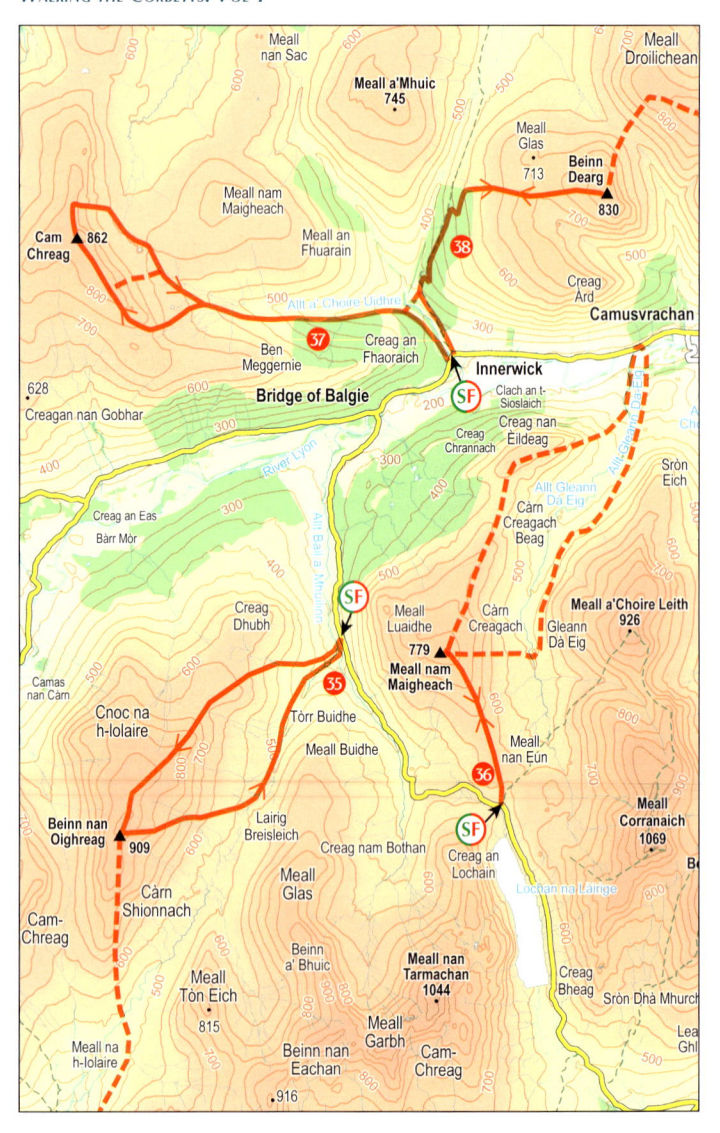

Route 35 – Beinn nan Oighreag

remember although GPS measures horizontal position very accurately, vertical height is probably not measured to better than 5–10m.

Cross the **Allt Bail a' Mhuilinn** by the bridge. If you look carefully you may be able to imagine a faint grassy track up the hillside. Assuming you can locate this old vehicle track it will take you easily to a minor summit on the ridge, avoiding heather and peat hags (1hr, 705m, 55540 43070). The old track continues and leads easily to the impressive cairn on the N top (899m, 54350 41820) of **Beinn nan Oighreag**. Head S to the middle top (54300 41410) and then SSW to the S top, a tiny cairn on a rock outcrop (1hr 50min, 909m, 54170 41190).

Cut diagonally (roughly E) down grass slopes and then through heather and peat hags in **Lairig Breisleich** to the source of the Allt Breisleich (2hr 25min, 550m, 55980 41540). Descend the left bank of the burn. You will occasionally have to climb high above the water to avoid landslips. Continue back to the Allt Bail a' Mhuilinn and back to the parking area (3hr 15min).

Allt Breisleich on Beinn nan Oighreag

Walking the Corbetts: Vol 1

ROUTE 36
Meall nam Maigheach
ROUNDED HILL OF THE HARE

Start	Lochan na Lairige (NN 59360 41580)
Distance	5km (3 miles)
Total ascent	260m (900ft)
Difficulty	The ridge is pathless heather and peat hags, but at this altitude the growth is rather stunted and although the going is a little rough in places it is not particularly difficult.
Time	1hr 35min
Summit	Meall nam Maigheach (779m, 2558ft)
Map	OS Landranger 51
Access	From Killin go E along the A827 and turn left along the minor road W of Ben Lawers. Just after the N end of Lochan na Lairige you will see a large cairn above the road, below which there is very limited parking.
Note	You could start at Camusvrachan to the NE and ascend Gleann D-Eig, climb the E ridge of Meall nam Maigheach, then descend the NE ridge.

Meall nam Maigheach, an outlier of the well-known Munro Ben Lawers, is a featureless tract of moorland. It appears on older maps as Meall Luaidhe (hill of lead) but this is now the name given to the W top, which is 3m lower than the E summit. The best walk is probably the suggested alternative, but the route described here is the shortest and would make a good walk for a sunny evening.

Lawers Dam was constructed across the S end of Lochan na Lairige in 1951–1956 as part of the Breadalbane hydroelectric scheme, raising the water level by 27m. The reservoir is fed by a system of tunnels and aqueducts from a 45 km^2 catchment area, and from it the water drops 415m to the Finlarig power station on Loch Tay.

Ben Lawers seen from the cairn above the parking area

▸ Climb to the cairn above the road and head roughly N to **Meall nan Eun** (635m, 59390 42020). Cross an easy peat hag and head NNW, veering NW to the summit cairn on **Meall nam Maigheach** (55min, 779m, 58560 43600).

Return by the same route (1hr 35min).

See map in Route 35.

ROUTE 37

Cam Chreag CROOKED CRAG

Start	Innerwick (NN 58650 47510)
Distance	13km (8 miles)
Total ascent	660m (2200ft)
Difficulty	There are some short sections of tough heather and care will be needed with navigation if descending in mist.
Time	3hr 25min
Summit	Cam Chreag (862m, 2823ft)
Map	OS Landranger 51
Access	From Killin go E along the A827 and turn left along the minor road W of Ben Lawers to Bridge of Balgie. Turn right to Innerwick where there is a car park and picnic site.
Note	In bad weather it would make sense to follow the access track as far as the final bend (54670 48660) before the hut and then follow an old vehicle track that reaches the ridge a little S of the summit.

WALKING THE CORBETTS: VOL 1

> Cam Chreag, in Glen Lyon, has a nice ridge but is surrounded by tough heather moorland. Route 37 shares the car park with Route 38 and the routes are short enough to climb both routes in one day.

Meggernie Castle, built around 1585 with later additions, is believed by many to be haunted. Menzies of Culdares murdered his wife in a fit of rage and concealed her body in a chest one of the castle towers. He went away for some time and when he returned spread the story that his wife had drowned while they were travelling in Europe. It was time to dispose of the body, so he cut it in two, burying the lower half in the graveyard and leaving the upper part still in the chest. Unfortunately, before he was able to bury the upper half, he was murdered himself.

Most ghost sightings have involved guests staying at the castle who claim to have seen the upper part of a woman's body floating through the air. One visitor to the castle claims to have been awakened one night by a kiss on his cheek. When he sat up in bed he saw the ghostly form of a woman's torso moving away from him, before passing through the wall.

See map in Route 35.

◀ Take the estate road from the car park and follow it W up the **Allt a' Choire Uidhre**, ignoring unmapped tracks off to the right. Continue until the second sharp right-hand bend (1hr, 560m, 55400 48240). Head WSW over rough moorland towards the SE ridge of **Cam Chreag** and then head, with increasing ease, NW up the ridge, which has some interesting rock formations. Continue NNW along the summit plateau to the cairn on the summit (1hr 55min, 862m, 53680 49120).

Continue NW for about 7min then N to a shallow pass (820m, 53550 49500). Descend the grass and heather slopes to the right. You may be able to pick up an old faint vehicle track on the descent; otherwise pick it up

Allt Choire Uidhre on Cam Creag

by some big boulders (2hr 15min, 670m, 53990 49300). Follow the old vehicle track (occasionally marked by posts) to a corrugated iron shed at the end of the main track (2hr 30min, 640m, 54700 48700). Follow the track 5km back to the car park (3hr 25min).

ROUTE 38
Beinn Dearg RED HILL

Start	Innerwick (NN 58650 47510)
Distance	10km (6 miles)
Total ascent	620m (2000ft)
Difficulty	There are sections of relatively easy, pathless, heather and peat hags.
Time	2hr 50min
Summit	Beinn Dearg (830m, 2702ft)
Map	OS Landranger 51
Access	Parking as for Route 37
Note	Beinn Dearg could be included in a traverse of Carn Gorm and possibly more of the Munros to the E.

Beinn Dearg is a heather-covered dome, better seen from a distance than close-up! It is actually just the W peak on the ridge stretching along the N side of Glen Lyon which includes four Munros.

Innerwick War Memorial is a tall cairn built by Alex McCallum in 1921 in memory of the men of Glen Lyon who died in World War I. His son, John McCallum, a private in the Black Watch (Royal Highlanders), died in France on 17 October 1918 in the last month of the war.

See map in Route 35.

◀ Return to the road, cross the bridge, pass the large war memorial cairn and then turn left up a forestry track signed 'Path to Loch Rannoch'. Keep straight on at a double gate, then veer right when a track goes off left (58260 48530). ◀ Continue until there is a track going off sharp right (465m, 58670 49550).

This track could be used to combine Routes 37 and 38 without returning to Innerwick.

Turn right up this track and follow it to the edge of the forest (50min, 560m, 58960 49720). Pick up a ribbon of grass that leads easily to the pass S of **Meall Glas**. At this point **Beinn Dearg** comes into view and you should head E towards it across peat hags and heather moorland. A line of old fence posts joins from the left and this is followed more easily to the summit plateau. When the fence line bends left, veer slightly right to the summit cairn, which may be the highest point on this flat plateau (1hr 40min, 830m, 60880 49710).

Return by the same route (2hr 50min).

Beinn Dearg

ROUTE 39

Creagan na Beinne

HILL OF THE CRAGS

Start	Ardtalnaig (NN 70200 39270)
Distance	18km (11 miles)
Total ascent	840m (2800ft)
Difficulty	Easy, but care is needed with navigation in mist
Time	4hr 55min
Summit	Creagan na Beinne (888m, 2909ft)
Maps	OS Landranger 51 and 52
Access	From Killin take the minor road along the S shore of Loch Tay. There is limited parking at Ardtalnaig.
Note	The route could be completed with an ascent of Beinn Bhreac. It could also be combined with an ascent of Creag Uchdag (see Route 25).

Walking the Corbetts: Vol 1

Creagan na Beinne is the highest point on the vast moorland plateau SE of Loch Tay. It would appear to fit naturally into Section 4, but it is easier to climb when based at Killin rather than Crieff. It has remarkably few crags for a hill named 'hill of the crags'.

Two **long-distance routes** follow the minor road along the S shore of Loch Tay. The Rob Roy Way is a 79-mile (126km) walk from Drymen to Pitlochry and links together many of the places associated with Rob Roy Macgregor, the popular hero and outlaw who lived in these parts from 1671 to 1734. National Cycle Route 7 is a long-distance cycle route between Sunderland and Inverness via Penrith, Carlisle, Dumfries, Ayr, Glasgow, Pitlochry and Aviemore.

Take the road signed 'Footpath to Glen Almond' on the S side of the Allt a' Chilleine at **Ardtalnaig**. The road

Crannog on Loch Tay

ROUTE 39 – CREAGAN NA BEINNE

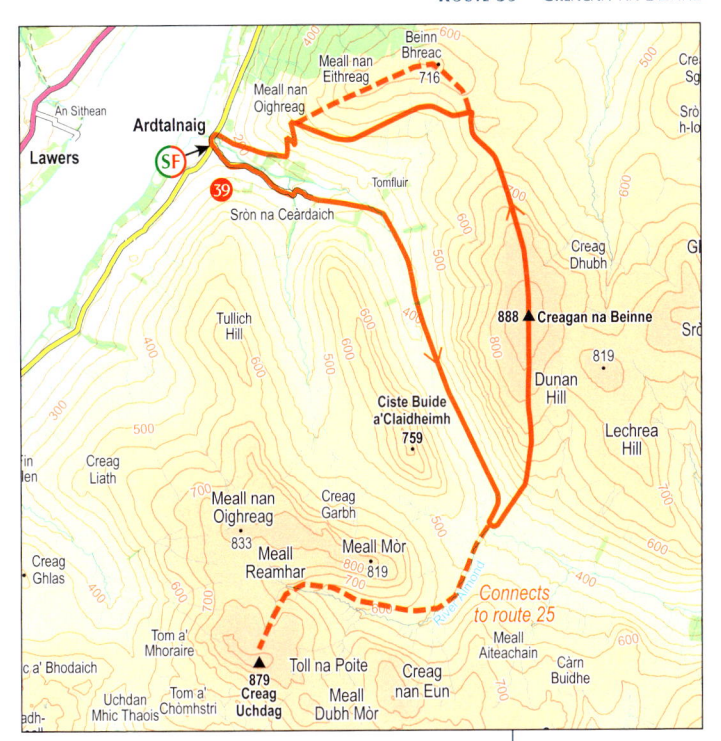

becomes a track at Claggan Farm (30min, 295m). After passing through the farmyard fork left up Gleann a' Chilleine, a typical U-shaped valley, and follow the track to the locked bothy at Dunan (1hr 45min, 435m, 74020 34090). Go left of the sheepfold and pick up a faint grass track up the hillside and onto the broad summit plateau. When the track fades continue N to the summit cairn on **Creagan na Beinne** (3hr 10min, 888m, 74450 36850).

Head N along the line of fence posts that pass about 40m E of the summit cairn. Keep straight on at a fence corner and follow the fence as it curves left and right to avoid peat hags, before curving round Hill 658. A grassy track crosses the pass after this small peak (3hr 55min,

645m, 73810 39730). You could continue over Beinn Bhreac to the NW, but it is easier to follow the sometimes boggy grass track left until it appears to end at a wall junction (4hr 35min, 365m, 71040 39370). The track actually switchbacks left through a gap in the wall, and continues to switchback down the hillside to come out at the road (70210 39310). The parking area is 70m to the left across the bridge (4hr 55min).

7 THE WESTERN GRAMPIANS (GLEN COE AND KINLOCHLEVEN)

NW ridge of Creach Bheinn (Route 40)

The Western Grampians: Bases and facilities

Base for Routes 40–50: Glencoe and Ballachulish

Glencoe Village at the foot of Glencoe and the villages of Ballachulish and North Ballachulish, on Loch Leven, are extremely popular and provide excellent facilities for tourists. Glencoe village has two campsites.

There are two large hotels: The Glencoe Hotel (Tel: 01855 811 245) and the Isles of Glencoe Hotel (Tel: 0844 855 9134 www.islesofglencoe.co.uk). There are also guesthouses and B&Bs.

Just N of Glencoe is the Clachaig Inn, which has been frequented by climbers for many years. Tel: 01855 811 252 www.clachaig.com

Kings House Hotel is a remote inn at the head of Glen Coe and is popular with walkers and climbers. Tel: 01855 851 259 www.kingshousehotel.co.uk

Ballachulish Visitor and Tourist Information Centre has a gift shop and cafe as well as exhibitions. Ballachulish, PH49 4JB Tel: 01855 811 866 info@glencoetourism.co.uk

Ballachulish has a co-op and Glencoe has a village store.

WALKING THE CORBETTS: VOL 1

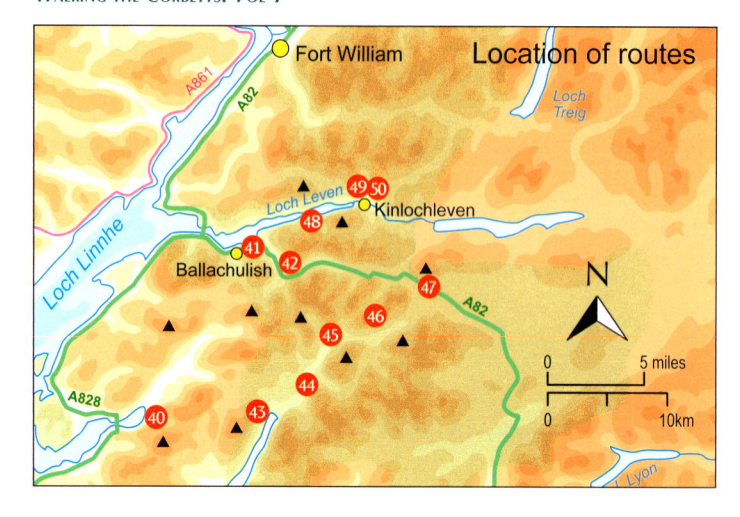

Glencoe Visitor Centre is on the A82 about 1 mile E of Glencoe Village has a gift shop selling local products and a cafe as well as superb exhibitions, video presentations and information for walkers and climbers. Tel: 0844 483 2222. The visitor centre access is shared with a large camping and caravan site.

Glencoe SYHA, Glencoe, Ballachulish, Argyll, PH49 4HX Tel: 01855 811 219

Glencoe Independent Hostel Tel: 01855 811 906 www.glencoehostel.co.uk

Local facilities for Routes 47–49: Kinlochleven

Kinlochleven is a large village with several hotels, a co-op, fish and chip shop, hostel, campsite and the Ice Factor (see below).

Blackwater Hostel and Campsite, Lab Road, Kinlochleven, Argyll, PH50 4SG Tel: 01855 831 253 www.blackwaterhostel.co.uk

The Ice Factor in Kinlochleven has the biggest indoor ice-climbing facility in the world, as well as a large rock-climbing wall. The instructors run courses suitable for beginners in climbing and mountaineering, using the facilities at the centre as well as in surrounding mountains. Experienced climbers can make independent use of the facilities. In addition there is a sauna, outdoor equipment shop, cafe, restaurant and bar.
Tel: 01855 831 100 www.ice-factor.co.uk

ROUTE 40
Creach Bheinn WINDSWEPT HILL

Start	Druimavuic, Loch Creran (NN 00900 45080)
Distance	15km (9 miles)
Total ascent	1020m (3400ft)
Difficulty	Easy in good weather, but care would be needed with navigation in mist, especially finding the best route through the crags in descent.
Time	4hr 25min
Summit	Creach Bheinn (810m, 2656ft)
Map	OS Landranger 50
Access	From Glencoe follow the A82, then A828, W round the coast to Loch Creran. After crossing the bridge over Loch Creran, turn left along the S shore to Druimavuic at the head of the loch. Park in a lay-by on the right just after Druimavuic.
Note	Creach Bheinn could be combined with an ascent of Beinn Sgulaird. The best way would be to climb the W ridge of Beinn Sgulaird and then follow the SW ridge to Creach Bheinn.

Creach Bheinn is a summit on the ridge stretching SW from the Munro Beinn Sgulaird. Access is limited by the forests to the W and the roadless Glen Etive to the SE. The NE ridge, which is climbed, is grassy with many crags, outcrops and erratic boulders, but it is not the fortress suggested by the OS map. There are very good views, particularly W to Mull and E across Loch Etive.

Until 1999 the **road bridge** across the River Creran at the head of Loch Creran was the main road from Oban to Fort William. It has now been replaced by the bridge across the narrows, which was built on the piers of a former railway bridge.

Head back towards **Druimavuic** and turn left along a track immediately N of the Druimavuic drive. Follow

WALKING THE CORBETTS: VOL 1

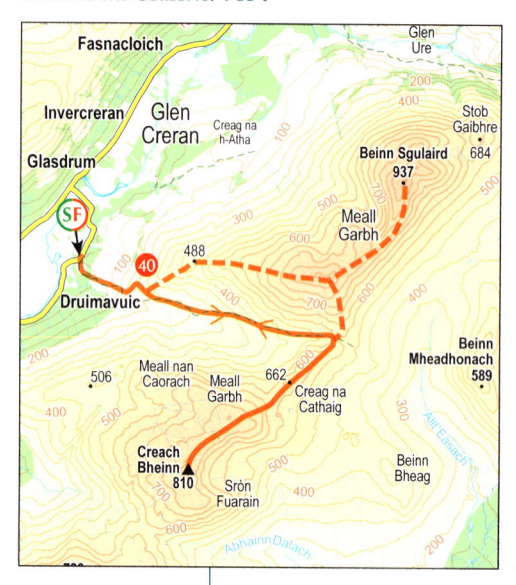

this track, ignoring a couple of right forks, all the way to the pass between Creach Bheinn and Beinn Sgulaird at the head of Coire Buidhe (1hr 20min, 565m, 04430 44060). Head SW to **Creag na Cathaig** (662m, 03790 43390) and descend to a pass (610m, 03510 43150). Pick a route through the crags up the steep grass slope to the multi-topped NE summit of **Creach Bheinn** and head SW along the knobbly summit plateau to the trig point on the summit (2hr 35min, 810m, 02380 42240).

Return by the same route to the track (3hr 30min) and the parking area (4hr 25min).

Trig point on the SW summit of Creach Bheinn

ROUTE 41

Fraochaidh HEATHERY HILL

Start	Ballachulish (NN 08380 58460)
Distance	21km (13 miles)
Total ascent	1250m (4100ft)
Difficulty	Easy, but rather boggy in places
Time	6hr 30min
Summit	Fraochaidh (879m, 2883ft)
Map	OS Landranger 41
Access	From Glencoe, head W along the A82 to Ballachulish and park at the Tourist Information Centre.
Note	There are probably shorter routes up through the forest from Glen Duror or Glen Creran, but with so much forestry work going on these routes could change dramatically over the next few years.

Fraochaidh, hidden away S of Beinn a' Bheithir, is surrounded by forest that is reaching maturity and is gradually being clear-felled. The long ridge walk suggested gives very good views back to Glen Coe and forward to Loch Linnhe.

The **Ballachulish Bridge** was opened in 1975 replacing the Ballachulish ferry, which crossed the narrows separating Loch Leven from Loch Linnhe on the main west coast route between Glasgow and Inverness. The alternative to the ferry was a 30km diversion along the narrow road round the head of Loch Leven.

Head S from the visitor centre, forking left at the co-op. Cross the River Laroch, turn left past the primary school and continue as the road becomes a track and then an increasingly boggy footpath. Continue above the River Laroch to a prominent cairn (1hr 5min, 240m, 06860 54810). ▶ Just beyond the cairn a faint path leads down

The paths shown on the OS map around here no longer exist.

173

WALKING THE CORBETTS: VOL 1

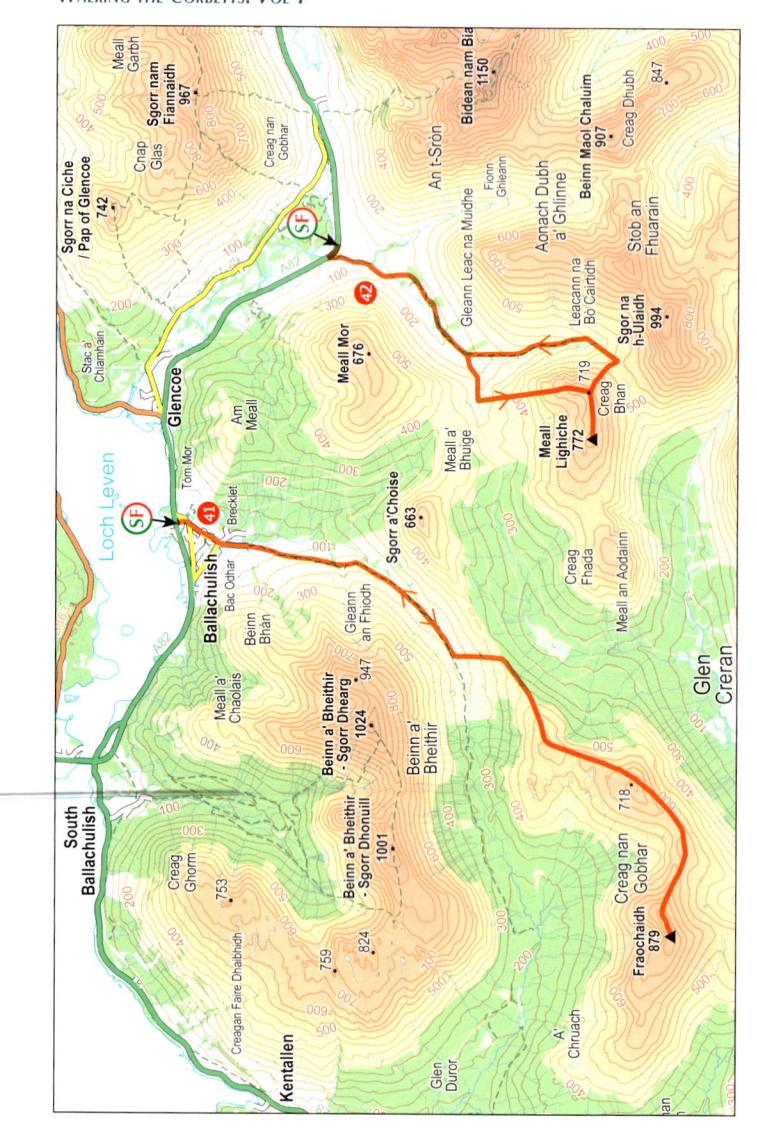

Burn in Gleann an Fhiodh, Fraochaidh

to the river and along its N bank. A pair of cairns mark the point to cross the river (06600 54610). From here a faint path leads up a line of boggy grass to reach the original path further up the slope and onto the ridge at a stile into Glen Creran Forest (1hr 30min, 395m, 06540 53980).

Turn right on a path that follows the fence. At 590m you must climb the fence as it crosses the ridge and continue along the path, which now follows an old fence line. You pass over three summits (626m, 05370 53330; 718m, 04870 52190; and 671m, 04090 51560) before a steeper final climb and narrow final ridge leads you to the cairn on the summit of **Fraochaidh** (3hr 45min, 879m, 02920 51710).

Return by the same route to the River Laroch (5hr 30min) and then back to **Ballachulish** (6hr 30min).

ROUTE 42

Meall Lighiche ROUNDED HILL OF THE DOCTOR

Start	Glencoe Mountain Cottages (NN 12000 56360)
Distance	12km (7 miles)
Total ascent	800m (2600ft)
Difficulty	Care must be taken in descent down the grassy SE ridge of Creag Bhan, which has many bands of crags, none of which are shown on the OS map. The Allt na Muidhe could be difficult to ford if it is in flood.
Time	3hr 55min
Summit	Meall Lighiche (772m, 2468ft)
Map	OS Landranger 41
Access	Take the A82 E from Glencoe. About 1 mile after the Glencoe Visitor Centre there is a private road on the left signed 'Glencoe Mountain Cottages'. Continue to a parking area on the left a little further up the A82.
Note	If the Allt na Muidhe is in flood then it would be possible to ascend and descend by the recommended descent route.

Meall Lighiche, which is hidden from view among the hills to the S of Glencoe village, is really the NW summit of the Munro Sgorr na h-Ulaidh. Meall Lighiche was below 2500ft on the OS 1 inch:1 mile maps, but is shown about 20m higher on the newest maps.

The name **Glen Coe** is often thought to mean Glen of Weeping, after the infamous Massacre of Glencoe. However, it is actually named after the River Coe, which bore this name long before that incident.

In early February 1692, 120 men under the command of Captain Robert Campbell of Glenlyon were billeted on the MacDonalds in Glencoe and received with the hospitality traditionally given in the Highlands. On the excuse that Alastair Maclain, 12th Chief of Glencoe, was late in pledging

ROUTE 42 – MEALL LIGHICHE

allegiance to the new monarchs, William and Mary, Campbell was ordered 'to fall upon the rebels, the McDonalds of Glencoe, and put all to the sword under seventy'. Early in the morning of 13 February 1692 his troops murdered 38 MacDonalds, and at least 40 women and children died from exposure after their homes were burnt.

In those days few Scots would have had any concern about the murder of so many MacDonalds, but this was considered to be a heinous crime because the rules of hospitality had been broken.

▶ Return to and follow the private road. Shortly after the track crosses the Allt na Muidhe by some cottages, take a path to the left which rejoins the track after passing some houses. Continue to the end of the track (35min, 165m, 10610 54570). Continue to the stream junction and cross the Allt na Muidhe, possibly getting wet feet. Follow the right-hand tributary to a fence, which is followed until it crosses the burn again (250m, 10140 54290). Head S up the ridge, which steepens as crags are easily bypassed. When the flat summit of **Creag Bhan** (719m, 10160 52990) is reached, continue to an old fence line and turn right along it to the summit of **Meall Lighiche**, which is marked by a tiny cairn on a rock outcrop (2hr 5min, 772m, 09490 52830).

See map in Route 41.

Lambs in Gleann-Leac-na-muidhe

Walking the Corbetts: Vol 1

Retrace your steps along the fence line and follow it down the SE ridge of Creag Bhan. There are many bands of crags, but these are fairly easy to bypass before the pass between Creag Bhan and Sgor na h-Ulaidh is reached (2hr 40min, 530m, 10390 52430). Head NE down to the Allt na Muidhe (10740 52910), cross the burn and descend the wild glen. You will soon pick up a path, which is followed down to the track end (3hr 25min); then follow the track back to the parking area (3hr 55min).

ROUTE 43

Beinn Trilleachan SANDPIPER MOUNTAIN

Start	Kinlochetive (NN 11160 45340)
Distance	8km (5 miles)
Total ascent	1050m (3500ft)
Difficulty	It is necessary to pick a way through the crags on Meall nan Gobhar and on the steep 70m descent through crags on the summit ridge. There is no great difficulty but care is needed.
Time	4hr 10min
Summit	Beinn Trilleachan (839m, 2752ft)
Map	OS Landranger 50
Access	From Glencoe head E up the A82, then turn right down Glen Etive to a car park at the end of the public road beside Loch Etive.

Beinn Trilleachan dominates the view as Loch Etive is approached down Glen Etive. There are granite crags and slabs all over the mountain which is best known for the Etive slabs (Trilleachan slabs on the OS map), which have attracted rock climbers for generations.

The **common sandpiper** is a small short-legged wader which breeds in the Highlands and will often be seen along the stony shorelines of upland lochs and shingle beds of the burns and rivers in

ROUTE 43 – BEINN TRILLEACHAN

Beinn Trilleachan and Glen Etive seen from Stob Dubh

the Highlands. You will probably see the bird flying low over the water with flickering wings and a shrill 'twee-wee-wee' call.

Head up to the left of the forestry (possibly clear-felled by the time you read this), aided by the remains of the old path between Loch Etive and Loch Creran. Continue until the ground levels as the forest boundary veers left (25min, 180m, 10800 46130). Turn left up the ridge, easily finding grassy ramps through the crags. From about 500m, rock slabs replace the crags and it is easy going to the NE summit of Beinn Trilleachan (1hr 55min, 767m, 09600 44680). Descend SW carefully over crags. If you go slightly left or right of the direct line to the pass (700m, 09460 44580) this can be done on grassy ramps. Continue easily to the well-built main summit cairn on **Beinn Trilleachan** (2hr 30min, 839m, 08650 43890).

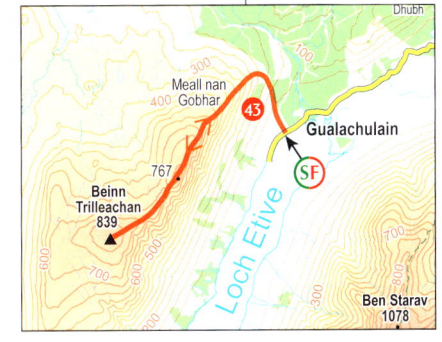

179

Return to the NE summit (3hr) and then descend the NE ridge. It may be an idea to go a bit left of the ascent line to make it easier to find lines through the crags. Descend to the forest and then turn right back to the car park (4hr 10min).

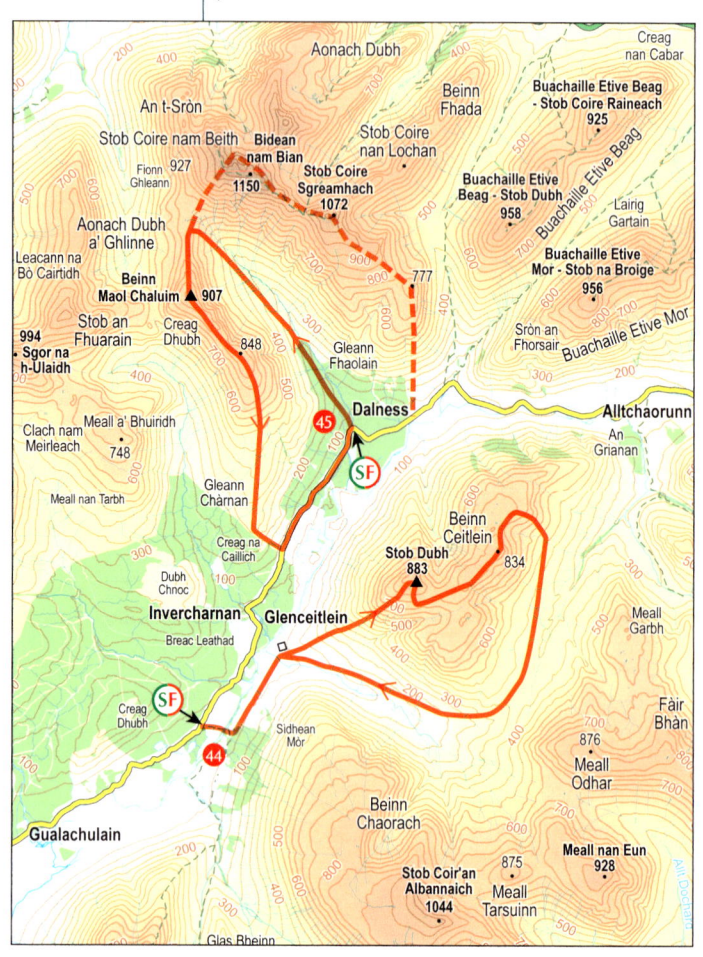

ROUTE 44
Stob Dubh BLACK PEAK

Start	Glen Etive (NN 13650 46800)
Distance	14km (9 miles)
Total ascent	1100m (3600ft)
Difficulty	Inexperienced walkers should not attempt this mountain in poor weather. Route-finding in descent on the steep crag-bound slopes that surround Stob Dubh could be difficult in mist and could lead the walker into dangerous situations. The going is actually relatively easy if the route described is followed accurately.
Time	5hr 15min
Summit	Stob Dubh (883m, 2897ft)
Map	OS Landranger 50
Access	From Glencoe head E up the A82 and turn right down Glen Etive. When about 3km from the head of Loch Etive there is a gated track that goes sharp left, signed 'Hill path – bridge'. There are several parking spots close to the gate.
Note	The peak-bagger might want to descend by the ascent route. Finding the easy way through the crags from above won't be straightforward and it is not recommended that you attempt the descent of the SW ridge unless you climbed the ridge first and fixed the descent route in your mind.

A rival guidebook suggests a direct descent SE from Beinn Ceitlein, but this route is well guarded by crags (not all shown on the OS map) and this appears to be a dangerous option.

The peak described here is Stob Dubh to the S of Glen Etive, not the Munro with the same name to the N of the glen. Stob Dubh is a steep grassy peak, well protected by crags. The suggested route is designed to allow you an excellent view of the Munros that seem to surround this Corbett, as well as to provide an easy, safe descent off this intimidating mountain.

The **Glen Etive** road meanders for some 14 miles to the head of Loch Etive where the derelict pier

Glen Etive seen from Stob Dubh

has recently been renovated to allow timber to be shipped out, now that harvesting the forests in the glen has started, with the intention of replanting with native trees such as oak and Scots pine. Glen Etive hasn't always been so quiet: in 1750 there was a good track running down the S side of the loch as far as Taynuilt and from 1847 a steamer service operated from Oban to the pier.

Follow the track across the bridge, then fork left along a track to a bridge over the Allt Ceitlein (20min, 35m, 14810 47710). Before you head up the ridge try and get a picture of the crags and the easy breaks through them. Fork left past Glenceitlein Cottage and, when the track levels out, head right up the ever-steepening ridge. There is a path developing on the lower slopes and also through the crags. If in doubt, turn crags on their left to avoid the more continuous crags on the right of the ridge. Once through the band of crags at about 600m the gradient eases a little and it's an easy climb to the summit cairn on **Stob Dubh** (2hr 10min, 883m, 16640 48820).

The direct descent to the ESE is rocky and difficult. Instead, head S on grassy slopes, then veer E to the pass (765m, 16970 48630) between Stob Dubh and Beinn Ceitlein. Head easily to the SW top (850m, 17410 48840) on the knobbly summit plateau of **Beinn Ceitlein** and then head NE to the NE top (2hr 50min, 834m, 17800 49240). Head down the N ridge for about 15min, veering a little to the right until there appears to be an easy descent over grass (at about 750m, 18090 49710). Descend SE down a steep but manageable slope, easily avoiding a number of crags. Aim to cross the burn on your right just below the crags that are across from the burn (3hr 25min, 480m, 18390 49360).

Head roughly S, diagonally downhill. At some point (probably about 18330 48120) you should pick up the remains of an old stalker's path, which is followed easily through boggy rough pasture. This path eventually fades away (at about 17970 47240) but by then you are just above the source of the Allt Ceitlein. This burn is followed downstream, at some stage picking up the path descending from the Munro Meall nan Eun, and descending down to shielings where the path is shown starting on the OS maps (4hr 40min, 85m, 15810 47370). Continue down the path to the bridge, turn left and retrace your steps to your starting point (5hr 15min).

Walking the Corbetts: Vol 1

ROUTE 45
Beinn Maol Chaluim
Calum's bare mountain

Start	Glen Etive (NN 15790 50830)
Distance	11km (7 miles)
Total ascent	960m (3200ft)
Difficulty	The ascent is relatively easy. On the descent it is necessary to search for easy routes through the many bands of crags (not shown on OS map) on the S ridge of Beinn Maol Chaluim. The final descent to the road is uncomfortably steep.
Time	4hr
Summit	Beinn Maol Chaluim (907m, 2967ft)
Maps	OS Landranger 41 and 50
Access	Take the A82 E from Glencoe and turn right down Glen Etive. About a mile after Dalness House there is a parking area on a sharp bend.
Note	A circuit of the peaks surrounding Gleann Fhaolain could be attempted, starting with the ascent of the Munros Stob Coire Sgreamhach and Bidean nam Bian and descending over Beinn Maol Chaluim. This would be rough and tough.

Beinn Maol Chaluim is a summit on the S ridge of Bidean nam Bian, a complex mountain lying between Glen Coe and Glen Etive. Bidean nam Bian is best known for the 'Three Sisters of Glen Coe' (Aonach Dubh, Gearr Aonach and Beinn Fhada), which form the impressive S wall of Glencoe.

We usually like to climb mountains in **good weather**, but it can be equally rewarding in bad weather. After heavy rain the ascent of Gleann Fhaolain is special with the burns in flood and the many waterfalls are magnificent. It isn't very interesting to climb the ridges in the cloud, but sudden clearances in the cloud can give spectacular views.

ROUTE 45 – BEINN MAOL CHALUIM

▶ Cross the river and head about 50m down the glen, then turn sharp right up a forest track which isn't very obvious from the road. Follow this track easily to the top of the forest (25min, 205m, 15050 51950). Continue along the track until it ends (255m, 14860 52220) and then continue up **Gleann Fhaolain**. When the glen steepens follow the main burn and climb to the pass at the top of the corrie (1hr 40min, 700m, 13550 53560). Turn S, following a line of fence posts to the foot of a boulderfield. Climb this to the summit of **Beinn Maol Chaluim**, which is honoured with two cairns (2hr 5min, 907m, 13500 52580).

Head easily SE down the narrow ridge to the SW top (848m, 14210 51820) and then descend SSE. Care will be needed to bypass the many crags. At the bottom of the steep slope head S over rough pasture, aiming for the high point of the forest (3hr 20min, 290m, 14340 49470). Follow the fence down the steep grassy slope to the road (14800 49240), where there is parking for a couple of vehicles. Turn left along the road back to your starting point (4hr).

See map just before Route 44.

Beinn Maol Chaluim and Bidean nam Bian from Stob Dubh

Walking the Corbetts: Vol 1

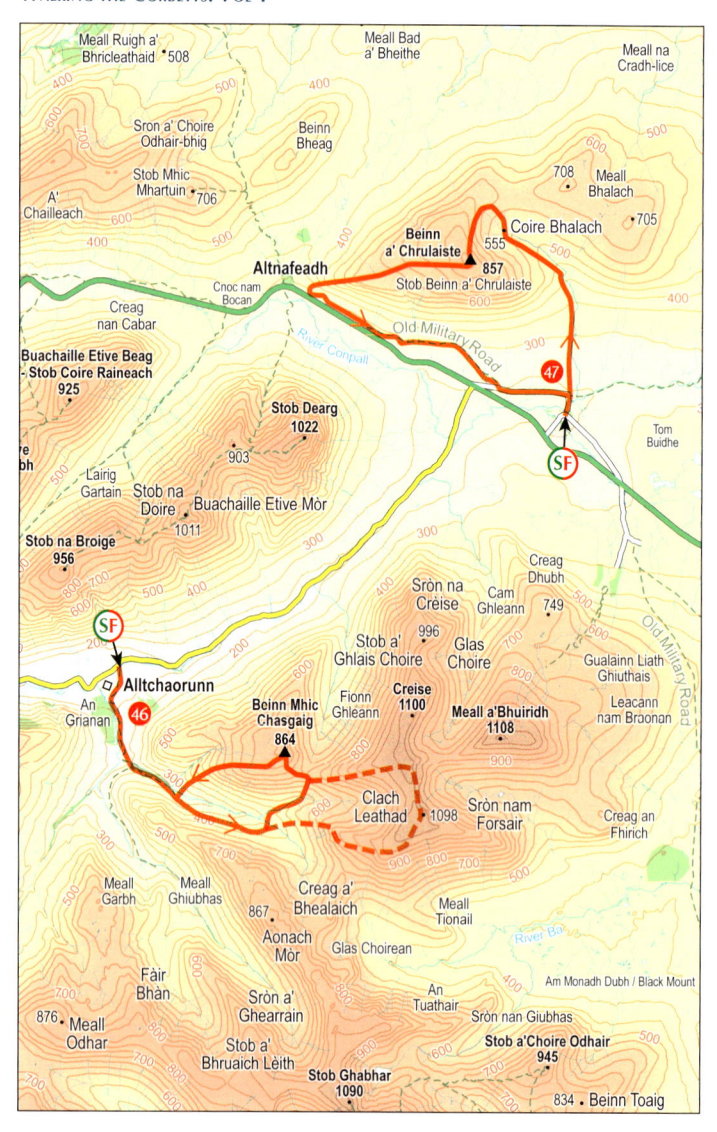

ROUTE 46
Beinn Mhic Chasgaig
MACCHASGAIG'S HILL

Start	Glen Etive (NN 19790 51280)
Distance	9km (6 miles)
Total ascent	780m (2600ft)
Difficulty	This Corbett is not recommended for inexperienced walkers in poor weather. The experienced mountaineer will want to follow this route when the Allt Coire Ghiubhasan is running high, when the river cascades dramatically down granite slabs and over many waterfalls. The downside of this is that there are three river crossings where it is necessary to ford the streams. Great care is needed with navigation in descent to find the route that avoids the steep slopes and crags.
Time	3hr 30min
Summit	Beinn Mhic Chasgaig (864m, 2820ft)
Maps	OS Landranger 41 and 50
Access	From Glencoe head E up the A82 and then turn right down Glen Etive. Continue down the glen until there is a gated bridge across the river on the left. There is parking for one vehicle and further parking just down the road.
Note	It's not a good idea to do this route in reverse as the descent would be uncomfortably steep and the best line would not be obvious from above. It would be natural to continue from Beinn Mhic Chasgaig with a traverse of the Munro Clach Leathad, round the head of Coire Odhar.

Beinn Mhic Chasgaig may just look like a little peak on the W ridge of Creise, but it is a fine mountain in its own right. It is well protected by the River Etive to the N and crags on its N, W and S faces.

River Etive has a series of fantastic rock pools, which make it an exciting place for wild swimming. Many of these pools are at the foot of waterfalls and this is a play area for expert canoeists who like to

Allt Coire Ghiubhasan on Beinn Mhic Chasgaig

shoot the rapids and jump the falls. The annual Etive River Race covers 2.5km with a total drop of over 50m and seven drops/rapids to overcome.

Cross the river and follow a boggy waymarked path SSW, which bypasses **Alltchaorunn Lodge**. This path soon joins the good stalker's path up Allt Coire Ghiubhasan. Continue about 100m upstream of the confluence with the Allt a' Chaorainn, where there is a footbridge hidden in the gorge (30min, 195m, 19990 50000). Cross the bridge and head uphill to pick up the path up the right bank of the gorge of the Allt Coire Ghiubhasan. Continue up the gorge as it opens out until the burn splits at a waterslide above a waterfall (1hr 10min, 395m, 21780 49230).

Head slightly upstream to find a safe crossing place, ford the burn and follow the NE branch up Coire Odhar. When the gradient eases, ford this burn and continue up its left-hand side until it enters a bit of a gorge below a waterfall. Head steeply up grassy slopes, aiming for the pass between Beinn Mhic Chasgaig and Clach Leathad. There are some small waterslides obstructing the direct route and these are safer to cross higher up the mountain, after which you veer right to the pass (1hr 40min, 700m, 22410 49860). Head easily NW up grass slopes, veering right to the small cairn on the summit plateau of **Beinn Mhic Chasgaig** (2hr, 864m, 22110 50180).

Head SW, gradually veering W to pick up the grassy ridge to the left of the burn, which is in a deep gully draining the S slopes of Beinn Mhic Chasgaig. Keep clear of the crags on the S face: it would not be safe to descend this face. The grassy ridge leads SW to the Allt Coire Ghiubhasan (2hr 50min, 245m, 20630 49610). Ford the burn, turn right and follow the path back to the parking area (3hr 30min).

ROUTE 47

Beinn a' Chrulaiste ROCKY HILL

Start	Kings House Hotel (NN 25950 54630)
Distance	11km (7 miles)
Total ascent	660m (2200ft)
Difficulty	The ascent is easy. Care would be needed in the descent of the W ridge in mist to avoid the dangerous crags on the S face of the mountain.
Time	3hr 30min
Summit	Beinn a' Chrulaiste (857m, 2811ft)
Map	OS Landranger 41
Access	From Glencoe head E up the A82 to the Kings House Hotel at the head of Glen Coe. Parking is permitted at the hotel.

Beinn a' Chrulaiste does not look very impressive when viewed from the Kings House Hotel, but the ascent up the cascading Allt a' Bhalaich and the views back to Rannoch Moor, to the magnificent Buachaille Etive Mor and down Glen Coe make this a very good walk.

Beinn a' Chrulaiste seen over the Kings House Hotel

The **Kings House**, on the W edge of Rannoch Moor, was built in the 17th century and is one of Scotland's oldest licensed inns. The Wade military road crosses the River Etive at the inn, before heading towards Glen Coe and ascending the Devils Staircase to Kinlochleven and on to Fort William. The name 'King's House' was acquired when the inn was used as a base by troops conducting operations to crush the Jacobites in the Western Highlands in 1746. When the troops eventually left, The Kings House reverted to being a coaching inn.

See map just before Route 46.

◀ Head N from the hotel, up the old road and then along boggy paths to the Allt a' Bhalaich. Follow a small path along this burn until the burn splits in the floor of **Coire Bhalach** (1hr, 555m, 25130 57070). Head roughly NNW to reach the ridge (at about 675m, 24850 57470), which is grassy with a multitude of small rock outcrops. Turn left, SW, gradually veering to SSE, to the trig point on the summit of **Beinn a' Chrulaiste** (1hr 45min, 857m, 24630 56680).

Descend the W ridge. If in doubt turn crags on their right to avoid the dangerous slopes on the S face of the mountain. There is a path developing in places on this ridge, which can be useful when the gradient steepens as the end of the ridge is approached. Continue down the ridge until a fence is reached, then turn left along the fence as it cuts back below the crags down to the

West Highland Way (2hr 40min, 285m, 22500 56160). Turn left and follow the West Highland Way along the old military road back to the Kings House Hotel (3hr 30min).

ROUTE 48
Garbh Bheinn ROUGH HILL

Start	Caolasnacon, Loch Leven (NN 14220 60770)
Distance	6km (4 miles)
Total ascent	840m (2800ft)
Difficulty	There is a path all the way to the summit, but it winds through rock outcrops with an occasional straightforward rockstep.
Time	3hr 40min
Summit	Garbh Bheinn (867m, 2835ft)
Map	OS Landranger 41
Access	From Glencoe take the B863 towards Kinlochleven. Park by the second bridge about 250m after the Caolasnacon Camping and Caravan Site.
Note	It would be worth traversing the ridge E to W from Kinlochleven, but it would be advisable to have cars at either end of the route as there is fast traffic along the road. An E to W traverse also means you are walking towards the magnificent view down Loch Leven, past the Pap of Glencoe, to Loch Linnhe and Ardgour.

Garbh Bheinn is squeezed between Loch Leven and the Aonach Eagach ridge. The W ridge has many rock outcrops and makes a fine half-day walk.

Looking S from Garbh Bheinn you will see the rocky **Aonach Eagach ridge** which runs along the N of Glencoe. Aonach Eagach is regarded as the most difficult 'scrambling' ridge in mainland Scotland and is a magnificent expedition in summer. In winter conditions the ridge is considerably harder than in summer and many parties will treat it as a roped climb.

Walking the Corbetts: Vol 1

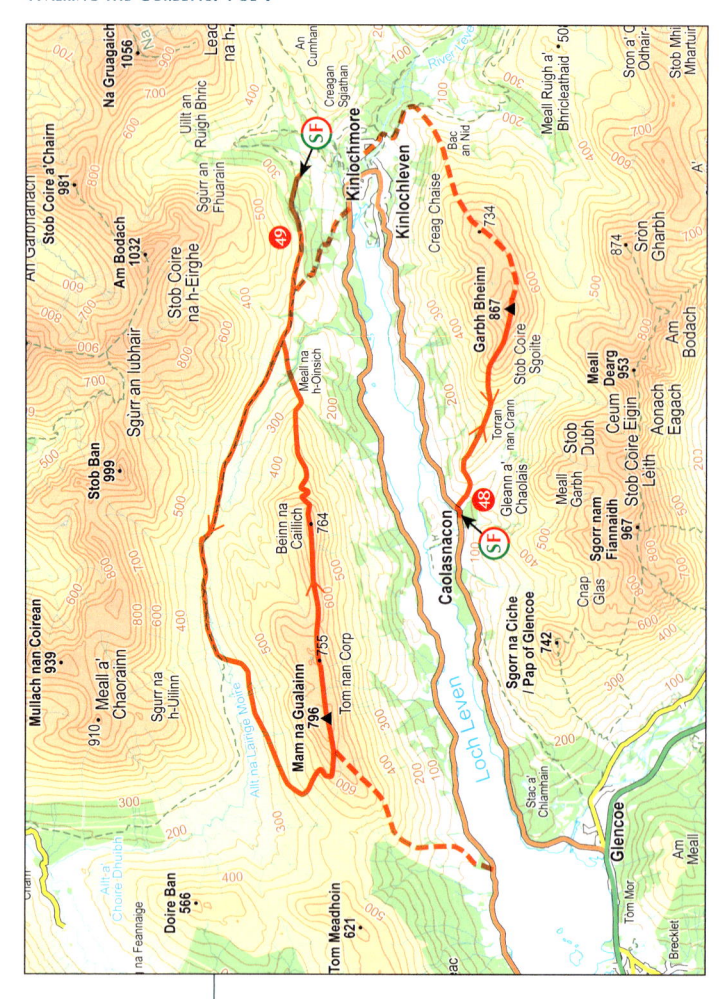

Take the path up the E bank of the Allt Gleann a' Chaolais (all the strands of the path go in the same direction). After about 15min (155m, 14650 60520) there is a faint path to the left – follow this to crags on the ridge. The path winds past the crags and up to a minor summit (765m, 16490 60160). Avoiding some more crags, continue to the small summit plateau. The high point of **Garbh Bheinn** is a dilapidated cairn constructed from red rocks rather than the large red cairn, the quartzite cairn or one of the other random cairns on the plateau (2hr 20min, 867m, 16930 60090).

Return by the same route (3hr 40min).

ROUTE 49

Mam na Gualainn PASS OF THE SHOULDER

Start	Mamore Lodge (NN 18610 62950)
Distance	18km (11 miles)
Total ascent	1040m (3400ft)
Difficulty	The ascent is easy. The descent from Beinn na Caillich is down a steep path. The route would be a little easier if done in reverse so you climb steeply and descend gently.
Time	5hr 20min
Summits	Mam na Gualainn (796m, 2611ft), Beinn na Caillich (764m)
Map	OS Landranger 41
Access	From Glencoe take the B863 to Kinlochleven, There is a small tarmac road on the right about 1km after Kinlochleven, which leads to Mamore Lodge. At the time of writing Mamore Lodge Hotel has closed down but parking is possible. If parking is no longer available at the Mamore Lodge you could park in Kinlochleven and follow the West Highland Way, which leaves the B863 just W of Kinlochleven (NN 18240 62300) to join the recommended route.
Note	The peak-bagger will probably climb the SW ridge from Callert (NN 09550 60300) but this misses the essence of this fine mountain.

Mam na Gualainn and Beinn na Caillich dominate the N side of Loch Leven. Of the two, the lower, Beinn na Caillich, is the finer mountain but it doesn't make Corbett status as there is only about a 400ft drop between the mountains. There are impressive views of the Mamores and the serrated Aonach Eagach ridge from these mountains.

The track between the ruins at Lairigmor and Callert on Loch Leven was a **coffin road** used to carry the dead to the graveyard that existed on the small island of Eilean Munde in Loch Leven. Eilean Munde was the site of a chapel built by St Fintan Mundus, who travelled here from Iona in the 7th century. The Stewarts of Ballachulish, MacDonalds of Glen Coe and Camerons of Callert shared the graveyard, even when there was conflict between them.

See map in Route 48.

◀ Just above Mamore Lodge, turn left along a good track and follow it to the top of the pass (330m). Descend past one ruin to the ruin at Lairigmor. There is a path signed to Callert just before the ruin (1hr 30min, 275m, 12290 64040). Turn left along the path and ford the Allt na Lairige Moire and follow the path until a small cairn marks where a small path goes off left (425m, 10820 63010). Turn left along this old stalker's path, which fades away in places. You may be able to follow the line of the path all the way to the ridge, but if you lose it just head uphill. You should reach the ridge at a gate (720m, 11160 62440) in a fence. Go through the gate and follow the path to the trig point on the summit of **Mam na Gualainn** (2hr 50min, 796m, 11510 62540).

Head E along the ridge using intermittent paths. Be careful to follow the E ridge, not the NE ridge from the E top of Mam na Gualainn. Descend to a col (649m, 12800 62650) and then E along the fine ridge to **Beinn na Caillich** (3hr 40min, 764m, 14070 62790).

There is a path down the steep E ridge of Beinn na Caillich but it is not obvious where it starts. It can be found a little left of the direct line. This path takes you easily down the steep slope. Stay on the path to find the old stalker's path that switchbacks down the lower slopes of the mountain to reach a bridge over the Allt Nathrach (4hr 40min, 200m, 15920 63240). Cross the burn and continue up the path, which climbs 60m back to the West Highland Way. Turn right along the track back to Mamore Lodge (5hr 20min).

Route 49 – Mam na Gualainn

Double rainbow from Beinn na Caillich

WALKING THE CORBETTS: VOL 1

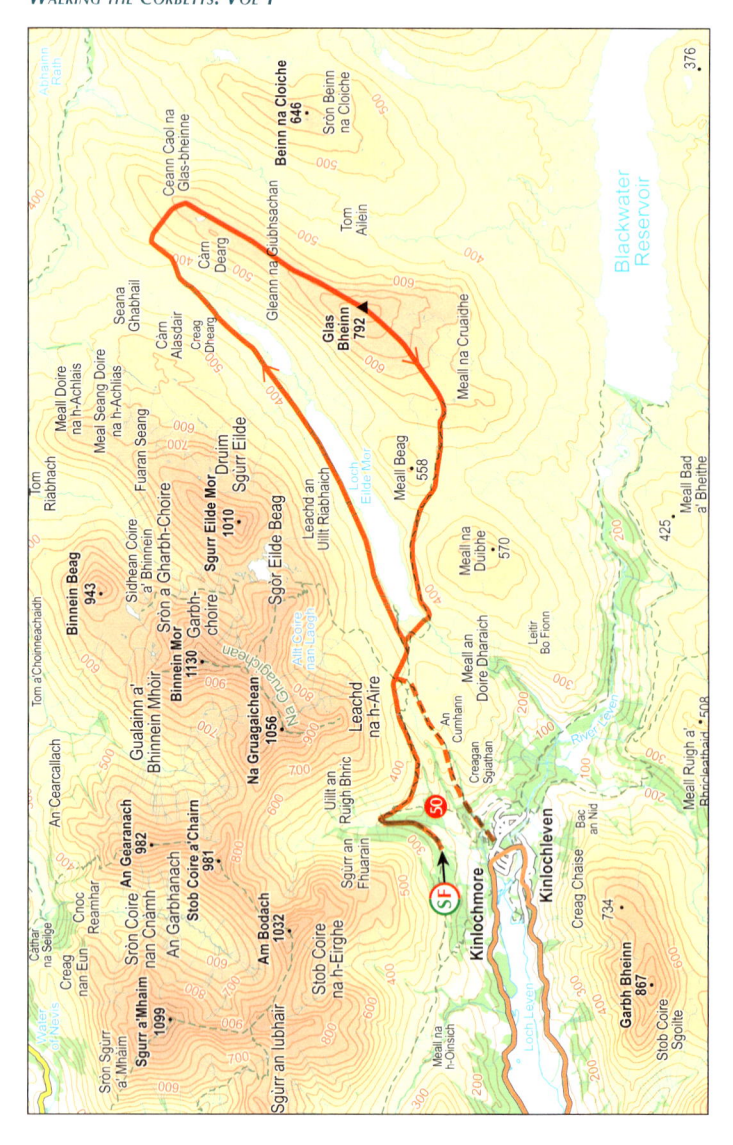

ROUTE 50

Glas Bheinn GREENISH-GREY HILL

Start	Mamore Lodge (NN 18610 62950)
Distance	24km (15 miles)
Total ascent	880m (2900ft)
Difficulty	There are some sections of rough moorland, but the going is generally fairly easy. Navigation on the descent would need care in mist.
Time	6hr 5min
Summit	Glas Bheinn (792m, 2587ft)
Map	OS Landranger 41
Access	Parking as for Route 49. If parking becomes unavailable at Mamore Lodge then it would be best to park at the Grey Mare Waterfall car park in Kinlochleven and follow a good path that joins the suggested route about 800m W of Loch Eilde Mor.
Note	This is a good peak to do on a backpacking trip from Corrour Station to the E.

Glas Bheinn is an isolated peak in the moorland between Loch Eilde Mor and the Blackwater Reservoir. The peak itself isn't very interesting, but the recommended ridge walk gives magnificent views in all directions.

The massive dam for the **Blackwater Reservoir** is, at 914m, the longest in the Highlands. It was constructed in the early 1900s for the British Aluminium Company to provide water for a hydro-electric scheme to power their aluminium smelting plant in Kinlochleven (now closed). The dam was built using hand tools, without the benefit of mechanical earth moving machinery, by 3000 navvies (mainly from Ireland) and created a reservoir 9 miles long and 75ft deep, drowning the glen which had contained three lochs.

Turn right along the good track just above Mamore Lodge, follow a short signed diversion round the Stalker's Cottage, then follow the track to a memorial seat with superb views down Loch Leven. Continue along the track along the N shore of **Loch Eilde Mor** and Loch Eilde Beag and continue until there is a faint grassy vehicle track on the right just before the high point of the track (2hr 5min, 360m, 26190 66610). Follow this boggy track until it levels off (470m, 26810 67020) then head straight up the hill over rough moorland to reach the ridge (at about 630m, 27300 66590). Turn right along the ridge, aided by the remains of an old vehicle track, to the well-built cairn on the summit of **Glas Bheinn** (3hr 40min, 792m, 25900 64100).

Head SW down rough moorland, aiming for a stalker's path (somewhere near 24620 62970). Wherever you hit the path, turn right to cross a stream (4hr 20min, 445m, 24050 63030). The path leads you over the pass between Meall Beag and Meall na Duibhe and down to Loch Eilde Mor. Follow the path to a dam at the SW corner of the loch (5hr 5min, 350m, 21760 63180). Cross the dam and follow the path up to the main track (21340 63490). Turn left back to Mamore Lodge (6hr 5min).

Glas Bheinn seen across Loch Eilde Mor

8 THE CENTRAL GRAMPIANS (PITLOCHRY AND LOCH RANNOCH)

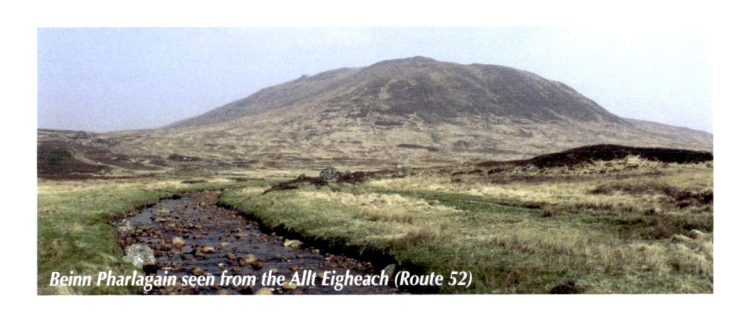

Beinn Pharlagain seen from the Allt Eigheach (Route 52)

The Central Grampians: Bases and facilities

Base for Routes 51–64: Pitlochry

Pitlochry is a major tourist resort on the A9 N of Perth and has all the facilities a tourist might need.

Pitlochry Tourist Information Centre, 22 Atholl Road, Pitlochry, PH16 5BX
Tel: 01796 472 215 www.pitlochry.org

Local facilities for Route 51

Corrour Station House has a good cafe (open 8.00am–10.00pm) as well as offering bed and breakfast. Tel: 01397 732 236

Loch Ossian SYHA is 1.5km from Corrour Station at the W end of Loch Ossian. Tel: 01397 732 207

Local facilities for Routes 51–53: Rannoch Station

Moor of Rannoch House at Rannoch Station: Accommodation and restaurant. Booking essential. Tel: 01882 633 238 www.moorofrannoch.co.uk

Local facilities for Routes 51–55: Kinloch Rannoch

Kinloch Rannoch has hotels and a store.

Location of routes

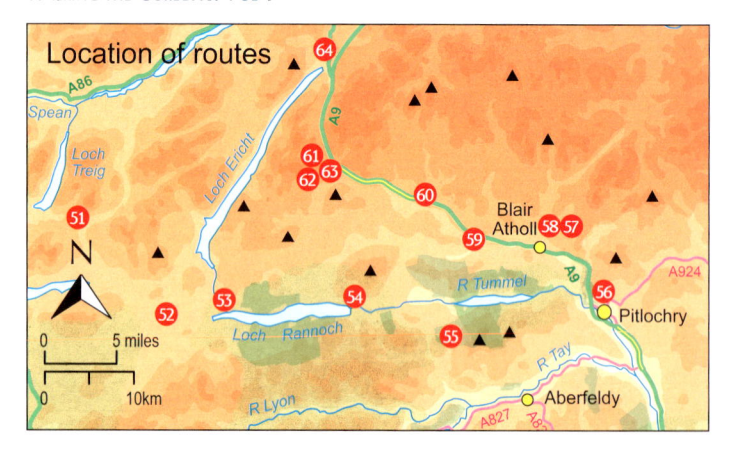

Loch Rannoch Hotel Tel: 0844 879 9059 www.MacdonaldHotels.co.uk/LochRannoch

Kilvrecht Caravan and Camping site is 3 miles away on the S shore of Loch Rannoch. Tel: 01350 727 284

Local facilities for Routes 51–55: Tummel Bridge

Loch Tummel Caravan site at Ardgualich Farm on Loch Tummel takes tents and touring caravans. Tel: 01796 472 825

Tummel Valley Holiday Park, Tummel Bridge has all the facilities you would expect of a holiday park, including shop, restaurant, bar and take-away. Tel: 0844 381 9146 www.parkdean.com

Local facilities for Routes 57 and 58: Blair Atholl

Blair Atholl has two big hotels, two cafes, two caravan and camping sites, a small shop and Blair Castle, which claims to be Scotland's most visited historic house. www.blairatholl.org.uk

Local facilities for Routes 61–64: Dalwhinnie

The petrol station has very limited supplies as well as hot snacks.

ROUTE 51

Leum Uilleim WILLIAM'S LEAP

Start	Corrour Station (NN 35610 66420)
Distance	9km (5 miles)
Total ascent	510m (1700ft)
Difficulty	Rough and boggy moorland on the lower slopes
Time	2hr 45min
Summit	Leum Uilleim (909m, 2971ft)
Map	OS Landranger 41
Access	It's a long way to the nearest road but Leum Uilleim is easily accessed by train. Corrour Station is on the Glasgow to Fort William rail line, with about three trains a day in each direction. The nearest station is Rannoch Station, which is accessed along the B8079, B8019 and then B846 N then W from Pitlochry. Tel: 0845 601 5929 www.scotrail.co.uk
Note	The route described here makes a good wet weather route or a route to do if you need to rush to catch the next train. In good weather it makes sense to climb the An Diollaid ridge to Beinn a' Bhric en route to Leum Uilleim.

Leum Uilleim is an isolated peak on the N edge of Rannoch Moor. The hill is surrounded by boggy heather moorland, but the ridges are easy going.

Corrour Railway Station on Rannoch Moor is the most remote in Scotland, the nearest public road being 10 miles away! The station, which opened on 7 August 1894, was originally built to serve the Corrour sporting estate, whose owners were investors in the railway. Guests visiting the estate for deer and grouse shooting were taken from the station to the head of Loch Ossian by horse-drawn carriage and then a small steamer transported them to shooting lodge at the far end of the loch.

Walking the Corbetts: Vol 1

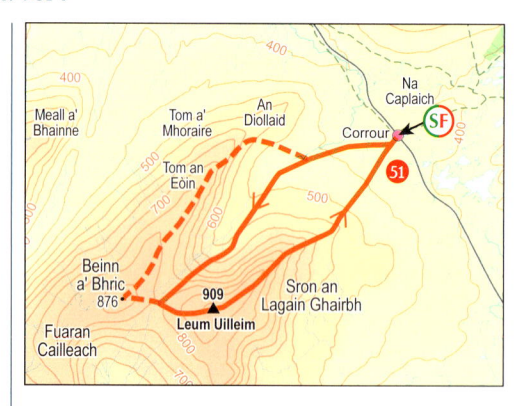

There is no sign of the path shown on the OS map leading to the An Diollaid ridge.

Corrour Station House

Take the boggy track SW from the NW end of **Corrour Station**. When this tracks turns left after 300m keep straight on along a small footpath. Follow this path to Allt Coire a Bhric Beag. ◀ Follow the faint path that continues up the burn and when this fades away continue to follow the burn to the pass between Beinn a' Bhric and Leum Uilleim (1hr 30min, 800m, 32370 64230). Ignore the old grassy track and head E to the large summit cairn on **Leum Uilleim** (1hr 45min, 909m, 33080 64130).

Head ENE down the ridge. A path is developing which takes you easily through scattered crags on **Sron an Lagain Ghairbh**. When the path fades away as the gradient eases, head NE over boggy moorland to **Corrour Station** (2hr 45min).

ROUTE 52

Meall na Meoig of Beinn Pharlagain

ROUNDED HILL OF WHEY OF THE

MOUNTAIN OF THE GRASSY HOLLOW

Start	Loch Eigheach (NN 44650 57840)
Distance	19km (12 miles)
Total ascent	710m (2300ft)
Difficulty	Once the access track is left behind the going can be rough and boggy in predominantly pathless terrain. Navigation will be demanding in mist.
Time	5hr 30min
Summit	Meall na Meoig of Beinn Pharlagain (868m, 2836ft)
Map	OS Landranger 42
Access	Take the B8079, B8019 and then B846 N then W from Pitlochry to Loch Eigheach, 2km before the roadhead at Rannoch Station. There is limited parking by a track end signed 'Public footpath to Ft. William by Corrour'. There is more parking 350m up the road.
Note	If you want a long day out you could traverse the headwaters of the Allt Eigheach to include Meall na Meoig with the Munros Sgor Gaibhre and Carn Dearg.

Beinn Pharlagain is the S ridge of the Munro Sgor Gaibhre, which itself is just a summit on the ridge stretching SW from the commanding Ben Alder. Meall na Meoig is the highest top on Beinn Pharlagain. The whole range is a massive heather moor.

WALKING THE CORBETTS: VOL 1

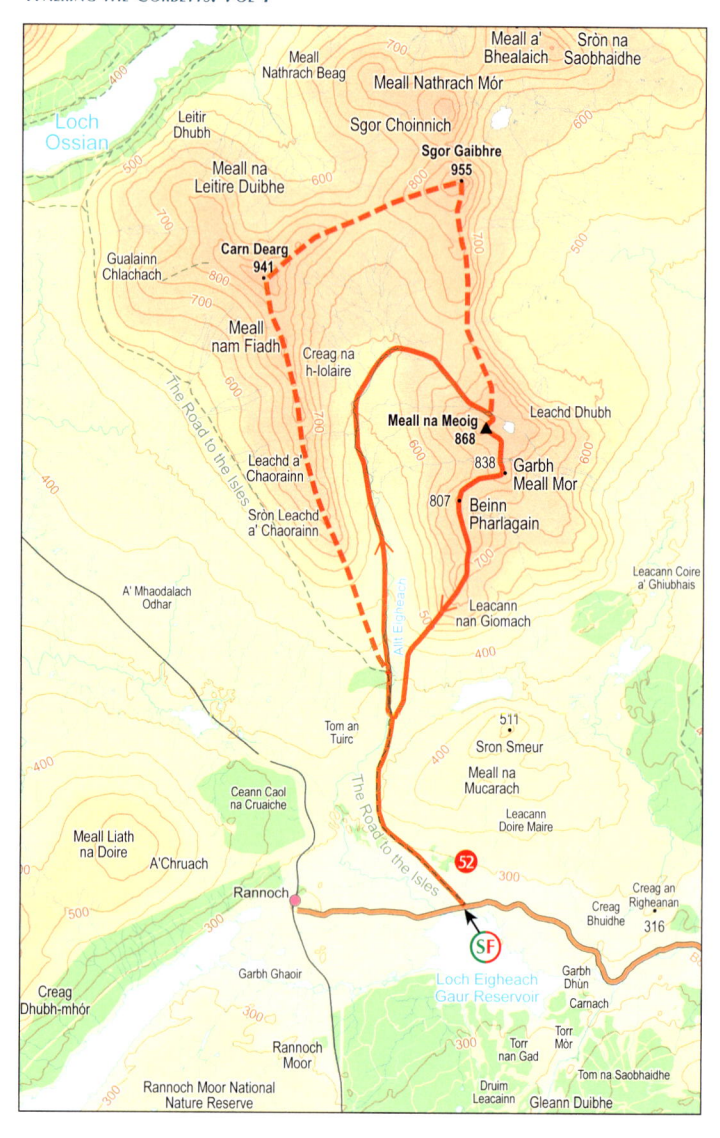

Route 52 – Meall na Meoig of Beinn Pharlagain

The route starts up the **'Road to the Isles'**, which was the main route to Fort William before the Military Road was built over Rannoch Moor. The original Road to the Isles referred to old cattle droving tracks (rather than the present A830 from Fort William to Mallaig), down which cattle from Skye were driven to the main markets in central Scotland.

Follow the track until a bridge is reached. Cross it and follow the left-hand bank of the Allt Eigheach to regain the track, which fords the river upstream. At the top of a recently planted wood the Road to the Isles turns left (50min, 370m 43500 60940). Keep straight on along a faint path up **Allt Eigheach**. This path becomes a rough, sometimes boggy track (43520 62370), which is followed until the burn veers right and the track continues away from the burn (2hr, 560m, 43060 64490). Follow the

Walker and companion on summit of Meall na Meoig

205

burn NE and continue up it until the main stream veers left (N) (2hr 20min, 600m, 43650 65200).

Cross the burn and head up the right-hand tributary heading SE. This burn can be followed to its source at a small lochan just below the summit of Meall na Meoig (3hr 15min, 820m, 44840 64350). There are crags above the lochan so it is best to continue to the far end of the lochan and swing right to climb the E ridge to the summit cairn on **Meall na Meoig** (3hr 25min, 868m, 44840 64160).

Descend ESE to a minor top (840m, 45320 63970) and then SW, veering SE, to **Garbh Meall Mo**r (838m, 45090 63560), which only has a few small crags despite its fortress-like appearance on the OS map. It is then WSW to **Beinn Pharlagain** (807m, 44500 63190) and over a few minor tops as you descend S down the ridge. Veer SW on the final steep descent, hopefully picking up a grassy track near the bottom, which takes you to the **Allt Eigheach** (4hr 50min, 365m, 43690 60890). Follow the burn down until the main track is regained and follow it back to the parking area (5hr 30min).

ROUTE 53

Stob an Aonaich Mhoir

PEAK OF THE BIG RIDGE

Start	Bridge of Ericht Cottage (NN 52190 58210)
Distance	28km (18 miles)
Total ascent	820m (2700ft)
Difficulty	Easy
Time	6hr 30min
Summit	Stob an Aonaich Mhoir (855m, 2805ft)
Map	OS Landranger 42
Access	Take the B8079, B8019 and then B846 N then W from Pitlochry to the River Ericht near the W end of Loch Rannoch. There is limited parking at an estate road signed 'Talladh-A-Bheithe Estate' beside the Bridge of Ericht Cottage.
Note	If you are walking rather than cycling the approach, you may prefer to climb Sron a' Chlaonaidh and follow the SW ridge of Stob an Aonaich Mhoir to the summit, or follow the burn up the S slopes of Stob an Aonaich Mhoir. Stob an Aonaich Mhoir could be included in a backpacking trip involving Beinn Mholach (Route 62) and the other Corbetts and Munros between the A9, Loch Ericht and Loch Rannoch.

The remote Stob an Aonaich Mhoir is the highest point on the ridge on the E side of Loch Ericht. The approach is through bleak heather moorland with some commercial forestry. There is a 13km walk along a tarmac road to the foot of the mountain and this could easily be done on bicycle rather than on foot.

Loch Ericht is 351m above sea level. We may think of the landscape as being natural, but this loch is man-made, as are many others in Scotland, and the loch is actually dammed at both ends as part of a hydroelectric scheme. Water flows into the NE end via the Cuaich Aqueduct. The SW end is linked to

WALKING THE CORBETTS: VOL 1

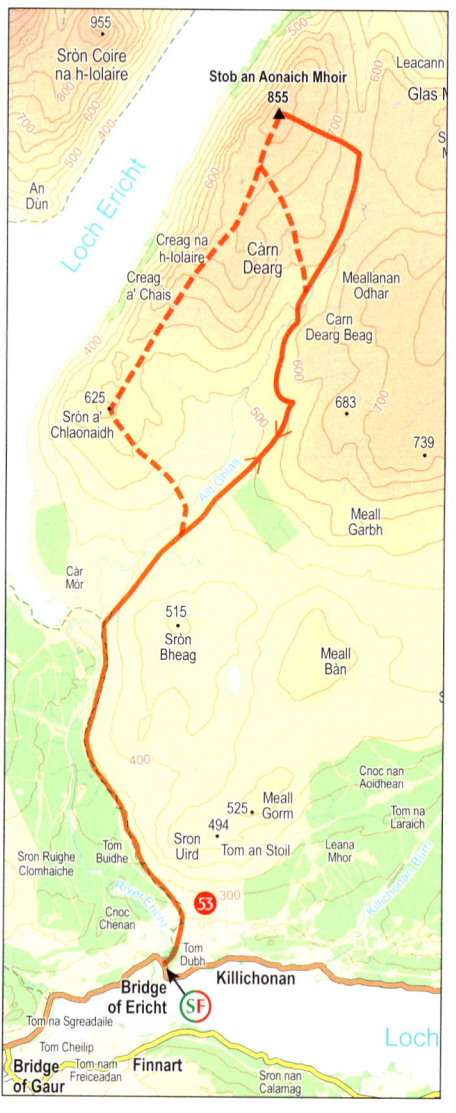

a hydroelectric power station at Loch Rannoch by the four-mile long River Ericht. The access road used to climb Stob an Aonaich Mhoir, like many of the roads into remote areas of the Highlands, was built as part of the hydroelectric scheme.

The main gate will probably be locked but the side gate should be unlocked. Follow the tarmac road, turning right when a road goes off left to Loch Ericht Dam after 5km and continue another 8km up the road to the high point of the road at the pass between Stob an Aonaich Mhoir and Stob Loch Monaidh (3hr, 640m, 54690 68840). Head WNW; initially there is some rough heather, but the going soon gets much easier as you approach the summit cairn on **Stob an Aonaich Mhoir** (3hr 40min, 855m, 53750 69420).

Return to the road (3hr 55min) and then down the road back to the parking area (6hr 30min).

The summit cairn on Stob an Aonaich Mhoir

ROUTE 54
Beinn a' Chuallaich HILL OF THE HERDING

Start	Kinloch Rannoch (NN 66180 58700)
Distance	15km (9 miles)
Total ascent	770m (2500ft)
Difficulty	The going is generally fairly easy, but there is some heather moorland and easy peat hags on the ascent and few useful paths above the mountain wall. Navigation could be tricky in mist.
Time	4hr 15min
Summit	Beinn a' Chuallaich (891m, 2925ft)
Map	OS Landranger 42
Access	Take the B8079, B8019 and then B846 N then W from Pitlochry to Kinloch Rannoch at the E end of Loch Rannoch. Park in the village centre.
Note	The easiest way to climb the mountain would be to ascend and descend by the suggested descent route.

Beinn a' Chuallaich has a delightful S ridge but is surrounded by heather moorland. There are superb views S to Schiehallion, one of the best-known Munros.

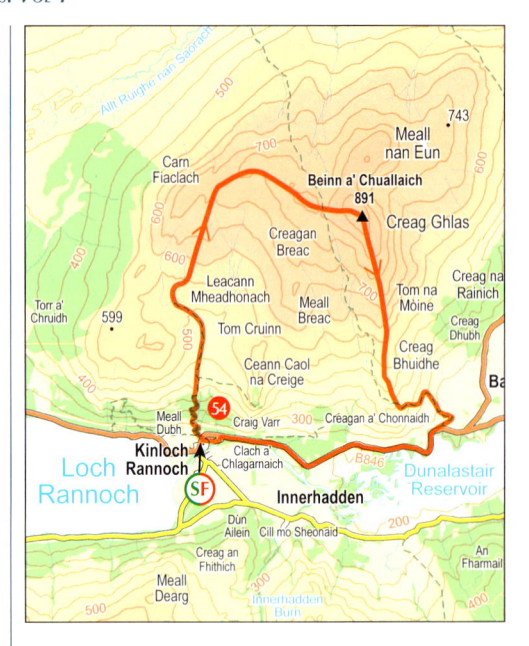

Schiehallion is a mountain well known to scientists and cartographers as a result of an experiment conducted in 1774 to measure the average density and therefore mass of the earth. The experiment involved measuring the tiny deviation of a pendulum caused by the gravitational attraction of the mountain. Schiehallion was chosen because it was a conical hill isolated from nearby mountains. The experiment showed that the average density of the earth was about twice that of the surface rocks, which led to the theories about the earth having a metallic core. The mountain is of particular significance for cartographers, as contour lines were invented by those surveying the mountain.

Head N past the church and, just after the garage, take a track signed 'Public footpath to Loch Rannoch Hotel'.

Route 54 – Beinn a' Chuallaich

Pass through the gate and stay on the main track signed 'Craig Varr', ignoring footpaths left and right. Fork right at the first track junction, keep straight on (left) at the second, either way at the third, and turn right at the fourth to reach a gate. Pass through and fork left when an unmapped track bridges the Allt Mor on the right (415m, 66190 59600) and continue uphill to cross the burn on stepping stones (40min, 475m, 66250 60260).

Continue up the track, which gradually deteriorates before ending at a burn (520m, 65840 60660). ▶ Follow the burn NNE until it fades away and then continue in the same direction until the ridge is reached among peat hags (1hr 25min, 715m, 66440 62310). Head ENE, veering SE up the heather-covered ridge to the pass W of **Beinn a' Chuallaich** (806m, 67940 61790) and climb easily E through scattered crags to the trig point and huge cairn on the summit (2hr 15min, 891m, 68460 61770).

Head SSE down a delightful ridge, veering right after the ridge flattens, dropping down to where an overgrown heathery path crosses the mountain wall (2hr 55min, 490m, 68790 59690). Continue S down the faint path until the path turns left (430m, 68780 59350) and becomes a poor, but clear track, which is easily followed down to Druimglas Cottage. Turn right at the cottage to reach the B846 (3hr 25min, 200m, 69550 58950).

The track shown on the OS map continuing N no longer exists.

Schiehallion seen from the summit cairn

There is very limited parking here. Unless you have organised transport there is now a 3km walk along the road to a parking/picnic area (66850 58820). From here there is a 1km riverside path back to Kinloch Rannoch (4hr 15min).

ROUTE 55

Meall Tairneachan THUNDER HILL
and Farragon Hill ST FERGAN'S HILL

Start	Foss Mine (NN 78030 56230)
Distance	17km (10 miles)
Total ascent	1060m (3500ft)
Difficulty	The ascent of Farragon Hill is over heather moorland. It is relatively easy as long as the visibility is good enough to pick the easiest route, but navigation and route-finding will be difficult in mist.
Time	4hr 40min
Summits	Meall Tairneachan (787m, 2559ft), Farragon Hill (783m, 2559ft)
Map	OS Landranger 52
Access	Take the B8079 and B8019 N then W from Pitlochry to Tummel Bridge. Turn left along the B846 to the entrance to Foss Quarry and Foss Mine where there is limited roadside parking opposite the mine entrance. Parking is discouraged on the area in front of the mine entrance. The mine road is good enough for road bikes to be used to access the Corbetts.
Note	If transport could be arranged it would be a good idea to continue E from Farragon Hill and drop down to the track connecting the River Tay to Loch Tummel and exit N or S along this track. This track would also be the way to approach Farragon Hill if you wanted to climb it on its own.

Meall Tairneachan and Farragon Hill are the highest points in the moorland to the W of Pitlochry. Barytes is mined at the mine just E of Meall Tairneachan. There are many small crags on Farragon Hill, but it isn't the fortress suggested by the OS map.

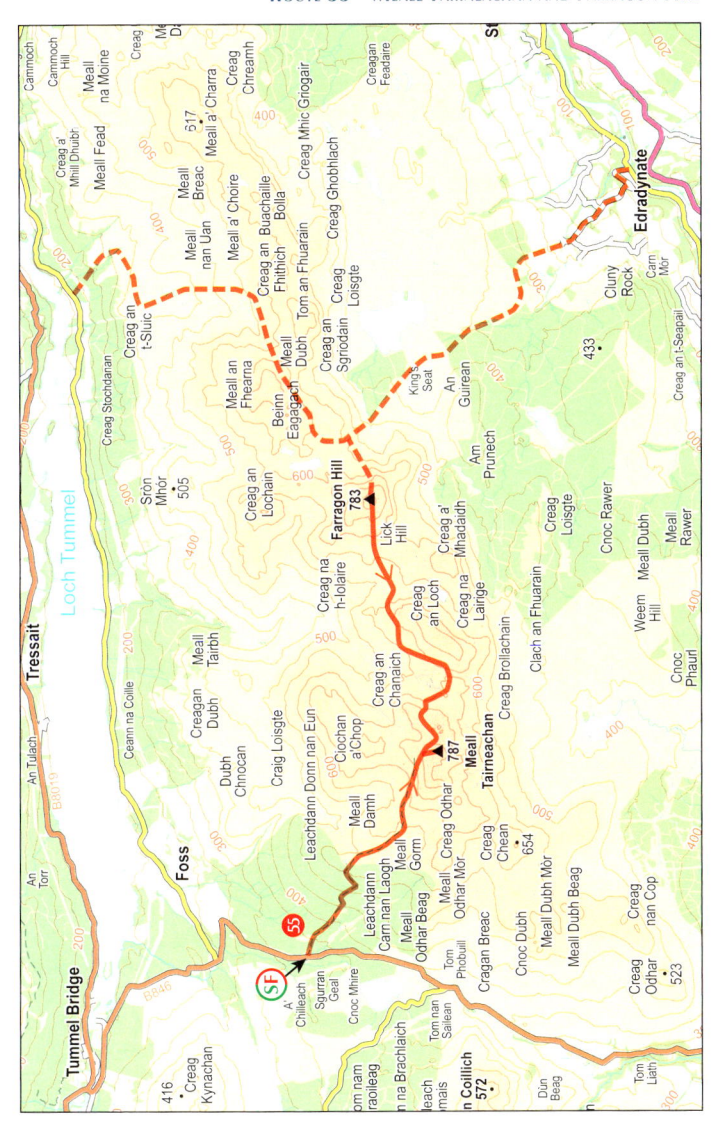

Route 55 – Meall Tairneachan and Farragon Hill

Tomphubil Lime Kiln

Limestone outcrops on the W slopes of Meall Tairneachan were mined in the 18th century to provide lime for mortar and fertiliser for Strathtay. In 1865 the Tomphubil Lime Kiln was built at Tomphubil as the need for lime to improve pastures and to crop yields increased. There is a car park beside the restored lime-kiln (NN 77840 54580).

Meall Tairneachan mine was opened to extract **barytes**, a mineral that is mostly barium sulphate. Barium-containing compounds are dense so this mineral is used as a component of 'mud', a heavy slurry, used to control the release of oil and gas from oil wells. The mine served the North Sea industry.

Pass through the gate to the mine and keep straight on for 2km up a good dirt road to the top of the forest (580m) and continue up the track until it flattens out just after a parking area (1hr, 740m, 80730 54660). Head up a faint path S to the stone-built trig point on the summit of **Meall Tairneachan** (1hr 10min, 787m, 80750 54370).

Return to the track, turn right and then keep straight on through an opencast mine. Beyond the mine the track deteriorates and becomes unsuitable for road bikes. Follow the track until it switchbacks left on the descent to

Frenich Burn (1hr 55min, 600m, 82770 54930). Descend ENE to cross the burn (555m) and pick a route W up the heather moorland to the summit cairn on **Farragon Hill** (2hr 45min, 783m, 84040 55300).

Return by the same route (4hr 40min).

ROUTE 56

Ben Vrackie SPECKLED HILL

Start	Moulin (NN 94440 59810)
Distance	8km (5 miles)
Total ascent	670m (2200ft)
Difficulty	Easy
Time	2hr 45min
Summit	Ben Vrackie (841m, 2760ft)
Maps	OS Landranger 43 and 52
Access	From the centre of Pitlochry, follow signs N to Moulin. Turn left up Baledmund Road immediately after the Moulin Hotel and follow the road as it swings right. When it turns sharp left, keep straight on, signed 'Ben-y-Vrackie', and follow this small road to a car park at the roadhead.

The impressive Ben Vrackie is one of the most popular Corbetts, with a well-engineered 'tourist path' to the summit of the mountain which is a magnificent viewpoint.

Moulin is well worth a visit. People lived here back in Neolithic times when the standing stones at Baledmund and Balnakeilly were erected. Moulin Kirk was founded by St Colm about AD700 and Moulin was a commercial centre with a market and fair. Moulin Hotel was established in 1695 and the Hotel opened a brewery in 1995 to produce real ale. The Church has now been converted to a heritage centre.

WALKING THE CORBETTS: VOL 1

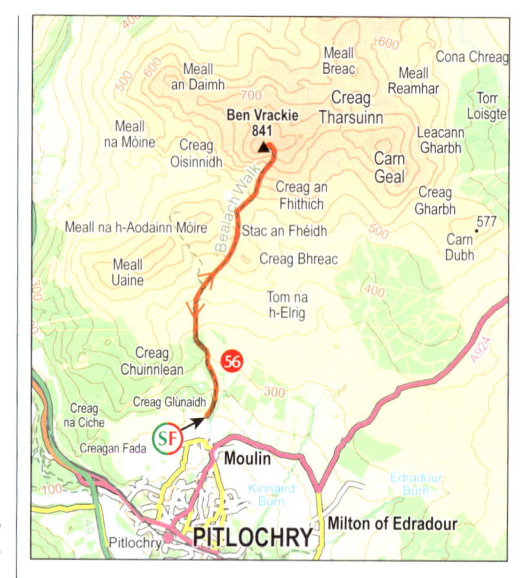

Tourist path to Ben Vrackie

Follow a good path N from the car park. The route should be obvious, but if in doubt look for the green waymarks. The path enters moorland (355m) and then forks right (445m), signed to **Ben Vrackie**, before crossing the Loch a' Choire dam (50min, 530m, 94850 62530). The path now steepens and becomes a staircase, which ends about 100m from the summit. At the summit there is a trig point and viewpoint indicator (1hr 35min, 841m, 95080 63240).

Return by the same route (2hr 45min).

ROUTE 57

Ben Vuirich HILL OF STAG ROARING

Start	Loch Moraig (NN 90560 67090)
Distance	23km (14 miles)
Total ascent	760m (2500ft)
Difficulty	The suggested route finds a relatively easy way through the pathless moorland, but there are still some rough sections. In mist it will be much harder, as it will be difficult to spot the easy lines through the heather, and navigation will be demanding.
Time	5hr 45min
Summit	Ben Vuirich (903m, 2961ft)
Map	OS Landranger 43
Access	From Pitlochry head NW to Blair Atholl and take the road to Old Bridge of Tilt, where you take the minor road signed to Monzie. Park at the cattle grid, just after reaching Loch Moraig.
Note	The main alternative route would be to follow Gleann Fearnach (from Strath Ardle on the A924 to the SE) all the way until N of Ben Vuirich and climb the N ridge.

Ben Vuirich is a remote peak to the S of the dominating Beinn a' Ghlo Munros. The approach is through improved pasture, after which you are on heather moorland. Despite the moorland, there is a lot of variety in this walk, which keeps the interest throughout the described route.

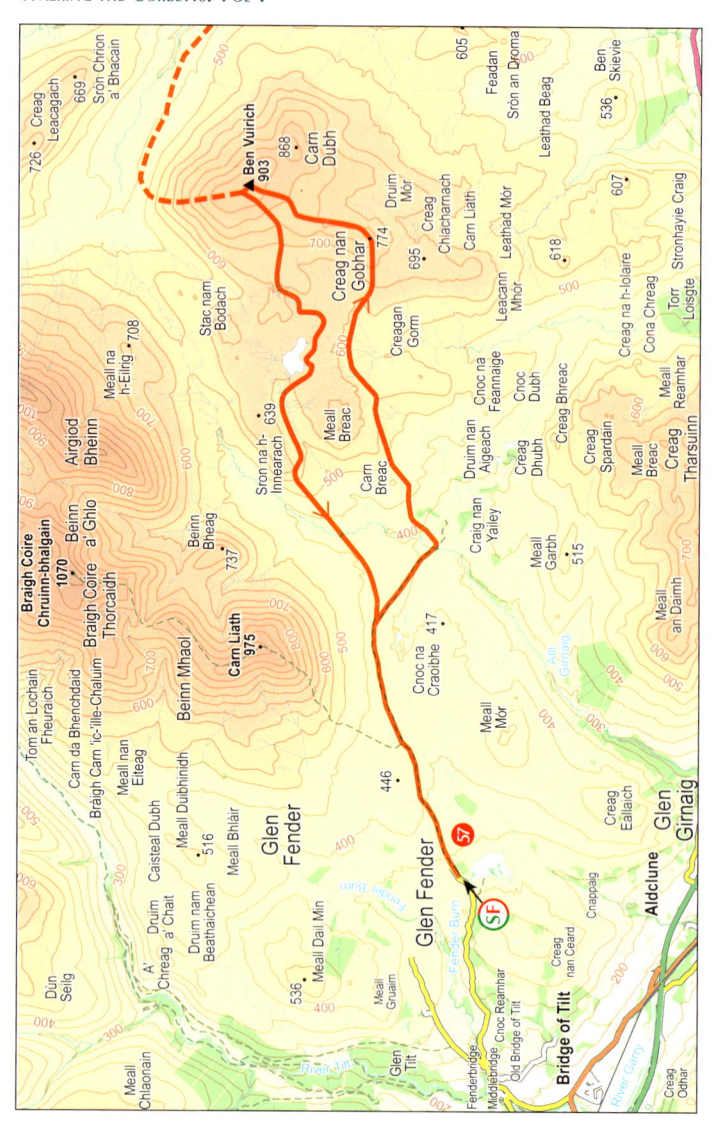

Walking the Corbetts: Vol 1

218

ROUTE 57 – BEN VUIRICH

Many people seem to think that the Corbetts are easier than the Munros, but have a look at the **scars** caused by the paths up Carn Liath and Carn nan Gabhar (both Munros) as you climb Ben Vuirich, where paths are little more than animal tracks. Without paths the going can be harder on the Corbetts and the navigation can be more demanding; what is more, you must be more self-reliant as there won't be so many other walkers around to help if you get lost or have an accident.

Continue up the road until it swings left towards Monzie Farm. Keep straight on through the gate, signed 'Shinagag', and follow the good track. Ignore the unmapped track to the right and then fork right after 4km along the main track towards Shinagag. Just before a gate and some farm buildings you have to imagine a grass track left up the improved pasture (1hr 5min, 375m, 95180 67320). Turn left up the 'track', which becomes

Airgiod Bheinn seen over Loch Valigan

a clear mountain track as it passes through a gate into the open moorland. Continue until the deteriorating track ends well beyond the point shown on the OS maps (1hr 50min, 595m, 97290 68490). A path continues for a short distance but you soon need to fight your way across the rough moorland, roughly E, to the summit of **Creag nan Gobhar** (774m, 99060 68350). Follow the ridge, generally NNE, over short heather to the trig point on the summit of **Ben Vuirich** (3hr 15min, 903m, 99720 69980).

Head SW, gradually veering W to pick up the green grassy ribbon that marks the course of a burn that is easily followed to the delightful Loch Valigan (3hr 55min, 605m, 97680 69180). Follow the S shore of the loch to its outlet, Allt Loch Valigan, and follow the burn downhill. When the going gets difficult (at about 96200 69100, 530m), cut across to the right under the nose of Sron na h-Innearach to where a path junction is marked on the OS map (4hr 35min, 510m, 95670 69110). The path you want to follow SW doesn't appear to exist anymore, but head SW anyway and you may be able to pick up the footpath as you head towards the track end you should be able to see across the Allt Coire Lagain. Ford the river opposite the track end (4hr 50min, 430m, 95100 68730). Follow the track, keeping straight on when you reach the main track (93970 68270) and following this back to the parking area (5hr 45min).

ROUTE 58
Beinn Mheadhonach MIDDLE HILL

Start	Old Bridge of Tilt (NN 87450 66260)
Distance	22km (14 miles)
Total ascent	1100m (3600ft)
Difficulty	Easy
Time	5hr 50min
Summit	Beinn Mheadhonach (901m, 2950ft)
Map	OS Landranger 43
Access	From Pitlochry follow the A9 NW, take the B8079 to Blair Atholl and then the minor road to Old Bridge of Tilt, where you turn left to a large car park.
Note	You could save a little time by completing the descent by the ascent route. This would be the best option if you cycled up to Gilbert's Bridge. If you want a long day you could continue round the head of Gleann Diridh to Beinn Dearg and return to the Bridge of Tilt via Glen Banvie.

Beinn Mheadhonach is a narrow ridge squeezed between the Munros Beinn Dearg and Carn a' Chlamain and separated from them by deep glens whose burns feed the River Tilt. There are twin tops which the author measures as being identical in height. The spot height on the OS map is shown as being on the N top but the bigger cairn is on the S top.

Blair Castle in Blair Atholl is the ancient home and fortress of the Dukes and Earls of Atholl. With its roots in the 13th century, Blair Castle has a long and illustrious history, throughout which it has accumulated many fascinating historical artefacts, including antique furniture, art, period dress, and arms and armour. The castle is open to the public and claims to be the most visited private historic house in Scotland (**www.blair-castle.co.uk**).

Walking the Corbetts: Vol 1

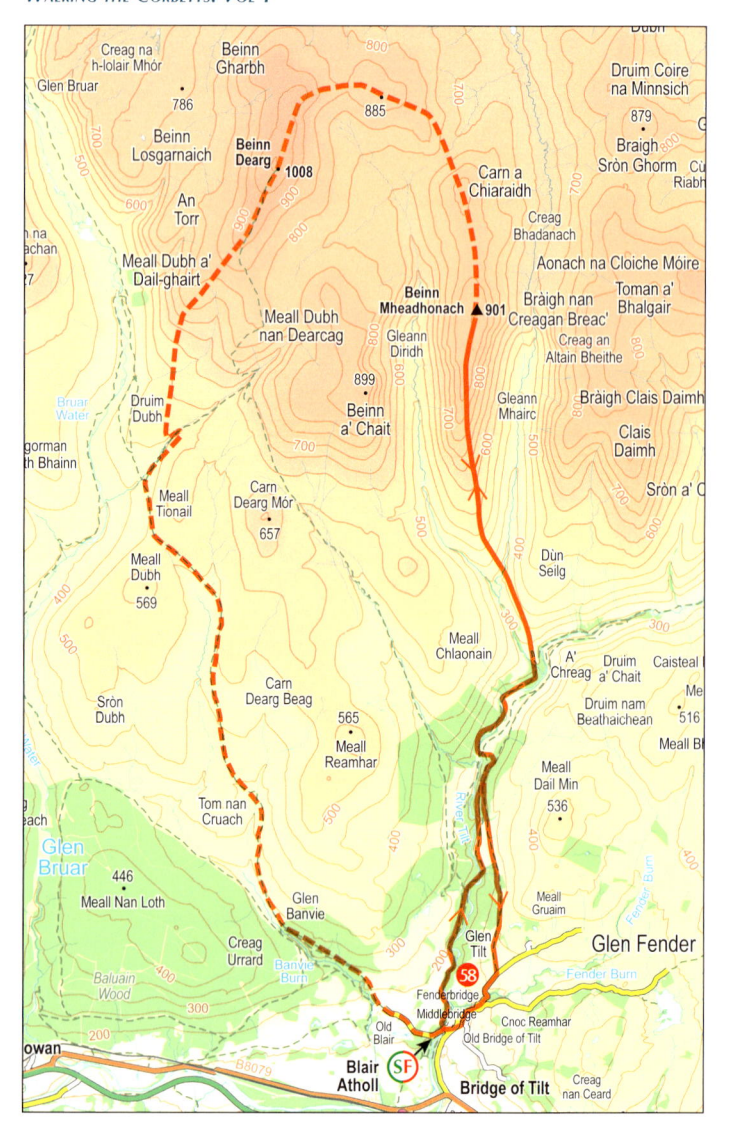

ROUTE 58 – BEINN MHEADHONACH

Bridge over Allt Mhairc

From the car park follow the path E inside the woods (not down the road) and turn left when the **River Tilt** is reached. Cross the road on an old stone footbridge (Wade's Bridge) and follow a path high above the gorge through which the river flows. Join an estate road and follow it, crossing a bridge over the river (88110 68470) and continuing up the E bank to Gilbert's Bridge (50min, 205m, 88100 70060).

Turn left over the bridge and then sharp right up a track through a gate in a deer fence and continue to an old bridge over the Allt Mhairc at a gorge (88840 71210). Cross the bridge and turn left along a faint path above the burn and on to another old bridge over the Allt Mhairc (1hr 35min, 325m, 88440 72460). Cross the bridge and follow small intermittent paths to the summit plateau on **Beinn Mheadhonach**. It is not clear whether the S top with a fairly large cairn (901m, 87980 75480) or the N top with a very small cairn (3hr 10min, 901m, 88010 75890) is higher.

Return to Gilbert's Bridge by the same route and follow the track downstream for about 200m to a small path on the left marked by a yellow arrow (4hr 55min, 215m, 88180 69900). You could return by the ascent route from here, but for variety, turn left, climb through the wood and then turn right along a grassy track which traverses pastures high above the river. Fork left at a track junction in a wood, then join a farm road at Kincraigie and soon reach a road junction (5hr 30min, 265m, 88330 67130). Turn right and follow the road to Old Bridge of Tilt. Turn right at the bottom of the hill back to the car park (5hr 50min).

ROUTE 59

Beinn Bhreac SPECKLED HILL

Start	Calvine (NN 80480 65740)
Distance	41km (26 miles)
Total ascent	1230m (4000ft)
Difficulty	The going is actually reasonably easy if the faint paths on the approach to Beinn Bhreac can be located, but it would be difficult to find them in mist.
Time	10hr 10min
Summit	Beinn Bhreac (912m, 2992ft)
Map	OS Landranger 43
Access	Follow the A9 W from Pitlochry and turn right to Bruar and left to Calvine along the B8079. There is limited parking in Calvine just before the track to the Bruar Lodge which is signed to the Minigaig Pass.
Note	It would be sensible to climb Beinn Bhreac as part of a backpacking expedition over the Munros and Corbetts between the Cairngorm Mountains and Glen Garry.

Beinn Bhreac itself is an easy mountain covered with short heather. The problem is that it is surrounded by a pathless boggy wilderness and is 20km from the nearest road! It is possible to cycle as far as Bruar Lodge, but the track is rather hilly and rough, so not really suitable for a road bike.

ROUTE 59 – BEINN BHREAC

The remote **Bruar Lodge**, constructed in 1789 with later Victorian additions, is a classic example of a Highland sporting lodge. It has developed luxury accommodation for outdoor and nature enthusiasts with plenty of opportunities for fishing, walking, birdwatching and photography.

Follow the track signed to the Minigaig Pass, soon turning right, crossing the busy A9 and then veering right and left. Follow this track for about 10km, ignoring all sidetracks, to the bridge over the **Bruar Water** in front of Bruar Lodge.

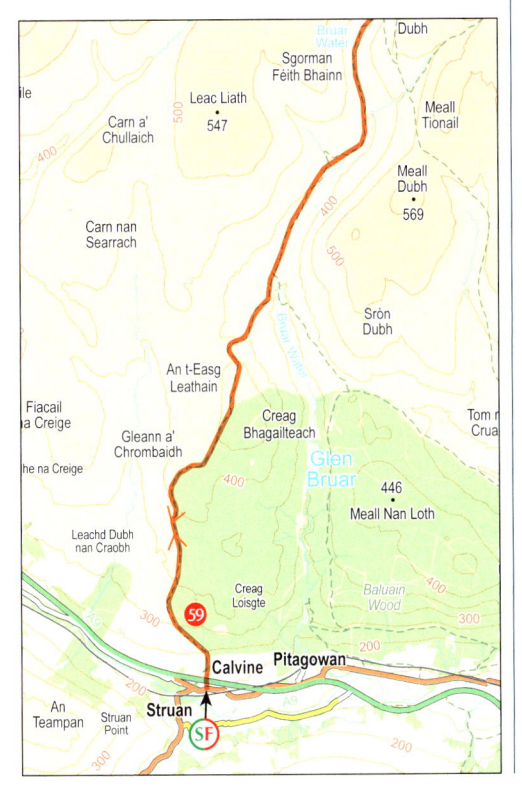

Map continues on page 226

WALKING THE CORBETTS: VOL 1

Beinn Bhreac

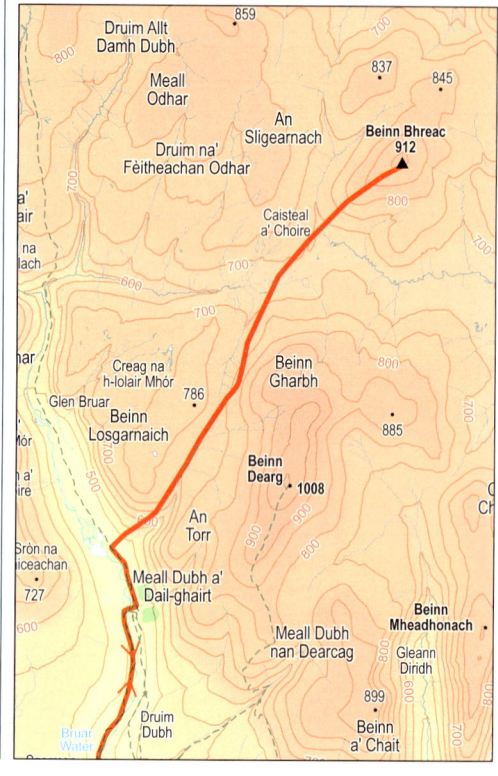

Route 60 – An Dun and Maol Creag an Loch (A'Chaoirnich)

Cross the bridge and pass left in front of the lodge, fork left and continue to a bridge over the Allt Beinn Losgarnaich by a lochan (2hr 45min, 480m, 82890 76910).

Cross the bridge and turn right up the burn to pick up an old stalker's path high above some big waterfalls. The path ends on a broad boggy saddle (3hr 15min, 715m, 84000 78180). Cross about 700m of peat hag and aim for a faint path (745m, 84370 78660) that is developing to the right of the burn that flows down the other side of the saddle. Follow this path past a small lochan, across a burn and then NE to reach the headwaters of the Tarf Water. You may get wet feet as you cross this burn (4hr 30min, 690m, 85700 81130). Now climb easily NE to the summit of **Beinn Bhreac** (5hr 10min, 912m, 86820 82050).

Return by the same route back to the track (7hr 15min) and **Calvine** (10hr 10min).

ROUTE 60

An Dun THE FORT and Maol Creag an Loch (A' Chaoirnich) HILL OF THE CRAG OF THE LOCH

Start	Dalnacardoch Lodge (NN 72330 70330)
Distance	30km (18 miles)
Total ascent	1090m (3600ft)
Difficulty	An Dun is uncomfortably steep, even by the S ridge route described here. Make sure you have a good tread on your shoes, and walking poles would be advised. Maol Creag an Loch is easy, but navigation would be difficult on the large plateau in mist.
Time	7hr 40min
Summits	An Dun (827m, 2707ft), Maol Creag an Loch (875m, 2844ft)
Map	OS Landranger 42
Access	From Pitlochry follow the A9 W to a minor road signed left to Trinafour. The estate road to An Dun, signed to Gaick Pass, is N of the A9 and has limited parking. It is possible to cycle the first 9km as far as Sronphadruig Lodge.

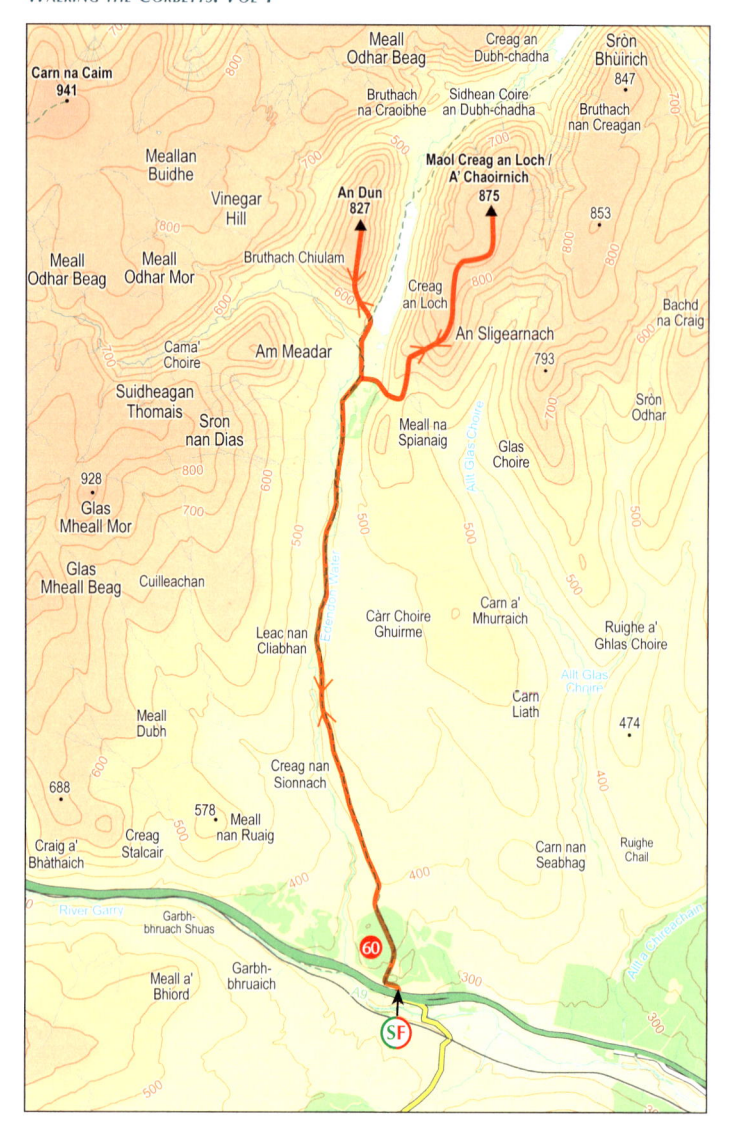

Walking the Corbetts: Vol 1

228

ROUTE 60 – AN DUN AND MAOL CREAG AN LOCH (A'CHAOIRNICH)

An Dun and Maol Creag an Loch are flat-topped hills separated by Loch an Duin. The flanks of the hills above this bleak loch are exceedingly steep. An Dun is an impressive mountain to look at, but uncomfortable to climb because of its steep slopes. An Dun has two tops which the author measures as being the same height so it would be wise to visit both to be sure of climbing the Corbett. Maol Creag an Loch is named as A' Chaoirnich on the OS map.

The ancient **Gaick Pass** was used as a route between Glen Garry and Strathspey. At the heart of the Gaick ('cleft' in Gaelic) it passes through a deep U-shaped valley alongside Loch an Duin between the Corbetts An Dun and Maol Creag an Loch. Loch an Duin is the source of the River Tromie and the through-route follows the river N past Gaick Lodge and down Glen Tromie to Speyside.

Head up the estate track, forking left in the forest and then right after leaving the forest. The track crosses the **Edendon Water** at a bridge, with a swimming hole, and recrosses at a ford. Just before derelict Sronphadruig

An Dun from Edendon Water

Lodge the track is washed away, but soon reappears. Continue past the lodge until the track crosses the burn (1hr 45min, 485m, 71790 78720). Follow the path, forking right, and follow intermittent paths up the very steep S ridge of **An Dun**. The S top (827m, 71660 80100) appears higher, but is actually about the same height as the N top, which is given the spot height on the OS map (2hr 45min, 827m, 71730 80490).

Return down the S ridge by the same route and continue down to the start of deer fence on the left of the track (3hr 30min, 485m, 71730 78520). Turn left along the deer fence over peat hags and head up a steep grassy gully to the saddle on the SW ridge of Maol Creag an Loch (571m, 72240 78200). Turn left up animal tracks, which eventually fade away, and veer right to the S top of Maol Creag an Loch (867m, 73480 80120). This top has a large cairn, but the higher top, **A' Chaoirnich**, is about 600m to the N and only has a tiny cairn (4hr 55min, 875m, 73530 80700).

Return to the track by the same route (6hr) and follow the track back to the A9 (7hr 40min).

ROUTE 61

Meall na Leitreach

ROUNDED HILL OF SLOPES

Start	Dalnaspidal (NN 64390 73380)
Distance	15km (9 miles)
Total ascent	510m (1700ft)
Difficulty	The ascent is straightforward, if a little boggy in places. The suggested descent is reasonably easy but it does involve some pathless heather and grass. It would be tougher in mist as it would be impossible to follow some of the faint paths and tracks.
Time	3hr 35min
Summit	Meall na Leitreach (775m, 2544ft)
Map	OS Landranger 42
Access	From Pitlochry follow the A9 N to Dalnaspidal (signed) just before the Pass of Drumochter. Turn left and immediately right and park above some cottages.
Note	Many walkers descend by the ascent route, which is quick and easy but lacks interest. It would be possible to continue on to Beinn Mholach (Route 62) after traversing Meall na Leitreach.

Meall na Leitreach is a heather-covered plateau. The mountain appears rather uninteresting from a distance, but the route suggested here has plenty of variety and interest.

The Royalist Rising of 1651–1654 took place between Scots loyal to King Charles II and English parliamentary forces loyal to Oliver Cromwell, who occupied Scotland. The Battle of Dalnaspidal, on the evening of 19 July 1654, brought an end to this uprising when the English cavalry surprised the Royalist cavalry at Dalnaspidal. The Royalist cavalry fled, leaving the infantry unprotected and they soon turned and ran.

Walking the Corbetts: Vol 1

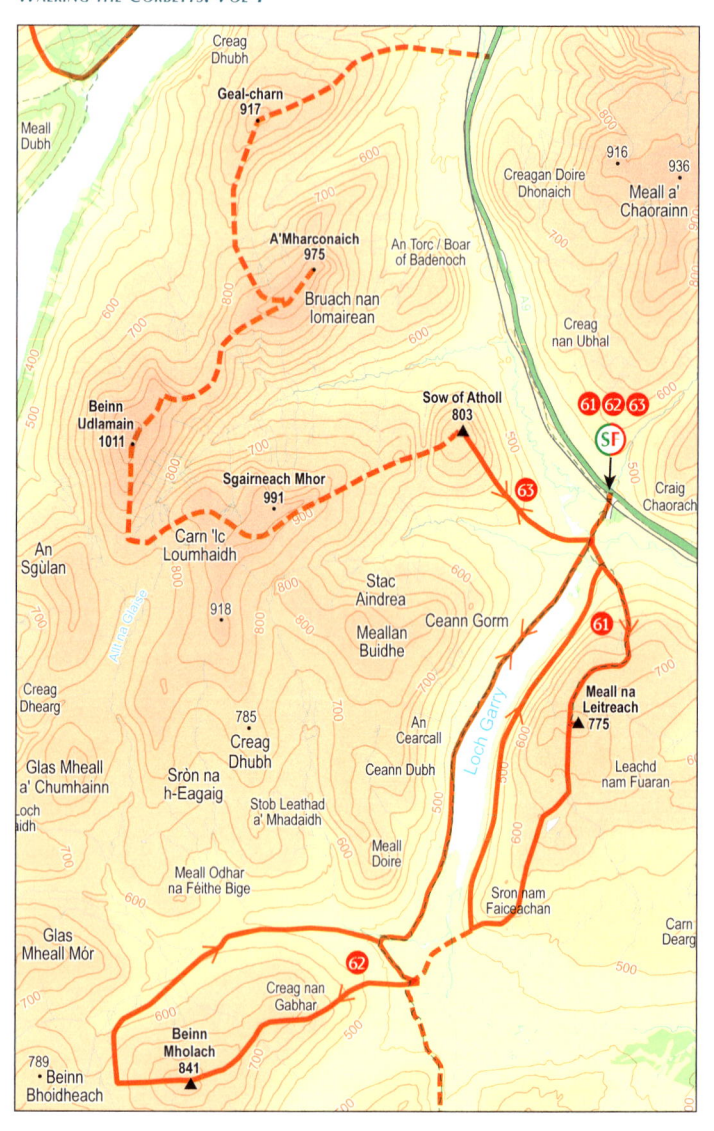

232

ROUTE 61 – MEALL NA LEITREACH

Meall na Leitreach

Take the road signed to Dalnaspidal Lodge, cross the railway and turn right along a good track opposite the farm. Continue to a small dam and bridge then turn left along the embankment to the left of the canal. Cross a small dam and a short track takes you to a newly bulldozed estate track (15min, 425m, 64390 72380). Turn left and immediately right up a peaty vehicle track, through a gate (470m, 64620 72150) and then follow the right-hand of multiple tracks to the left of a gully to the N ridge and turn right to the N top of **Meall na Leitreach** (748m, 64290 71010). The track continues to the W side of the summit plateau, but the summit cairn is about 150m away on the E edge of the plateau (1hr 20min, 775m, 64090 70270).

Return to the track and turn left along it to pass below Loch Meall na Leitreach. When the track fades away continue along the ridge with the help of animal tracks, then veer right after passing the crags of **Sron nam Faiceachan** to the end of the newly bulldozed track beside a newly planted small plantation (2hr 10min, 465m, 62650 67540). Follow the track down to the end of **Loch Garry** and along its E shore to reach the track junction above the small dam at the N end of the loch (3hr 15min, 425m, 64390 72380). Turn left and back to the parking area (3hr 35min).

233

ROUTE 62

Beinn Mholach SHAGGY MOUNTAIN

Start	Dalnaspidal (NN 64390 73380)
Distance	26km (16 miles)
Total ascent	640m (2100ft)
Difficulty	Once the approach tracks are left behind, the terrain is boggy and there is rough going on the suggested descent route. Care would be needed with navigation on the summit ridge in mist.
Time	6hr 40min
Summit	Beinn Mholach (841m, 2758ft)
Map	OS Landranger 42
Access	Parking as for Route 61
Note	It would be quicker, but less interesting, to descend by the ascent route. It would be possible to combine Beinn Mholach with Meall na Leitreach (Route 61). Beinn Mholach could also be approached from Annat on Loch Rannoch and it might be possible to cycle as far as Duinish.

Beinn Mholach is a remote peak to the N of Loch Rannoch. The broad summit ridge is a mixture of peat hags, rocky outcrops, grass and heather, and it is topped by an enormous cairn.

The **River Garry** used to be one of the finest salmon rivers in Scotland, but now Loch Garry is dammed and the water that used to flow out of the loch is taken in underground pipes under Meall na Leitreach to Loch Errochty to the S and further tunnels take the water to Loch Tummel and down the River Tummel to Pitlochry, passing through several hydroelectric power stations. The River Tummel itself is strongly controlled and is only likely to be flowing at the weekend when water is released to provide a playground for canoeists and rafters.

ROUTE 62 – BEINN MHOLACH

▸ Take the road signed to Dalnaspidal Lodge, cross the railway and turn right along a good track opposite the farm. Follow this track along the W shore of **Loch Garry** until its end (1hr 5min, 420m, 62250 68620). Cross the burn and continue on a faint, grassy, often boggy vehicle track along the edge of the flood plain to reach Allt Shallainn. Turn right to a bridge high over the burn (61350 67460) and continue along a good track until there is a faint vehicle track going off sharp right (W) just before reaching Duinish Bothy (1hr 50min, 435m, 61700 66910). Turn right up the track, which fades away in a peat hag on **Creag nan Gabhar**. Continue WSW up the ridge to the trig point and large cairn on the summit of **Beinn Mholach** (3hr 10min, 841m, 58750 65480).

Continue just S of W along the ridge, veering right and picking a route down the heather slopes to a small burn. Turn right down the burn and on reaching a faint vehicle track either follow it or continue down the burn to a junction with Allt Cro-chloich (3hr 45min, 575m, 57700 66440). It's best to follow the right-hand side of this burn to avoid awkward river crossings if the burns are in flood. The Allt Cro-chloich joins the Allt Shallainn, which is followed back to the bridge (5hr 5min, 445m, 61350 67460). Return to Dalnaspidal by the same route (6hr 40min).

See map in Route 61.

The large summit cairn on Beinn Mholach

ROUTE 63
The Sow of Atholl

Start	Dalnaspidal (NN 64390 73380)
Distance	7km (4 miles)
Total ascent	420m (1400ft)
Difficulty	The ridge is pathless, apart from a few animal tracks, but the ascent over grass and heather is relatively easy.
Time	2hr 15min
Summit	The Sow of Atholl (803m, 2500ft contour)
Map	OS Landranger 42
Access	Parking as for Route 61
Note	It would be possible to climb the Sow of Atholl and then continue over the four Munros Sgairneach Mhor, Beinn Udlamain, A'Mharconaich and Geal Charn and descend to Balsporran Cottages. There is then a cycle path that could be taken back to Dalnaspidal.

The Sow of Atholl is a rounded hill overlooking the Pass of Drumochter. It is a distinctive mountain as it is approached along the A9 from the N and it gives good views of the Munros on either side of the pass. The OS 1 inch:1 mile map didn't give a height for the Sow of Atholl, but it was shown with a 2500ft contour, which is about 40m lower than shown on the OS 50,000 map.

The hill's **anglicised name** is a response to match the hill known as the Boar of Badenoch (An Torc), which lies 2.5km to the N. Its more ancient and correct Gaelic name is Meall an Dobharchain, which translates as 'rounded hill of the watercress' and this refers to the marshy ground on the lower SE flanks of the hill where watercress would have grown in the past. Although 'watercress hill' is the accepted translation today, in 1854 'The New Statistical Account of Scotland' referred to the hill as Carnan Dobhrain, which can be translated as 'small cairn of the otters'.

Route 63 – The Sow of Atholl

The Sow of Atholl

▶ Take the road signed to Dalnaspidal Lodge, cross the railway and turn right along a good track opposite the farm. Continue to a small dam combined with a bridge (10min, 420m, 64230 72700). Cross the bridge and turn right along a faint path to the left of a fence and pick a route up the SE ridge of the **Sow of Atholl** to the summit cairn (1hr 15min, 803m, 62520 74110).

Return by the same route (2hr 15min).

See map in Route 61.

ROUTE 64

The Fara THE LADDER

Start	North of Dalwhinnie (NN 63610 86240)
Distance	24km (15 miles)
Total ascent	940m (3100ft)
Difficulty	Easy. The summit ridge is mainly short grass and moss with a few rocky outcrops and provides easy walking.
Time	6hr
Summit	The Fara (911m, 2986ft)
Map	OS Landranger 42
Access	From Pitlochry follow the A9 N and take the A889 through Dalwhinnie to the track signed 'Old drover's route to Fergour' (this is the track at the top of the hill after Dalwhinnie). There is only parking here for one vehicle so you should park at the village hall (63750 84920) or at the end of the route (63360 84630), unless you are arranging transport at either end.
Note	The quickest way to climb the mountain is to descend by the ascent route but this misses most of the interest. It would be more interesting to approach The Fara from the N up Allt an-t-Sluic and Uisge Geal or Dirc Mhor.

The Fara is the highest point of a fine ridge stretching 10km along the N side of Loch Ericht from Dalwhinnie to Ben Alder Lodge. There are magnificent views over the Munros between Loch Ericht and Loch Laggan, including Ben Alder.

Dalwhinnie, at 360m, is one of the highest villages in Scotland. It was once an important centre as the drover's road was the only easy route for driving cattle from the north of Scotland to the markets in the south. Dalwhinnie is the Gaelic for 'meeting place'. General Wade built his military road through the village, in 1863 the railway arrived and now the A9 is the main highway through the Highlands. Dalwhinnie it is best known for its whisky distillery, which is the highest in Scotland.

Route 64 – The Fara

Follow the track to the W and, before reaching the lodge, turn left up a newly bulldozed track (62920 86390) to its end (35min, 545m, 61550 85730). Continue up faint vehicle tracks. When these fade away continue up to the NE ridge of **The Fara** and turn left to the summit, which is a small cairn, with a big cairn nearby (1hr 40min, 911m, 59840 84380).

Continue over the S top (904m, 59540 82940, 900m) and Peak 901 (58640 81940) to **Meall Cruaidh** (2hr 50min, 897m, 57810 80850). Veer W to the **Meall Leac na Sguabaich** (850m, 57000 80900) and descend its SW ridge, veering SSE to a gate in the deer fence at a gap

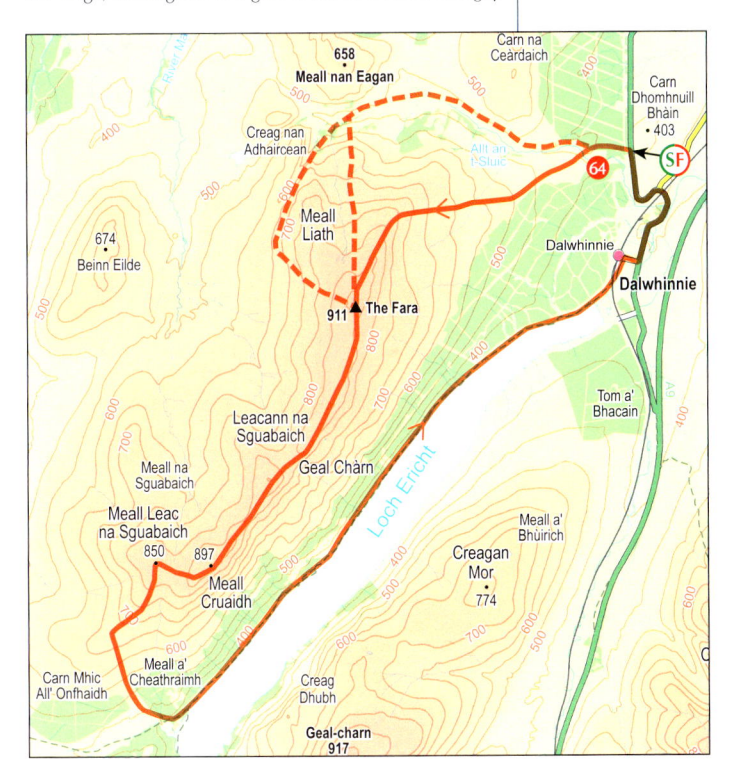

Walking the Corbetts: Vol 1

Dalwhinnie Distillery, the highest in Scotland

in the forestry (3hr 40min, 515m, 56630 79160). Drop down the grassy slope to the estate track (405m, 57010 78740) turn left, then left across a bridge and down to **Loch Ericht** (57610 79150). Follow the track left along the shore of Loch Ericht and keep straight on by the dam to cross the railway at a level crossing (5hr 30min, 360m, 63360 84630).

It is possible to park on the E side of the level crossing. Unless you have arranged transport you should walk along the road to the station and turn right to the A889 and left back to the start (6hr).

9 BADENOCH (SPEAN BRIDGE TO KINGUSSIE)

Turret Bridge in Glen Turret (Routes 67 and 68)

Badenoch: Bases and facilities

Base for Routes 65–69: Fort William

Fort William, nestling under the slopes of Ben Nevis, is the premier tourist resort in the Western Highlands and has all facilities for walkers and climbers.

Fort William Tourist Information Centre, 15 High Street, Fort William, PH33 6DH Tel: 0845 22 55 121 www.visitscotland.com

Glen Nevis SYHA, Fort William, PH33 6SY Tel: 01397 702 336

Local facilities for Routes 65–69: Spean Bridge and Roybridge

These small villages both have small stores as well as a variety of accommodation, including camping and caravan sites.

Spean Bridge Tourist Information Centre, Woollen Mill Car Park, Spean Bridge, PH34 4EP Tel: 01397 712 576

Roy Bridge Hotel has bunkhouse as well as normal hotel facilities.
Tel: 01397 712 236 www.roybridgehotel.co.uk

Local facilities for Route 69: Fort Augustus

Fort Augustus has good facilities for tourists.

Fort Augustus Tourist Information Centre, Car Park, Fort Augustus, PH32 4DD Tel: 0845 22 55 121 www.visitscotland.com

Stravaiger's Lodge, just up the B862 from Fort Augustus, has a hostel as well as a camping and caravan site. Tel: 01320 366 257
www.stravaigerslodgecumberlandscam.epageuk.com

SW of Fort Augustus along the Great Glen there are two independent hostels:

Saddle Mountain Hostel Tel: 01809 501 412
www.saddlemountainhostel.co.uk

Great Glen Hostel at Laggan Tel: 01809 501 430 www.greatglenhostel.com

Base for Routes 70–74: Kingussie or Newtonmore

Kingussie is a small town with several hotels and B&Bs. The seasonal tourist information office is housed in the Highland Folk Museum: Kingussie Tourist Information Office, King Street, Kingussie, PH21 1HP
Tel: 01540 661 297 www.visitscotland.com

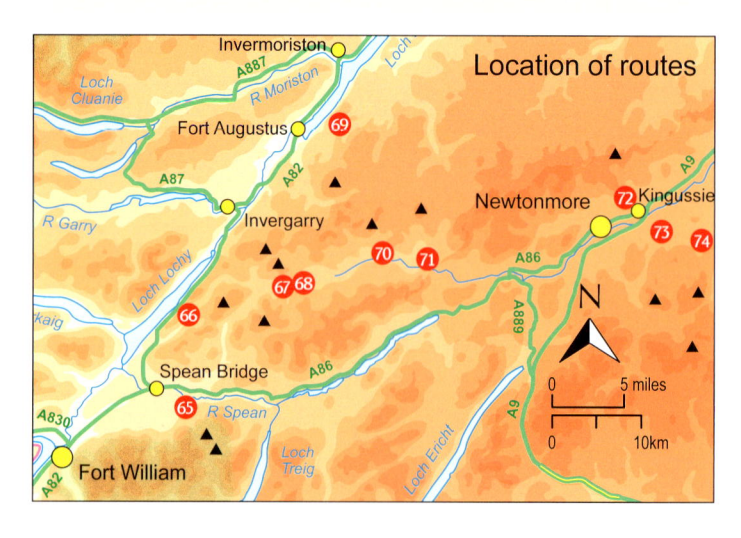

Newtonmore, about 3 miles W of Kingussie, has additional accommodation. Newtonmore Grill and a caravan and camping site are on the B9150 SW of Newtonmore.

Local facilities for Routes 70 and 71: Laggan

Laggan has a small shop, two hotels and a bunkhouse.

Laggan Country Hotel Tel: 01528 544 250 www.lagganhotel.co.uk

The Pottery Coffee Shop: The pottery has a bunkhouse and a tearoom serving delicious homemade cakes. Tel: 01528 544 231 www.potterybunkhouse.co.uk

ROUTE 65

Sgurr Innse ROCKY PEAK OF THE MEADOW
and Cruach Innse STACK OF THE MEADOW

Start	Corriechoille Lodge (NN 25560 78860)
Distance	13km (8 miles)
Total ascent	890m (2900ft)
Difficulty	The summit ridges look difficult from a distance, but paths take the walker relatively easily through the crags.
Time	3hr 45min
Summits	Sgurr Innse (809m, 2600ft), Cruach Innse (857m, 2850ft)
Map	OS Landranger 41
Access	From Fort William take the A82 E to Spean Bridge, and then take a minor road signed to Corriechoille, which is followed to a junction at the end of the tarmac road. Turn right up a good track past Corriechoille Lodge, through a gate and to limited parking just before the forest.

Cruach Innse and Sgurr Innse are two rocky peaks to the E of the 'Grey Corries' overshadowed by the big Munros Stob Coire na Ceannain and Stob Coire Easain.

WALKING THE CORBETTS: VOL 1

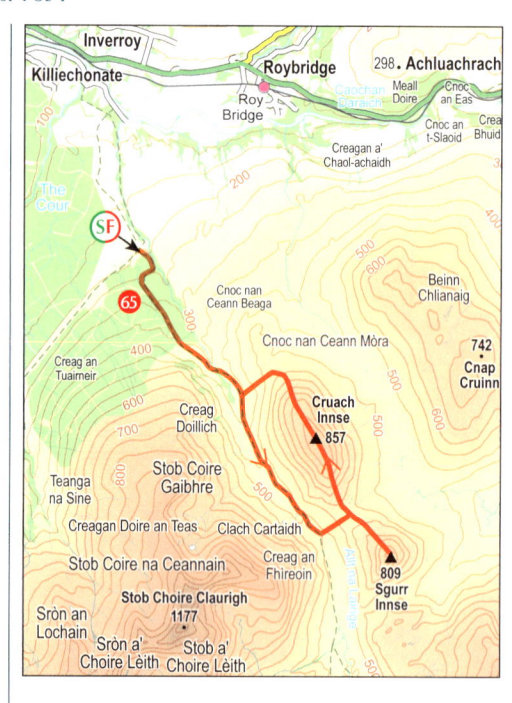

The Wee Minister carving on the approach to Chruach Innse

About 300m into the route you will come across a **wooden carved statue** entitled 'The Wee Minister'. A plaque affixed to the flat base of a tree stump states: 'A stone statue of the Wee Minister dating from the 1900s once stood on a site near here and was said to bring good luck to climbers and walkers. The statue, believed to be of the Rev John McIntosh, was destroyed in the 1970s. However, in May 2010 the local tourism group decided to resurrect him and replace him with this replica crafted in cedar wood by Peter Bowsher, champion wood carver. Good fortune to all who pass this way'.

Head up the track to its high point (1hr 10min, 505m, 28020 75090). Head left (ENE) up rough moor to the pass

Route 65 – Sgurr Innse and Cruach Innse

between Cruach Innse and Sgurr Innse (590m, 28480 75210) and turn right along a small path towards the main crag on the NW face of **Sgurr Innse**. The path follows a right to left ramp below the crag and then cuts back to the cairn on a rock outcrop on the summit (1hr 50min, 809m, 29020 74810).

Descend carefully back to the pass and climb the S ridge of **Cruach Innse** up small paths which easily bypass the crags. Pass many quartzite outcrops and boulders on the summit plateau before reaching the summit cairn (2hr 45min, 857m, 28000 76380).

Descend NNW down the grassy ridge, passing to the right of crags that are not shown on the OS map and then veering WSW when below the crags down to the track (3hr 15min, 380m, 26980 77010). Turn right and follow the track back to the parking area (3hr 45min).

Cruach Innse seen from Allt Leachdach

245

ROUTE 66
Beinn Iaruinn IRON MOUNTAIN

Start	Glen Gloy (NN 25780 88760)
Distance	10km (7 miles)
Total ascent	700m (2300ft)
Difficulty	This route does involve an ascent of the steep-sloped Glen Fintaig where the Allt Fintaig flows through a gorge. At one stage an exposed path is followed and the uncomfortably steep grass slope must be traversed with the aid of sheep tracks.
Time	3hr 25min
Summit	Beinn Iaruinn (803m, 2636ft)
Map	OS Landranger 34
Access	From Fort William take the A82 E to Spean Bridge and then N. Turn right up the minor road into Glen Gloy to the roadhead where there is limited parking.
Note	Inexperienced walkers might prefer to ascend easily by the recommended descent route. The other main option is to climb the steep SE ridge from Glen Roy.

Beinn Iaruinn dominates the W side of Glen Roy from which it is normally ascended by its steep SE ridge, but a gentler and more interesting ascent can be made from Glen Gloy to the W.

One mile NW of Spean Bridge is the **Commando Memorial** dedicated to the men of the original British Commando Forces raised during World War II. The monument is a cast bronze sculpture of three Commandos, sculpted by Scott Sutherland and unveiled by the Queen Mother in 1952.

Cross the bridge on the right and follow the track up **Glen Fintaig** to the track end (25min, 295m, 27470 88660). The direct ascent up the Meall Breac ridge to Beinn Iaruinn is possible, but it would involve a difficult

Glen Fintaig

crossing of the Allt Fintaig, which runs through a gorge. Instead head upstream and pick up an exposed path that passes just above the gorge, then head up Glen Fintaig on steep grass slopes, aided by sheep tracks. At some ruins it is easier to climb higher up the slope to reach a fence (at about 485m, 28110 89830). Continue up the glen, rejoining the burn as the gradient eases and continue to a grassy flat (1hr 20min, 605m, 28950 90460). Follow the burn up, through some peat hags and then up a grassy slope to the source of the Allt Fintaig (770m, 29490 90140). Head SE to the cairn of the summit of **Beinn Iaruinn** (1hr 55min, 803m, 29700 90040).

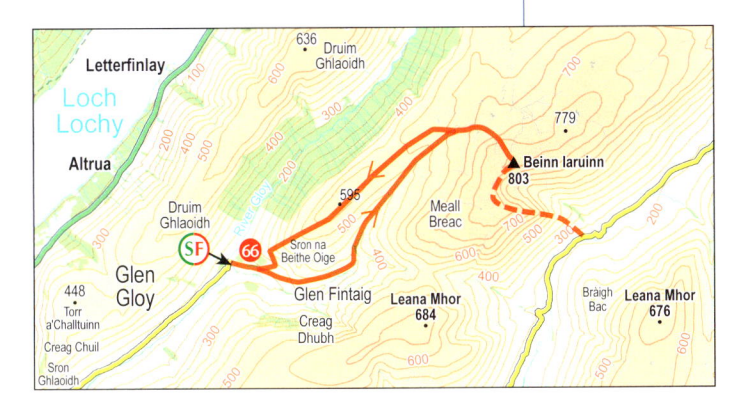

Head back to the grassy flat and then W, veering WSW to a fence junction (540m, 27930 90000) and follow the deer fence to Peak 595 (2hr 45min, 27300 89520). Continue along the deer fence and when it goes off right, continue WSW down the grassy ridge, bypassing a few crags as the slope steepens, to reach some woodland. Turn left down to the track and then right back to the parking area (3hr 25min).

ROUTE 67

Carn Dearg (Glen Roy)

RED CAIRN-LIKE PEAK

Start	Brae Roy Lodge (NN 33400 91120)
Distance	12km (7 miles)
Total ascent	660m (2200ft)
Difficulty	There is pathless moorland and rough pasture, but the going is generally easy. Crossing Canal Burn on descent could be difficult when it is in flood, at which time it might be better to descend by the ascent route.
Time	3hr 35min
Summit	Carn Dearg (Glen Roy) (834m, 2736ft)
Map	OS Landranger 34
Access	From Fort William take the A82 E to Spean Bridge then head E along the A86 to Roybridge and turn left up Glen Roy. There is limited parking at the end of the public road just before a plantation.
Note	It would be possible to ascend or descend the N or NW ridges of Carn Dearg, but these ridges are rather steep – the recommended descent has better views and is gentler.

This is the Carn Dearg to the S of Glen Roy. It should not be confused with two other Corbetts, also named Carn Dearg, at the head of Glen Roy, featured in Route 68. Glaciation in Coire na Reinich and Glen Roy has left this mountain protected by very steep slopes to the N and W.

ROUTE 67 – CARN DEARG (GLEN ROY)

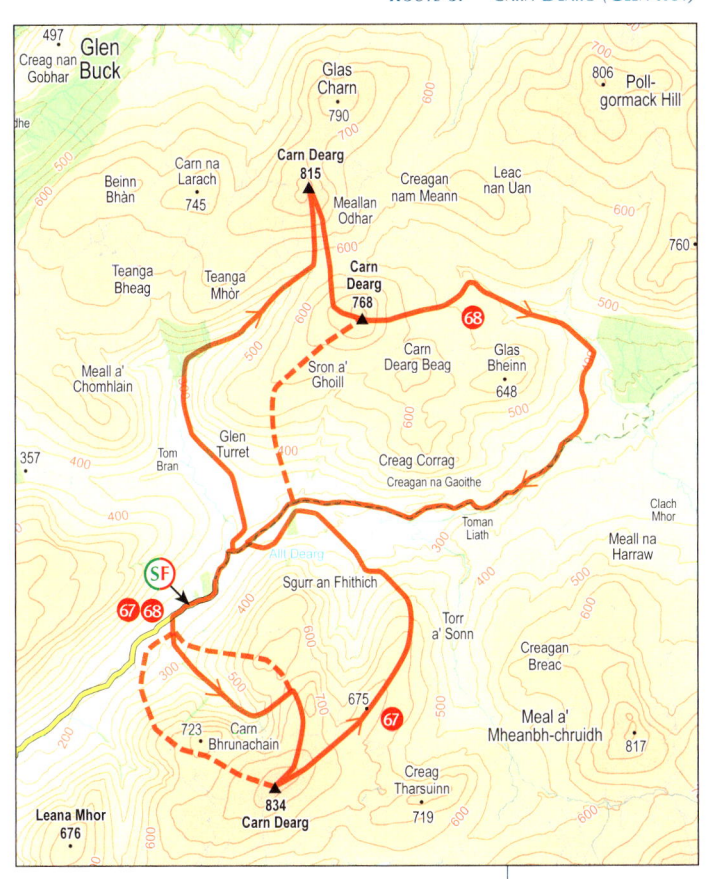

Glen Roy has world-wide fame among geologists for its **Parallel Roads**, a series of horizontal lines along the hillside at 261, 325 and 350m. They are actually the beaches that formed during the ice ages when huge lochs formed in the glen when massive glaciers flowing from the SW dammed the entrances to Glen Spean and Glen Roy.

The 261m beach was formed when the 'dam' was W of Roybridge and the level was limited by the loch occupying Glen Roy and Glen Spean draining over the pass to the E of Glen Spean, approximately where the outlet to Loch Laggan is today. The 325m beach formed when the glacier dammed the entrance to Glen Roy and the outlet of the resulting loch would have been to the S into Glen Spean over a pass to the E of Creag Dubh. The 350m beach formed when the glacier pushed further up Glen Roy and the level was set by the height of the pass at the head of Glen Roy and the loch would have drained E into the River Spey.

It is unclear why the OS has mapped them as tracks.

Head down the glen and cross the bridge over the River Roy. Head up rough pasture beside the burn which drains Coire na Reinich, continuing until the burn splits into three (45min, 460m, 34140 89650). Cross the left-hand tributary and climb easily up the grass slope to the right

Coire na Reinich

of the burn to reach the broad heather-covered N ridge of Carn Dearg. Continue to an old fence line (665m, 34770 90010) and turn right along it. When the fence line turns left, you should head right (roughly SSW) to reach the small summit cairn on the rocky ridge of **Carn Dearg** (1hr 50min, 834m, 34510 88690).

Head ENE, veering NE at the fence line (690m, 35440 89240) to reach Peak 675 (35780 89730). Head down the ridge, veering left as it steepens to drop easily down to a stalker's path, which is followed left to Canal Burn (2hr 50min, 285m, 35680 91640). Either boulder hop or ford the burn and continue down the path to Annat Cottage from where a good track leads down to and along the River Roy to a bridge. Cross the bridge and turn left back to the parking area (3hr 35min).

ROUTE 68

Carn Dearg (N of Gleann Eachach)
RED CAIRN-LIKE PEAK
and Carn Dearg (S of Gleann Eachach)
RED CAIRN-LIKE PEAK

Start	Brae Roy Lodge (NN 33400 91120)
Distance	21km (13 miles)
Total ascent	900m (3000ft)
Difficulty	The ascent is easy, assuming that you are able to locate the best sheep tracks up the steep grass slopes of Gleann Eachach. The descent of the Allt Dubh is rough in places.
Time	5hr 50min
Summits	Carn Dearg (N of Gleann Eachach) (815m, 2677ft), Carn Dearg (S of Gleann Eachach) (768m, 2523ft)
Map	OS Landranger 34
Access	Parking as for Route 67
Note	The quickest descent is SW from Carn Dearg (S), then veering S down the steep heather-covered slopes to Glen Roy, but this misses the magnificent waterfalls on the Allt Dubh, as well as the upper Glen Roy.

WALKING THE CORBETTS: VOL 1

There are two Corbetts named Carn Dearg either side of Gleann Eachach to the N of Glen Roy. These aren't to be confused with the Corbett to the S of Glen Roy. There doesn't seem to be any reason why any of these peaks should be called 'red cairn'!

One of Britain's rarer birds, the **ring ouzel**, breeds in Glen Roy. At first sight you may think you are looking at a blackbird, but the ring ouzel has a conspicuous white gorget (band) on its chest.

See map in Route 67.

◀ Follow the road through Brae Roy Lodge to Turret Bridge. Cross and fork left up a good track. When this track ends at a sheepfold continue up **Glen Turret** on a grassy, sometimes indistinct, track to a bridge over the Allt Eachach (45min, 305m, 33230 94070). Cross and head up the N side of Gleann Eachach. This is a steep grassy glen with the burn cutting a bit of a gorge. There are plenty of sheep tracks to ease progress and one of

Fresh snow on Carn Dearg (S)

252

these is developing into a path. When the gradient eases (at about 560m, 35080 95570) head N up the gentle slopes of **Carn Dearg (N)** to the cairn on its N top (2hr 10min, 815m, 34980 96650).

Head SSE, avoiding a few crags, to the pass at the head of Gleann Eachach (572m, 35320 95610). Cross a small peat hag and climb easily S, veering SE, up grass slopes to the summit cairn on **Carn Dearg (S)** (3hr, 768m, 35730 94870).

Head E down a grassy ridge and pick a grassy run through the heather moorland to reach the Allt Beithe Beag. Cross this burn and follow it down to the Allt Dubh (500m, 37150 95490). Descend this burn, with the help of animal tracks, down to a bridge (4hr 10min, 395m, 38900 94530). Turn right, initially uphill, along a stalker's path. When it fades away at a small burn, head downhill and you should pick it up again to reach a good track in Glen Roy (4hr 30min, 315m, 38670 93320). Turn right and follow the track back to Brae Roy Lodge and the parking area (5hr 50min).

ROUTE 69

Carn a' Chuillinn CAIRN OF HOLLY

Start	Loch Tarff (NH 43090 09860)
Distance	19km (12 miles)
Total ascent	860m (2800ft)
Difficulty	Rough pathless moorland in places, but not too tough
Time	5hr 25min
Summit	Carn a' Chuillinn (816m, 2677ft)
Map	OS Landranger 34
Access	From Fort William take the A82 NE to Fort Augustus and then the B862 S of Loch Ness and continue to the far end of the small Loch Tarff, where there is limited parking in a gateway on the left.
Note	The easiest way to climb the mountain is to ascend and descend the descent route.

Carn a' Chuillinn is the highest point in a vast heather moorland plateau in the Monadhliath Mountains E of Fort Augustus. The summit itself is worthy of a grander mountain.

At the time of writing there is a big construction project involving drilling tunnels for a hydroelectric scheme. This is due to be completed by the end of 2012; until then access from Glen Doe is restricted. It wouldn't be a surprise if the track was used for access to a wind-farm at a later stage. The route described here assumes that the track in Glen Doe will be useable by hikers after construction work is completed.

Fort Augustus Abbey was completed in 1880 on the site of the dismantled fort originally built in 1729 for the suppression of Highland Jacobites. The abbey has a place in the development of Highland landscape as, in 1890, the Benedictine monks installed an 18kW turbine in one of the burns to power the chapel organ. This was the first hydro-electric scheme in the Highlands. Excess energy was distributed to their secular neighbours and the hotels and houses of the village were to have the benefit of this local supply until nationalisation of the industry in 1948.

Follow a grassy track SE. This track soon deteriorates to a boggy path, which leads to the Allt Gleann nan Eun. Cross this burn, if necessary using a bridge 50m downstream. The path continues up the left bank of the Allt an Eich Dhuibh. The path has faded away in places, but there are animal tracks to help progress and the path becomes a decent stalker's path higher up the mountain. The path ends at an unnamed lochan (1hr 20min, 675m, 44640 07100). Continue over rough moorland along the left-hand shore of this lochan, then past Dubh Lochan and Lochan na Stairne and follow its outlet to the new dirt road built for the construction site (2hr 5min, 655m, 43990 05284).

Follow the road SW down to a sharp right-hand bend (725m, 42830 04180) and head SW up a bulldozed track

ROUTE 69 – CARN A' CHUILLINN

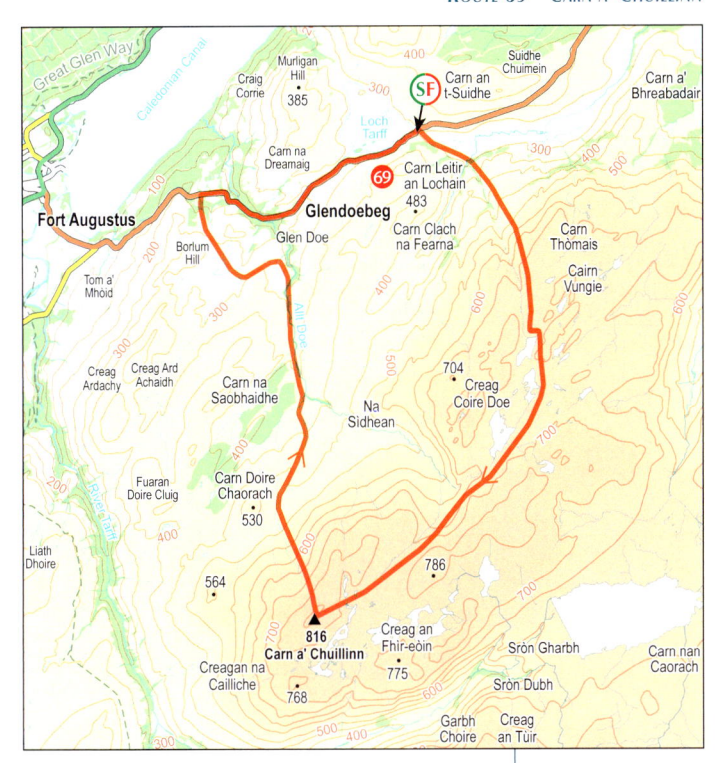

to the left of the burn. Continue as this track crosses the burn and until the track veers left at a grassy flat (2hr 45min, 730m, 42590 03920). Head WSW past one and between two more lochans (740m, 42130 03770) and climb easily up the rocky summit ridge to the well-built cairn on **Carn a' Chuillinn** (3hr 10min, 816m, 41680 03380).

Descend, initially NW, then N to pick up the S tributary of the Allt Doe. Cross the burn below **Carn Doire Chaorach** and soon pick up a path (at about 480m) along the W bank of the burn, which takes you down to the 'improved' track up **Glen Doe** (4hr 10min, 370m, 41580

Glen Doe | 06390). Follow the track back to the B862 (4hr 45min, 175m, 40250 09040). Turn right along the road back to **Loch Tarff** (5hr 25min).

ROUTE 70

Gairbeinn ROUGH HILL

Start	Melgarve (NN 46810 95910)
Distance	16km (10 miles)
Total ascent	830m (2700ft)
Difficulty	There are no paths between leaving the road and arriving at Corrieyairack Hill, but the going is generally fairly easy. Navigation should be easy as there is an old fence line from Gairbeinn to Corrieyairack Pass.
Time	5hr 5min
Summits	Gairbeinn (896m, 2929ft), Geal Charn (876m), Corrieyairack Hill (896m)
Map	OS Landranger 34
Access	From Kingussie follow the A86 W to Laggan and then the minor road signed to Garva. At Garva Bridge continue up the single-track road with very few passing places to the roadhead at Melgarve where there is limited parking.
Note	A really strong walker could combine Routes 70 and 71 by climbing Meall na h-Aisre from Garva Bridge and continuing across rough terrain to Gairbeinn and then completing Route 70.

Gairbeinn and Corrieyairack Hill are grassy hills to the N of the upper Spey Valley at the W end of the Monadhliath Mountains. They are both shown on the OS map at 896m and at one time they were both listed as Corbetts, but they don't quite meet the 500ft requirement. It is generally accepted that Gairbeinn is higher and is therefore listed as the Corbett but to be confident of climbing the Corbett you should climb both.

Corrieyairack Pass was an ancient drover's route over which General Wade's soldiers built a road in 1731 to enable the rapid movement of troops between Ruthven Barracks at Kingussie and Fort Augustus at the SW end of Loch Ness. Bonnie Prince Charlie and the Jacobite army camped on

WALKING THE CORBETTS: VOL 1

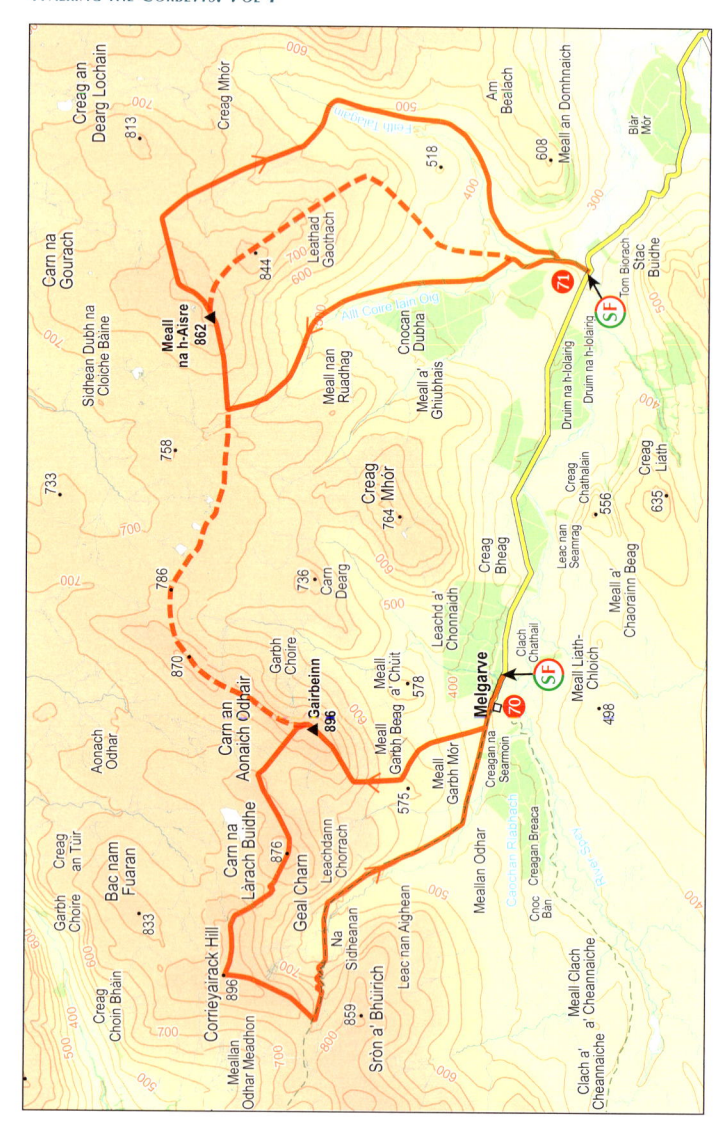

258

ROUTE 70 – GAIRBEINN

the pass during the 1745 uprising. It almost became the scene of a major battle when the English forces approached the pass, but they retreated when they saw the entrenched position of the Jacobite forces.

Head up the dirt road until a small burn about 200m past the cottage at Melgarve is reached (45990 96180). Turn right up the burn to the saddle N of **Meall Garbh Beag** (575m, 45370 97380). Turn right up the ridge, which has rocky outcrops to the summit outcrop on **Gairbeinn**, which is topped by a tiny cairn (1hr 40min, 896m, 46050 98520).

Continue about 200m along the ridge to a line of old fence posts (46080 98710). The fence line is followed to Corrieyairack Pass. Turn left, steeply downhill, and cross

Gairbeinn from the south

a saddle filled with peat hags (756m, 45640 98990) before climbing the opposite ridge and veering left to the summit of **Geal Charn** (2hr 35min, 876m, 44440 98840). Descend steeply WNW, crossing a couple of gullies and climbing the ridge of Corrieyairack Hill. The fence line passes left of the summit, so veer right to the summit cairn on **Corrieyairack Hill** when the route levels off (3hr 20min, 896m, 42820 99730).

Follow the fence line and a faint track SSW to the power lines that despoil Corrieyairack Pass (3hr 35min, 765m, 41990 98630). Turn left and follow the old military road back to the roadhead (5hr 5min).

ROUTE 71

Meall na h-Aisre HILL OF THE DEFILE

Start	Garva Bridge (NN 52220 94730)
Distance	17km (10 miles)
Total ascent	590m (1900ft)
Difficulty	Most of the route is over pathless terrain. Although the going is generally good, there are boggy or bouldery areas as well as small peat hags. Navigation is easy except that care is needed to pick up the burn on the descent.
Time	5hr 10min
Summit	Meall na h-Aisre (862m, 2825ft)
Map	OS Landranger 35
Access	From Kingussie follow the A86 W to Laggan and then the minor road signed to Garva. There is plenty of parking just before Garva Bridge.
Note	It would be possible to climb to the summit directly up the Leathad Goathach ridge. See note on Route 70 about combining Meall na h-Aisre with Gairbeinn.

Meall na h-Aisre is a featureless, mainly grassy hill to the W of the Monadhliath Mountains. Fortunately it is possible to ascend and descend from the plateau along delightful cascading burns.

ROUTE 71 – MEALL NA H-AISRE

Garva Bridge

The BBC television drama series **Monarch of the Glen** was set in the Scottish Highlands in fictitious Glenbogle, with much of the filming being done in Laggan and the surrounding area. The series was loosely based on Compton Mackenzie's Highland novels, set in the same location in the 1930s and 1940s.

▶ Cross the Garva Bridge and turn right up the track along the left bank of the **Allt Coire Iain Oig** to the second bridge (20min, 315m, NN 52210 95760). Cross the bridge and follow the right bank of the burn to Coire Iain Oig and continue until it starts levelling out on the W ridge of Meall na h-Aisre (2hr, 695m, NN 50180 99770). Turn right up the ridge to the trig point on the summit of **Meall na h-Aisre** (2hr 40min, 862m, NH 51530 00040).

See map in Route 70.

Follow the line of old fence posts E until the second set of peat hags is reached (3hr 10min, 800m, NH 52940 00720). Turn S and pick up the source of the Blackcorrie Burn. Follow the left bank of the burn down to the **Feith Talagain** burn (500m, NN 54340 98290) where you may get wet feet as you cross. Follow this burn down to a path end (435m, NN 54020 96740) and then down to a track and bridge over the burn (5hr 5min, 300m, NN 52380 95170). Cross the bridge and return to the Garva Bridge (5hr 10min).

ROUTE 72

Carn an Fhreiceadain LOOKOUT CAIRN

Start	Kingussie (NH 75580 00750)
Distance	18km (11 miles)
Total ascent	700m (2300ft)
Difficulty	Very easy. However, care is needed with navigation on the ascent as there are many new bulldozed tracks not shown on the OS maps.
Time	4hr 15min
Summits	Carn an Fhreiceadain (878m, 2879ft), Beinn Bhreac (843m)
Map	OS Landranger 35
Access	From Kingussie turn N up the road towards the golf club and park in the large Ardvonie car park after about 100m.

Carn an Fhreiceadain is a gentle heather-covered hill on the edge of the Monadhliath Mountains above Kingussie. The approach up the Allt Mor burn and the views across the Spey Valley make this a much more interesting walk than it appears on the map.

Just over 200 years ago, the **Duke of Gordon** drew up plans for a new town at Kingussie. This was one of the planned new industrial settlements created by landowners. The Duke intended that the water from Gynack Burn would power wool and flax (linen) mills and attract tradesmen, manufacturers and shopkeepers to live and work in Kingussie. The Duke's plans didn't work out and only a small village developed which has now developed into a small town.

In 1893 the Camanachd Association met in Kingussie to formalise the laws of shinty. This

ROUTE 72 – CARN AN FHREICEADAIN

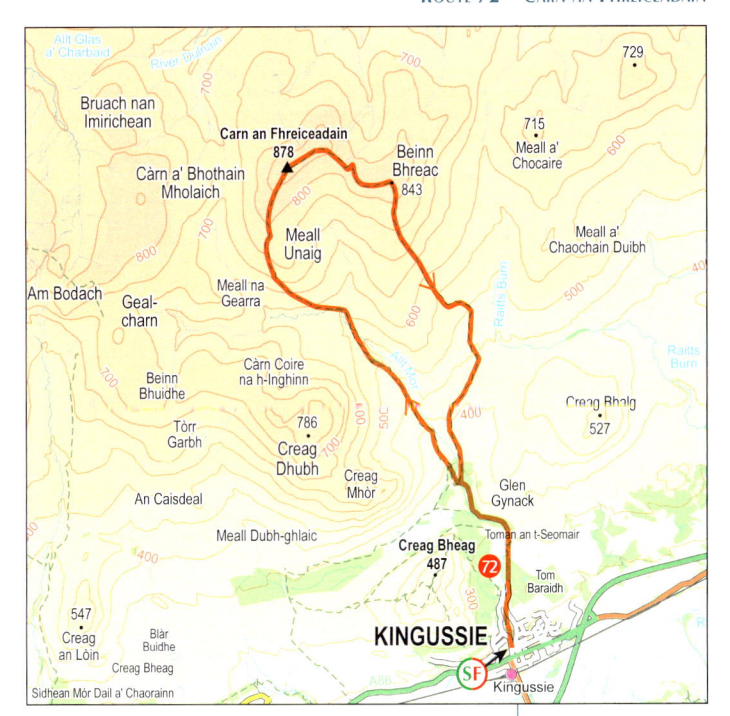

ancient sport was derived from the same root as the Irish game of hurling. Ice hockey was in turn derived from shinty when, in 1800, Scottish immigrants to Nova Scotia played a game on ice at Windsor. Kingussie has boasted the best team in Scotland, winning 20 consecutive league championships and even going four years in the early 1990s without losing a single fixture.

Walk N up the road then fork right down a path signed 'Gynack Mill Trail'. The path crosses the gorge of the Gynack Burn. Turn left and left again (don't recross the burn) to reach the paved Ardbroilach Road. Turn left and follow the road through the golf course and until the

Cairn on Carn an Fhreiceadain

tarmac ends at a bridge (30min, 330m, 74930 02920). Cross the bridge and pass in front of Pitmain Lodge and veer right up a good track. This track is followed up the **Allt Mor** burn to a bridge (525m, 73420 05030). After crossing the bridge continue up the track, forking right at the first junction and left at the second (1hr 45min, 730m, 72350 05760). Fork right when an old track goes off left (740m, 72300 05840) and pass a tall cairn before reaching the trig point on **Carn an Fhreiceadain** (2hr 15min, 878m, 72560 07120). There is a roofless stone shelter nearby.

Follow the track to the summit cairn on **Beinn Bhreac** (843m, 74010 06940) and turn S down the track to a new wooden shooting hut (possibly unlocked) (3hr 5min, 535m, 74750 05310). Continue down the track into the forest and on to the road by Pitmain Lodge (3hr 40min). Turn left and retrace your steps to the car park (4hr 15min).

ROUTE 73
Meallach Mhor BIG HUMP

Start	Tromie Bridge (NN 78930 99480)
Distance	25km (16 miles)
Total ascent	710m (2300ft)
Difficulty	Easy, except for a little deep heather on the descent
Time	5hr 50min
Summit	Meallach Mhor (769m, 2521ft)
Map	OS Landranger 35
Access	From Kingussie head E along the B970. There is limited roadside parking on the right just before Tromie Bridge.
Note	It would be possible to descend over the heather-covered Clach-mheall and Croid-la but that would be hard work. It would be possible to include Meallach Mhor on a backpacking trip involving Leathad an Taobhain and Carn Dearg Mor (see Route 74).

Meallach Mhor is a rounded peak at the head of Glen Tromie S of Kingussie. The isolated peak itself is rather uninspiring, but it is approached up the attractive Glen Tromie. The 10km approach to the foot of the mountain is up a paved estate road and it would be easy to cycle as far as Bhran Cottage.

The impressive **Ruthven Barracks** stands on a mound leftover by the retreat of the glaciers at the end of the last ice age. The first castle, built here in 1229, was destroyed in 1451, but rebuilt by 1459 as a much grander fortification. After the 1715 Jacobite uprising, the Government decided to tighten its grip on the Highlands by building four fortified barracks in strategic locations. Ruthven Barracks was one of them, and the earlier castle was removed to make way for the barracks you see today.

In August 1745 some 200 Jacobites tried to capture Ruthven Barracks, but a force of just 12 redcoats held out until February 1746 when a larger

WALKING THE CORBETTS: VOL 1

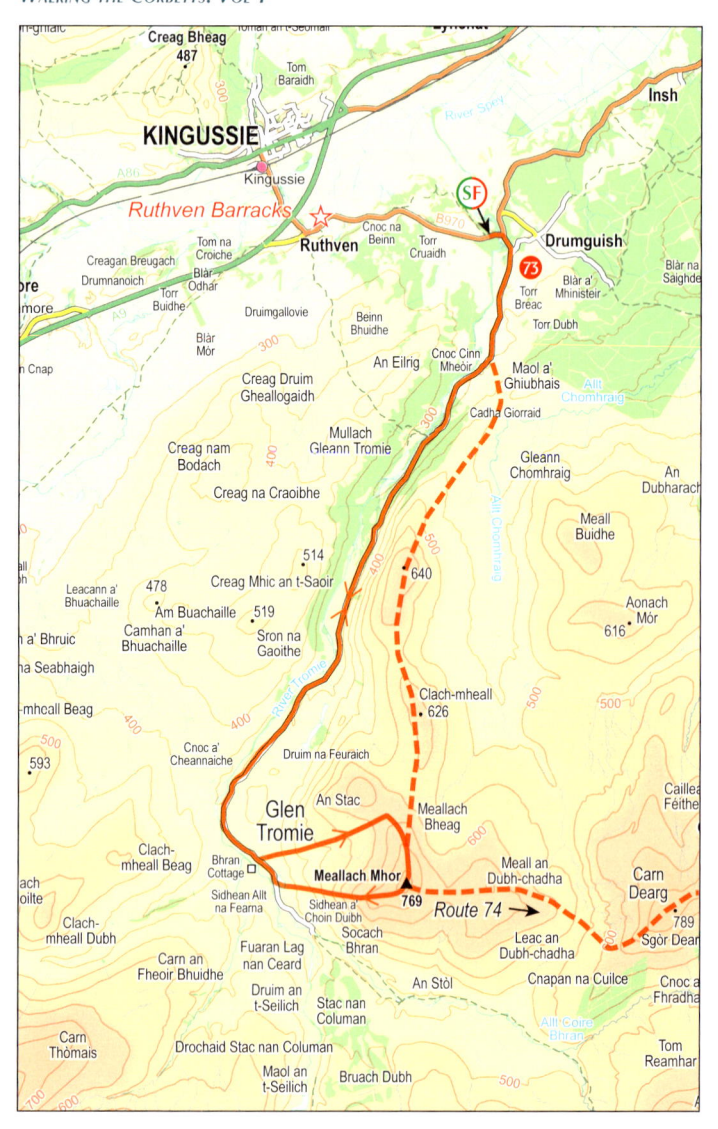

Route 73 – Meallach Mhor

Meallach Bheag from Glen Tromie

force of Jacobites arrived, this time equipped with artillery. The garrison was forced to surrender.

Follow the good track up the E side of **Glen Tromie**. This soon becomes a private paved estate road, which you follow for about 10km to **Bhran Cottage** (1hr 55min, 360m, 75390 91350). Just after the cottage turn left along a faint track. This becomes clearer after passing through the gate of a deer fence (75810 91350). Follow this track until it fades away on the saddle between Meallach Mhor and Meallach Bheag (619m, 77370 91780). Turn right up faint paths to the summit cairn on **Meallach Mhor** (3hr 10min, 769m, 77670 90870).

It is easiest to descend by the same route but instead follow the W ridge down to a memorial cairn (485m, 76420 90940) and on to the estate road (75800 91000) to the right of an artificial lochan. Turn right back to Bhran Cottage (3hr 55min). Return down the road to Tromie Bridge (5hr 50min).

WALKING THE CORBETTS: VOL 1

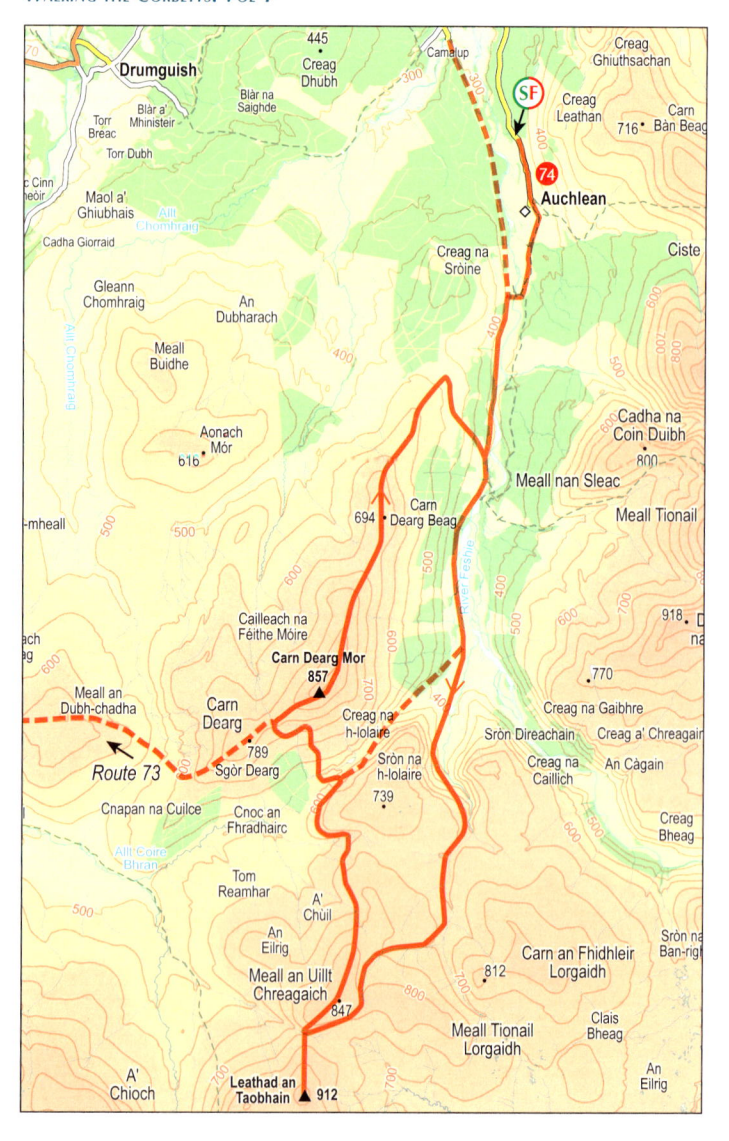

ROUTE 74

Leathad an Taobhain SLOPE OF THE RAFTERS
and *Carn Dearg Mor* BIG RED CAIRN

Start	Auchlean (NN 85070 98500)
Distance	33km (21 miles)
Total ascent	1200m (3900ft)
Difficulty	Once the access tracks are left behind small, sometimes boggy and often indistinct paths are followed. The going is generally good, although there are small sections of deep heather. Care will be needed with navigation in mist.
Time	8hr 25min
Summits	Leathad an Taobhain (912m, 2991ft), Carn Dearg Mor (857m, 2813ft)
Map	OS Landranger 43
Access	Follow the B970 E from Kingussie, then follow the minor road signed to Auchlean or Glen Feshie Hostel (this is not the road signed to Glen Feshie) and park at a large car park 900m from the roadhead at Auchlean.
Note	The easiest approach to the mountains is up the track to Lochan an t-Sluic. Another possibility is to backpack these Corbetts in combination with Meallach Mhor (see Route 73). If you are intending to cycle up Glen Feshie you may prefer to follow the road signed to Glen Feshie and park up that road (84220 00900). The approach is longer but it will be up a paved road.

Leathad an Taobhain is a remote, rounded hill on a vast featureless plateau to the SW of the Cairngorm Mountains. The shortest approach is from Glen Feshie when it can be combined with the rounded Carn Dearg Mor on the W side of Glen Feshie.

At Feshiebridge (84900 04550) on the B970 just W of the road to Auchlean there is the **Frank Bruce Sculpture Trail**. This short trail through the woods features a selection of sculptures created by Frank Bruce between 1965 and 2009. Most of the sculptures are carved from tree trunks and represent

WALKING THE CORBETTS: VOL 1

Frank Bruce sculpture

human or mythical characters. He has created a new style of sculpture known as 'Archetypal Abstraction'. The trail is well worth 30 minutes of your time.

Route 74 – Leathad an Taobhain and Carn Dearg Mor

Head up the road to **Auchlean** and follow a good footpath to the left of the cottage. Fork right to the bridge across the **River Feshie** (25min, 330m, 85050 96460). Cross the bridge and follow the track to the paved estate road. Turn left and follow the road until just before Glenfeshie Lodge (84360 93440). Fork left along a good track to a multiple junction by a ruin on a large grassy flat (1hr 25min, 375m, 84350 91780). The track going SW takes you to Lochan an t-Sluic; however, keep straight on along a grassy track between the ruins. The track deteriorates to an old shooting path as it enters and climbs the right wall of a canyon. At the top follow the deteriorating path up the Allt Lorgaidh burn and turn right up a tributary (2hr 50min, 665m, 84100 87880).

Follow the burn easily up to peat hags at its source and keep going a few yards to a vehicle track on the saddle (3hr 30min, 810m, 83020 86960). Cross the track and head WSW to another saddle and continue to a path (760m, 82380 86600). Follow the faint path up the ridge,

Allt na Cuilce on Leathad an Taobhain

veering right to the trig point on the summit of **Leathad an Taobhain** when the path fades away (4hr, 912m, 82180 85820). The lower W top is the one that is named as Leathad an Taobhain on the maps.

Return to the saddle and continue up a faint path to a track end on the summit of **Meall an Uillt Chreagaich** (847m, 82660 87080). Follow the good track until you reach the track coming up from Glen Feshie (5hr 25min, 580m, 82500 89990). Turn left and continue to a track on the right (690m, 81890 90540) about 100m after a line of shooting butts. Turn right to the ridge and veer right to the summit cairn on **Carn Dearg Mor** (6hr 10min, 857m, 82330 91180).

Continue along the faint track to the trig point on **Carn Dearg Beag** (694m, 83240 93500). Follow the path N, then NE. When the path fades away continue on the same line over heather to a good track (7hr 15min, 465m, 84100 95450). Turn right to the estate road (365m, 84570 94170) and return to the bridge over the River Feshie and on to the car park (8hr 25min).

10 THE SOUTHERN CAIRNGORMS

Looking across Glen Esk to the Hill of Wirren (Route 75)

The Southern Cairngorms: Bases and facilities

Base for Routes 75–77: Blairgowrie, Kirriemuir or Brechin

These three towns all have good facilities for tourists.

Blairgowrie Tourist Office, 26 Wellmeadow, Blairgowrie, PH10 6AS
Tel: 01250 872 960

Kirriemuir Tourist Office, Kirriemuir Gateway to the Glens Museum,
32 High Street, Kirriemuir, DD8 4BB Tel: 01575 575 479

Brechin Tourist Office, Pictavia Centre, Brechin Castle Centre, Haighmuir,
Brechin DD9 6LR Tel: 01356 623 050

Local facilities for Route 75: Edzell

Edzell is only a village but it has two hotels, several B&Bs, cafes and several small stores.

The Glenesk Caravan Park, just up Glen Esk from Edzell, provides camping and caravan sites. Tel: 01356 648 565

Local facilities for Route 76: Clova

Glen Clova Hotel also operates a bunkhouse and luxury lodges.
Tel: 01575 550 350 www.clova.com

The campsite marked on some maps up Glen Doll has closed.

Local facilities for Route 77: Kirkton of Glenisla

Kirkton of Glenisla is on the B951 NW of Kirriemuir. There is a small village store and the Glenisla Hotel. Tel: 01575 582 223
www.glenisla-hotel.com

Base for Routes 78–85: Braemar

Braemar is not much more than a village, but it has many hotels, B&Bs, cafes and small shops, as well as a good outdoor store. For the budget travellers there is also a SYHA hostel and a caravan and camping site.

Braemar SYHA, 21 Glenshee Road, Braemar, AB35 5YQ
Tel: 01339 741 659

Braemar Tourist Information Office, The Mews, Mar Road, Braemar, AB35 5YP Tel: 01339 741 600 www.braemarscotland.co.uk

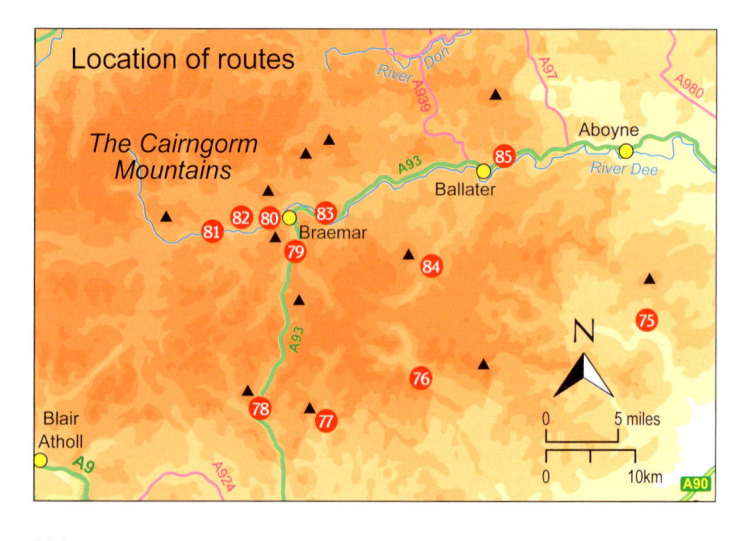

Local facilities for Routes 84 and 85: Ballater

Ballater is a small town with a good selection of hotels and B&Bs, as well as a caravan and camping site.

Ballater Tourist Information Office, The Old Royal Station, Station Square, Ballater, AB35 5RB Tel: 01339 755 306 www.ballaterscotland.com

ROUTE 75
Mount Battock
POSSIBLY DERIVED FROM BAD AG, MEANING LITTLE CHUMP

Start	Milden Lodge (NO 54030 78930)
Distance	16km (10 miles)
Total ascent	710m (2300ft)
Difficulty	This is an easy route, mostly on good shooting tracks, and navigation is aided by fences on the summit ridge.
Time	3hr 50min
Summit	Mount Battock (778m, 2555ft)
Map	OS Landranger 44
Access	From the A90 Brechin bypass take the B966 N through Edzell and follow the minor road up Glen Esk. At Milden Lodge turn right along a road signed to Mill of Auchen and park by the telephone box.
Note	A more direct route following one of the tracks up the Burn of Turret would be more sheltered in windy weather. The E approach up Glen Dye from the B974 might be the best route up the mountain, but it is longer and the access roads are more remote.

Mount Battock is the most easterly Corbett and gives wide views of the NE lowlands of Scotland stretching to the North Sea. The broad rounded ridges are covered with heather. There are numerous unmapped shooting tracks on this grouse moor.

WALKING THE CORBETTS: VOL 1

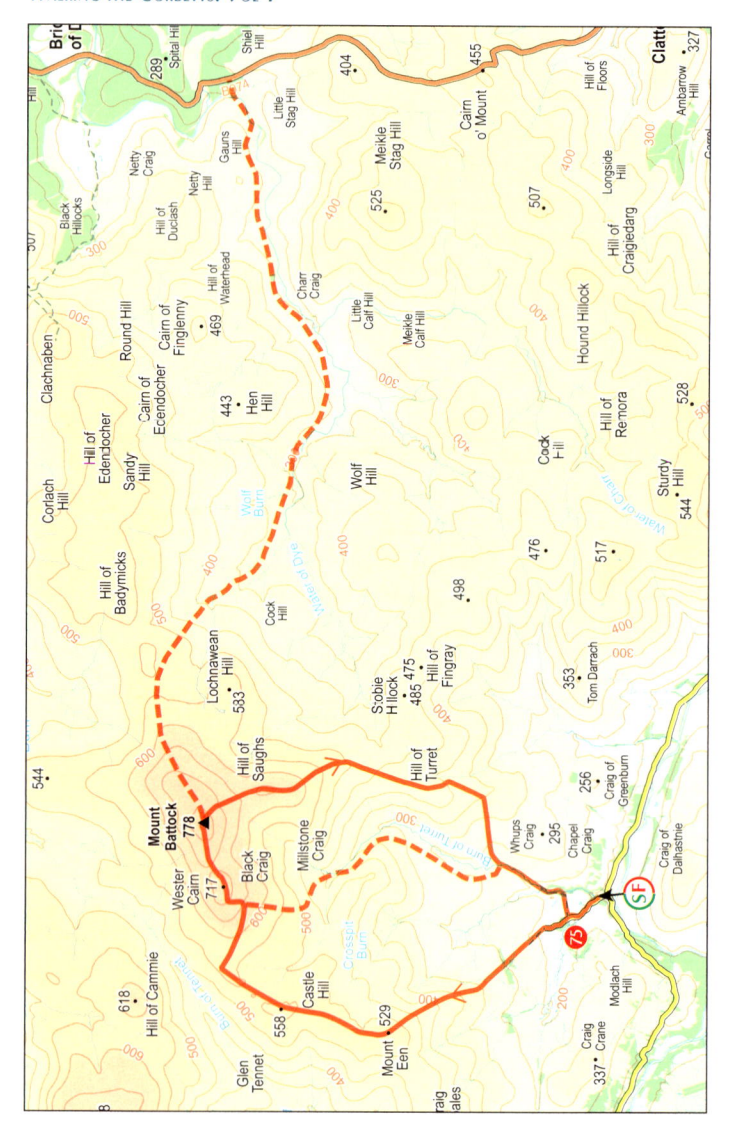

ROUTE 75 – MOUNT BATTOCK

Glen Esk has been settled for thousands of years. On the Hill of Rowan, above Tarfside, can be seen the outlines of Bronze Age settlements, 3000 years old. The Glenesk Folk Museum at 'The Retreat' has flint knives and arrowheads found in the glen and an axe head, thought to come from Switzerland. In the lower part of the glen, at Colmeallie, is a stone circle, said to be of Druidical origin. Little remains now of what were once two concentric circles, as many of the stones have been removed for building purposes.

Walk to the top of the paved road and continue up the farm track to Blackcraigs Farm. Keep straight on up an estate shooting track to a junction on **Mount Een** (55min, 529m, 52290 81860). Keep straight on, then fork right at another junction at the N end of Mount Een and continue to a junction at the N end of Bennygray (1hr 30min, 560m, 53030 84160). Fork right towards Wester Cairn and as you approach the top of the hill, the main track levels off (640m, 53910 83920). Fork left up an old disused track that leads over Wester Cairn to meet a fence, which is followed to the trig point on the summit of **Mount Battock** (2hr 10min, 778m, 54970 84460).

Wester Cairn

Turn right, SSE, and follow the fence to a saddle covered with peat hags. When the fence goes off to the right, cross it and keep straight across the boggy saddle to the **Hill of Saughs**. Cross a fence at its corner and soon reach the start of another shooting track (2hr 30min, 660m, 55390 83650). Follow the track, keeping straight on at a junction, and descend until you eventually reach another track junction (3hr 15min, 315m, 55150 80410). Turn right, then left across the Burn of Turret and follow the track left down to Hazel Burn. Cross this burn and follow the track to reach the road at Muir Cottage (180m, 53740 79400). Turn left down the road back to the parking area (3hr 50min).

ROUTE 76

Ben Tirran HILL OF HILLOCKS

Start	Glen Clova Hotel (NO 32650 73070)
Distance	16km (10 miles)
Total ascent	710m (2600ft)
Difficulty	The walking is relatively easy, but navigation on the plateau and on the descent could be difficult in mist.
Time	4hr 10min
Summit	Ben Tirran (896m, 2939ft)
Map	OS Landranger 44
Access	From Kirriemuir follow the B955 N into Glen Clova and up to the top of the road at the Glen Clova Hotel. There is public parking about 100m up the minor road towards Glen Doll.
Note	It will be a little quicker to climb direct to Green Hill by climbing the ridge to the right of Loch Brandy. You could extend the route by traversing the ridge to White Hill, Finbracks and Manywee and descending to Rottal Lodge. The peak-bagger could go up and down by the described descent route, but this misses much of the scenic beauty.

ROUTE 76 – BEN TIRRAN

Ben Tirran is the highest point on the vast plateau between Glen Esk and Glen Clova. Heather predominates on the lower slopes of this grouse moor, with grass and occasional peat hags covering the summit ridges. There are many sheep tracks, which are often more obvious than the indistinct paths marked on the OS maps. Two magnificent corries enclosing Loch Brandy and Loch Wharral to the W of Ben Tirran make this a spectacular walk. The OS maps label the highest point as 'The Goet' (the goat), with the name Ben Tirran given to the SW top.

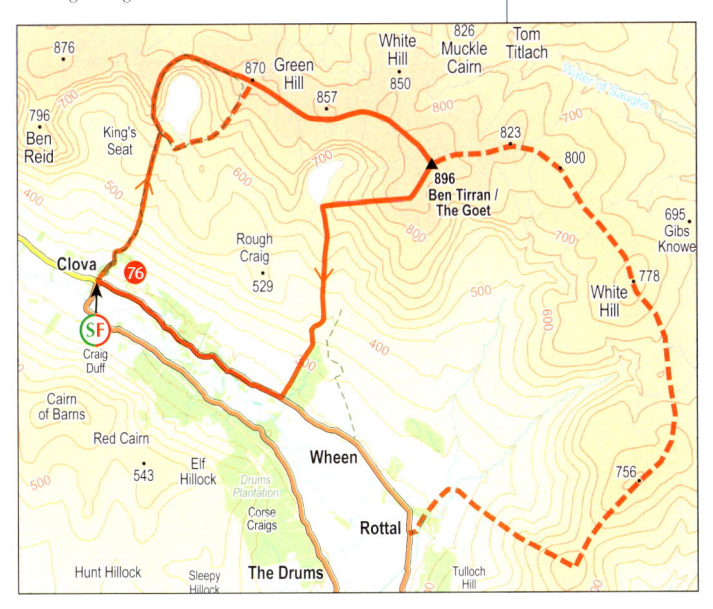

It is unusual to find such good **corries** as those occupied by Loch Brandy and Loch Wharral on a S facing slope. Corries normally form when snow accumulates in small hollows on N and NE facing slopes. In conditions of freeze and thaw this snow can turn into glacial ice, and freeze-thaw weathering and glacial erosion will cause erosion of the bedrock; if conditions are right, this glacial erosion can intensify and a deep basin with steep headwalls can be formed. When the glacier eventually melts the hollow fills with water to give the magnificent corrie lochs that we see today.

Walk back to Glen Clova Hotel and turn left through the hotel car park. After passing through a gate, fork right along a good footpath signed to Glen Esk. Follow this path until you get a good view of Loch Brandy (50min, 640m, 33590 75040). Fork left along a deteriorating path up the ridge to the left to The Snub (837m, 33580 75720). Follow indistinct paths, keeping above the crags surrounding Loch Brandy, to the summit of **Green Hill** (1hr 35min, 870m, 34870 75640).

In good visibility it will be easier to swing S of the direct line to avoid some peat hags as you aim for the small tarn (2hr 10min, 850m, 36840 75060) between White Hill and Ben Tirran. ◄ A new fence comes up from the N and heads up Ben Tirran. Follow the faint path to the right of this fence to the trig point on the summit on **The Goet** (2hr 20min, 896m, 37340 74610), about 50m to the right of the fence.

Descend the SW ridge of **Ben Tirran**, bearing W to a ruin at the outlet of Loch Wharral (635m, 35810

> In 2010 there were small piles of new wire and fence posts on this ridge, suggesting that there will be a new fence by the time you read this guide.

Loch Wharral

74010). Follow an old, often indistinct track S, veering left through a gate and right as you approach the burn coming down from Gowed Hole. Descend until a small path goes off to the right just above a conifer plantation (3hr 15min, 370m, 35870 72370). Turn right along the path and follow it down the right side of the plantation to the road (240m, 35300 71480). Unless you have organised transport you will have to walk 3km along the road back to the Glen Clova Hotel (4hr 10min).

ROUTE 77

Monamenach MIDDLE HILL

Start	Auchavan (NO 19130 69550)
Distance	14km (9 miles)
Total ascent	700m (2300ft)
Difficulty	The ascent of Monamenach is straightforward. There are some rough boggy sections further on as you cross the peat hags on Black Peak and descend from Mallrenheskein down pathless rough grassland. Navigation shouldn't present any problems.
Time	3hr 40min
Summit	Monamenach (807m, 2643ft)
Map	OS Landranger 43
Access	From Blairgowrie, head up the A9, turn right along the B957 and then left onto a minor road signed to Auchavan. There is very limited parking on the grass verge just before Auchavan at the top of the paved road.
Note	For a short easy walk you could descend by the ascent route. Those wanting a long walk should continue from Mallrenheskein over the Munros Creag Leacach and Glas Maol before descending into Glen Isla.

Monamenach is the highest point on the SE ridge of the Munro Creag Leacach. The recommended route takes you along the heather-covered ridge from Monamenach to Mallrenheskein before dropping down into the spectacular Glen Isla.

Walking the Corbetts: Vol 1

Forter Castle, about 5km S of Auchavan, was an outlying stronghold of the great Angus family of Ogilvie of Airlie, and would have been built both as a refuge and as a defence against Highland caterans. Caterans were originally bands of fighting men from a Highland clan, but the term was later used for marauders and cattle thieves. The castle fell into ruins but has been renovated by Robert Pooley and his daughter Katherine, a top London-based interior designer who, among her many exploits, has travelled by dogsled to the North Pole and climbed Antarctica's highest peak.

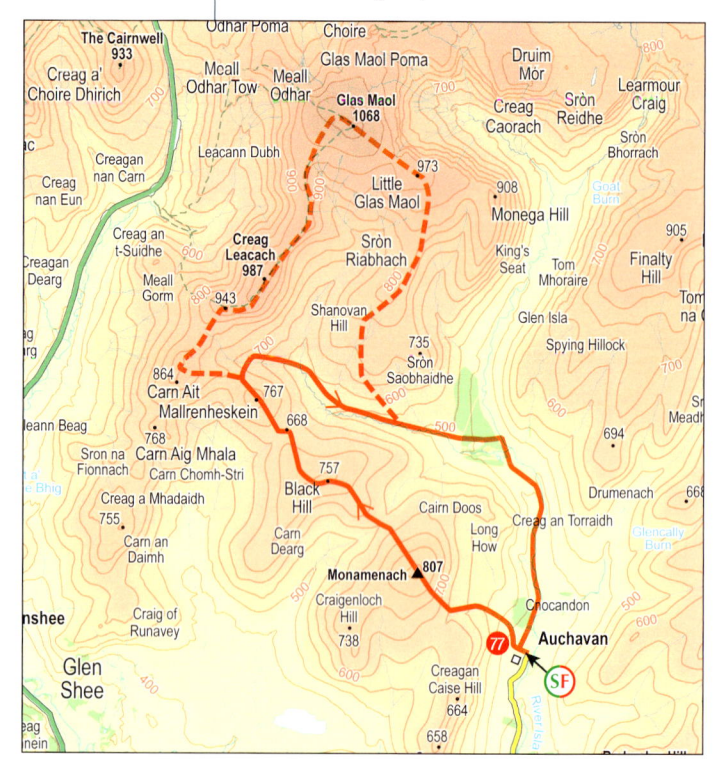

SE ridge, Monamenach

At the end of the paved road fork left up a private dirt road signed to Tulchan Lodge. Just after **Auchavan**, after the second cattle grid, turn left up a grassy track. This improves as it is followed to the crest of the ridge (30min, 625m, 17960 69960). Turn right up a faint track that leads to the summit of **Monamenach** (50min, 807m, 17600 70660).

A ruined fence joined from the right during the ascent and you should follow this NW down to Glack of Glengairney (608m, 17170 71290) and up to the summit of **Black Hill** (757m, 16470 71910). Follow the faint track heading off diagonally to the right until a fence is reached (16100 71780). Turn right along the ruined fence, descending over peat hags, to a saddle (668m, 15760 72510) and over the summit of **Mallrenheskein** (767m, 15350 72910) before descending to a saddle (2hr, 735m, 15140 73180).

Descend the slope on your right and then follow the burn down a pathless rough grassy valley to Glen Brighty (16010 73360). Cross over the burn and follow the left bank, with the aid of animal tracks. When the burn turns

W you should be able to pick up an old disused track, which leads to a good track descending from the left. Follow this into woods until there is a track junction just before Tulchan Lodge (3hr, 420m, 18630 72400). Fork left and then turn right along the track beside the **River Isla**, which is followed back to Auchavan (3hr 40min).

ROUTE 78

Ben Gulabin HILL OF THE BEAK

Start	Just N of the Spittal of Glenshee (NO 11410 71230)
Distance	6km (4 miles)
Total ascent	470m (1500ft)
Difficulty	Easy
Time	1hr 35min
Summit	Ben Gulabin (806m, 2641ft)
Map	OS Landranger 43
Access	There is a clearly visible track going diagonally up the mountain about 1km N of the Spittal of Glenshee on the A93 between Blairgowrie and Braemar. It is better to park in the rough lay-by about 200m S of the track, rather than park in the gateway.
Note	If you want a full day's walk you should follow the ridge N to the Munro Carn a' Gheoidh and descend to the Glenshee ski centre at Cairnwell Pass.

Ben Gulabin, part of a heather-covered deer forest, is the southernmost peak on the S ridge of the Munro Carn a Gheoidh. The view of the mountain from the Spittal of Glenshee is impressive and there are splendid views from the summit, but there is little else to recommend the route described here except that it is quick and easy. This is a peak to climb to stretch the legs on the drive N to the Cairngorms or to climb in the evening to see the sunset.

The megalithic **standing stone** behind the old kirk in Spittal of Glenshee and the Four Poster Stone

ROUTE 78 – BEN GULABIN

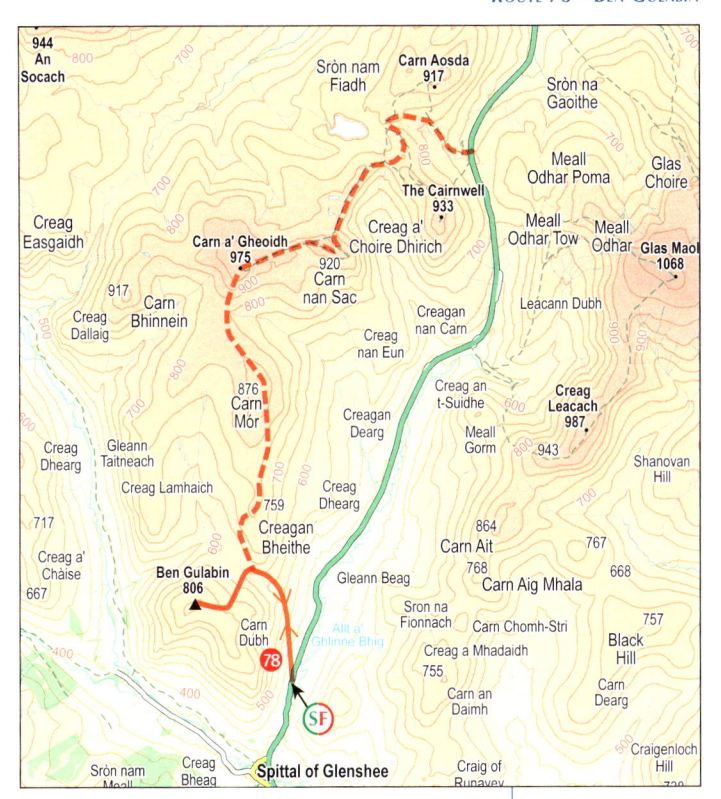

Circle on a nearby mound suggest the area has been inhabited for thousands of years, and there is evidence of a spittal (a hospital or refuge for the sick) at the site dating back to AD961. The Four Poster Stone Circle sits on top of a very artificial-looking mound on an otherwise flat plateau running along the base of Bad an Loin. In 1894 a shaft sunk into the mound proved that the mound was actually a glacial moraine deposited at the end of the ice ages.

Walking the Corbetts: Vol 1

Glen Shee seen from Ben Gulabin

Follow the small path along the road embankment to the gateway (11440 71400) and follow the good track to the saddle between Ben Gulabin and Creagan Bheithe (30min, 585m, 10830 72650). Turn left, SW, up a rough track to the summit plateau and turn right along a clear path to the summit cairn on **Ben Gulabin** (55min, 806m, 10040 72200).

Return by the same route (1hr 35min).

ROUTE 79
Creag nan Gabhar
CRAG OF THE GOATS

Start	Auchallater Farm (NO 15610 88190)
Distance	14km (8 miles)
Total ascent	530m (1700ft)
Difficulty	The ascent is easy. There is a short pathless section on the descent where care will be needed with navigation in mist.
Time	3hr 15min
Summit	Creag nan Gabhar (834m, 2736ft)
Map	OS Landranger 43
Access	Follow the A93 about 3km S from Braemar to a large car park by Auchallater Farm.
Note	It would be easy to descend the ascent route and this will give good views N to the Cairngorm plateau. If you can arrange transport you could turn right when you reach the track after Creag nan Gabhar and descend to the A93.

Creag nan Gabhar is the S top on a ridge squeezed between Glen Clunie and Glen Callater. It is a rounded, heather-covered ridge where you can expect to see red grouse, ptarmigan and red deer, as well as sheep in Glen Callater. There are fabulous views of the Munros that surround this Corbett.

Glen Callater SSSI is one of the richest and most diverse botanical sites in NE Scotland, including heath, grassland, rocks and cliffs, blanket bog, calcareous flushes and lochs. Some of Britain's rarest arctic-alpine plants are found on the cliff ledges, including woolly willow, alpine sedge and alpine sow-thistle. There are also important populations of nationally rare species of birds on this site, such as dotterel.

Walking the Corbetts: Vol 1

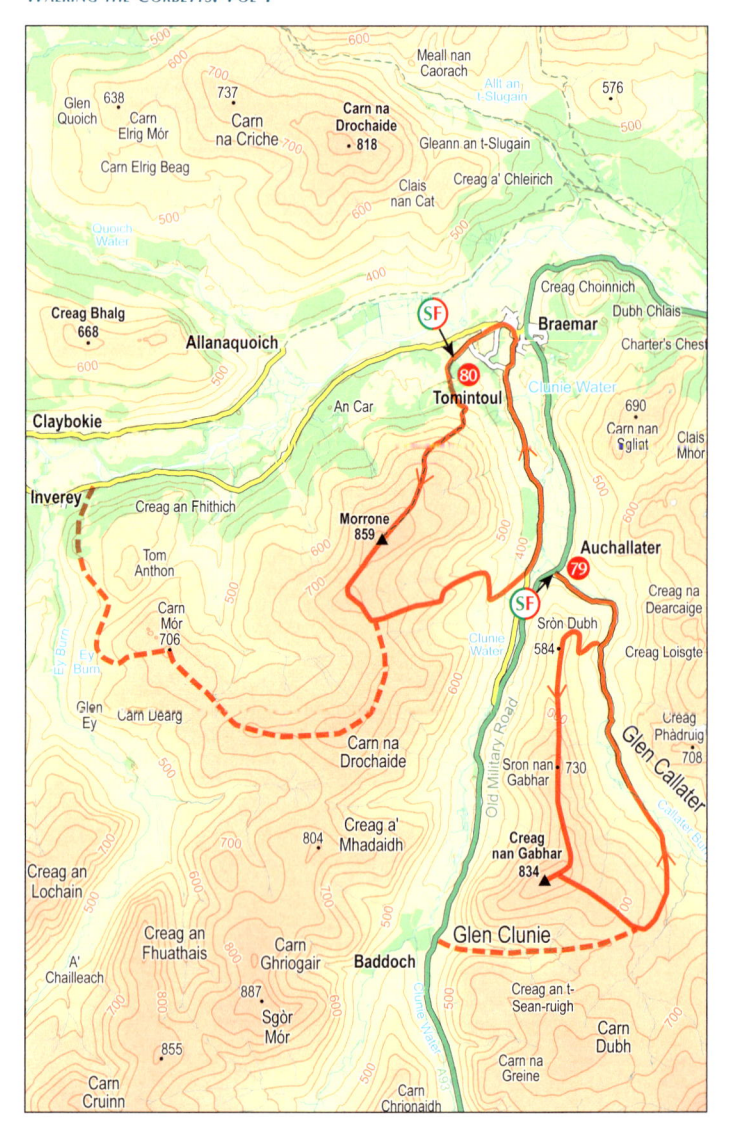

ROUTE 79 – CREAG NAN GABHAR

Creag nan Gabhar

Follow the good track up **Glen Callater** until you reach an old track turning back sharp right (20min, 435m, 16220 87250). Turn right and follow the track to the ridge (584m, 15670 87210) and on to the summit of **Sron nan Gabhar** (730m, 15530 85480) where the track fades away. Continue along the path, veering right just before the summit cairn on **Creag nan Gabhar** (1hr 40min, 834m, 15470 84100).

Retrace your steps until the faint path splits. Fork right, veering further right across a boggy saddle onto a minor top (740m, 16300 83760). The path fades away here, but continue SE to a good track (2hr 5min, 665m, 16570 83480). Turn left and follow the track down to **Callater Burn** where you will probably get wet feet at the easy ford. You soon reach the main track (480m, 16620 85370) descending from Lochcallater Lodge. Follow this track left to the car park (3hr 15min).

Walking the Corbetts: Vol 1

ROUTE 80

Morrone BIG NOSE

Start	Chapel Brae (NO 14320 91050)
Distance	12km (8 miles)
Total ascent	590m (1900ft)
Difficulty	Easy
Time	3hr
Summit	Morrone (859m, 2819ft)
Map	OS Landranger 43
Access	Take the road heading W through Braemar and fork left at the Taste Cafe. Follow the minor road to Chapel Brae where there is a big car park beside a pond at the head of the public road.
Note	Most people who climb Morrone will descend by the ascent route. If you want a longer day you could head S from Morrone over heather-covered ridges to Carn na Drochaide and W to Carn Mor before descending to Inverey in Glen Dee.

Morrone is the hill overlooking Braemar and is readily identified from a distance as there is a tall communication mast and associated buildings on the summit. While the mountain itself is uninteresting it does provide very good views.

The route approaches Morrone through the **Morrone Birkwood National Nature Reserve**. This is the best example in Britain of a sub-alpine birch-juniper wood and is how the first woodlands would have looked when the glaciers retreated. In the past the wood has been subject to high levels of grazing by deer, but since it was declared a conservation area, the wood has been fenced to exclude deer and natural regeneration is taking place.

See map in Route 79.

◀ Continue up the road through Morrone Birchwood National Nature Reserve. Fork left and veer right, then

ROUTE 80 – MORRONE

continue past a cottage, staying on the main track. Ignoring several track and path junctions, continue until the track flattens by a viewpoint, which is slightly hidden away on the left. ▶ From here follow a path that forks off right with a post labelled 'Morrone' (15min, 445m, 14310 90490).

Follow the good footpath, which becomes a bit of a scar on the summit plateau, to the trig point and communication mast on the summit of **Morrone** (1hr 15min, 859m, 13210 88630). Follow the good track SW to the S top of Morrone and follow it down to Glen Clunie (2hr 10min, 380m, 15230 88220). There is very limited parking where the track meets the road. Unless you have arranged transport you now turn left and walk down the road to **Braemar** and back to the car park (3hr).

Braemar seen from Morrone

Don't panic if you can't see all the points shown on the viewpoint marker as it was designed to be placed on a knoll a little higher up the hill!

ROUTE 81

Sgor Mor BIG PEAK

Start	Linn of Dee (NO 06340 89820)
Distance	20km (12 miles)
Total ascent	570m (1900ft)
Difficulty	There are no paths or tracks on the mountain once you leave the River Dee and although the ridges provide easy walking, the ascent and particularly the descent are tough, with knee-deep heather in places. Navigation will be demanding in mist.
Time	5hr 20min
Summits	Sgor Mor (813m, 2908ft), Sgor Dubh (741m)
Map	OS Landranger 43
Access	Follow the road W from Braemar to the Linn of Dee. There is a large car park about 200m after the River Dee is crossed.
Note	The recommended ascent route is the easiest route up the mountain and you could avoid the rough descent by retracing your steps. If you did this it would be possible to cycle as far as White Bridge.

Sgor Mor is a heather-covered mountain with broad ridges. The walk up the majestic Glen Dee with its scattering of Caledonian pines, an interesting ridge with many small granite outcrops, and a close-up view of the Cairngorms make this a worthwhile walk.

The **Mar Lodge Estate** has been owned and managed by the National Trust of Scotland since 1995 and is now being managed for nature conservation. As well as containing four of the five highest mountains in Scotland, it includes the upper watershed of the River Dee with its remnant Caledonian pine forest. Conservation work includes reducing the red deer population to allow regeneration of the native Caledonian pine forest, restoration of bulldozed tracks to footpaths, footpath repair and removal of deer fencing.

ROUTE 81 – SGOR MOR

Granite outcrops on Sgor Mor

Walk back to the Linn of Dee where you will want to view the falls. Head up the good track along the N bank of the **River Dee** to White Bridge (1hr 5min, 410m, 01880 88450). Just before the bridge turn right up a good path and follow it until you reach a burn descending from Sgor Mor (1hr 35min, 455m, 00300 89480). Follow the

293

burn to the right and continue along the same line to the ridge (725m, 01480 91570). Turn left up the ridge, passing numerous small granite outcrops, to the summit of **Sgor Mor** (2hr 55min, 813m, 00710 91420).

Retrace your steps and continue along the ridge over Top 744 to a shallow saddle (695m, 02610 91770) and continue on to the trig point on the summit of **Sgor Dubh** (3hr 40 min, 741m, 03380 92090). Head down the broad ridge SE to **Carn an 'Ic Duibhe** (630m, 05150 90680), then descend SW through increasingly deep heather until you reach a burn. ◄ Cross to the right bank and descend down to the track in **Glen Dee** (4hr 50min, 385m, 04540 89380). Turn left and follow the track back to the Linn of Dee and the car park (5hr 20min).

It is reported that there is now a deer fence 350m east of the burn. It will need to be climbed or an alternative descent route chosen.

ROUTE 82

Carn na Drochaide HILL OF THE BRIDGE

Start	Linn of Quoich (NO 11700 91000)
Distance	10km (6 miles)
Total ascent	500m (1600ft)
Difficulty	The paths are intermittent and there are times when you will need to traverse deep heather. Navigation could be difficult in mist and the going would be harder as you wouldn't be able to take full advantage of the faint paths.
Time	2hr 55min
Summit	Carn na Drochaide (818m, 2681ft)
Map	OS Landranger 43
Access	Take the road W from Braemar along the S side of the River Dee, cross the river at the Linn of Dee and continue along the N side to park at the road end.

Carn na Drochaide is a rather uninteresting heather-covered peak rising above the River Dee opposite Braemar. However, it is a fine viewpoint and the suggested route gives good views throughout.

Route 82 – Carn na Drochaide

On 6 September 1715, John Erskine, 24th Earl of Mar, raised the Standard for King James VIII and III in Braemar. The ceremony followed a great hunt held in the Forest of Mar. To entertain the guests, brandy was poured into **The Earl of Mar's Punchbowl**, a hollow worn in the rock by pebbles swirling fast in the stream above the footbridge at the Linn of Quoich. Queen Victoria was fond of this place and it became a popular attraction, but nowadays it is much quieter than the nearby Linn of Dee.

Cross the bridge over **Quoich Water** and follow the dirt road ahead until just before Allanquoich Cottage. Turn sharp left, forking right when a track heads into the woods and on to another junction just after you reach a plantation (30min, 440m, 10720 92450). Fork right and then left at another junction. The track eventually ends with multiple faint branches (55min, 570m, 10290 93800). Head NE up a faint path to the summit of **Carn na Criche** (737m, 11180 94390), then head along the ridge, assisted by some intermittent paths, to the summit cairn on **Carn na Drochaide**, ignoring several other cairns on the summit plateau (1hr 55min, 818m, 12740 93840).

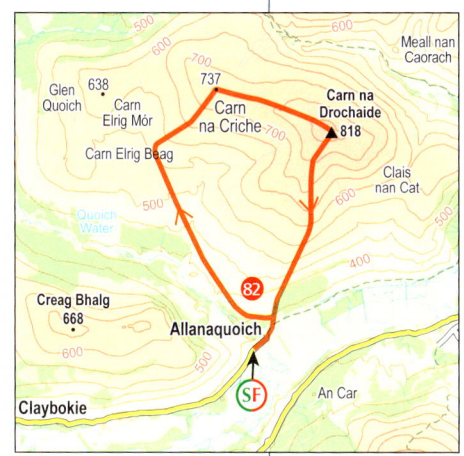

Head SSW to pick up a path, which takes you down to 590m before fading away. Continue down through deep heather in the same direction and hopefully you will pick up a faint path lower down that reaches the track at a gap in the trees (2hr 45min, 340m, 11910 91340). Return to the parking area (2hr 55min).

WALKING THE CORBETTS: VOL 1

ROUTE 83
Creag an Dhail Bheag and Culardoch BIG HIGH PLACE

Start	Invercauld Bridge (NO 18830 91260)
Distance	24km (15 miles)
Total ascent	950m (3100ft)
Difficulty	There are no paths once the access tracks are left behind, but the heather is relatively short and the only rough terrain is a few boulderfields on Carn Liath. Navigation could be tricky in mist.
Time	5hr 50min
Summits	Creag an Dhail Bheag (863m, 2831ft), Culardoch (900m, 2953ft)
Map	OS Landranger 43
Access	Head E along the A93 from Braemar and turn left to a large car park, up the Invercauld estate road, just after the A93 crosses the River Dee.
Note	The easiest route would be to walk (or cycle) directly up to Bealach Dearg and climb the two Corbetts from there, but this would be rather uninteresting compared with the route described here.

Carn Liath and Culardoch are situated between the Dee Valley and Ben Avon and are separated by the 650m Bealach Dearg. There are superb views across to Ben Avon and SE to Lochnagar. Carn Liath has twin summits given as 862m on the OS 50:000 map and there are a number of other tops which appear to be about the same height. The eastern summit, Carn Liath, was listed as the Corbett until accurate measurements in 2013 showed that Carn Liath (861.5m) was lower than Creag an Dhail Bheag (863m), which is now accepted as the Corbett.

The **Bealach Dearg** is the old route connecting Braemar to Tomintoul and was once the main droving road between Speyside and Deeside. Three hundred years ago, Highland drovers would have driven their cattle S to markets at Crieff and later Falkirk where they would sell their cattle to the lowlanders.

Route 83 – Carn Liath and Culardoch

Follow the estate road past Invercauld House and continue until the end of the paved road (340m, 17150 92750) where you fork right, then left and right again, signed to Inverchandlick. Go right at the next fork (40min, 355m, 16270 93250) then veer left through a gate in the deer fence and immediately fork right, climbing to a second deer fence (435m, 15810 94090) and then a third fence into open heather moorland. The good hill track ends beside the Glas Allt Beag burn (1hr 30min, 590m, 15610 96600).

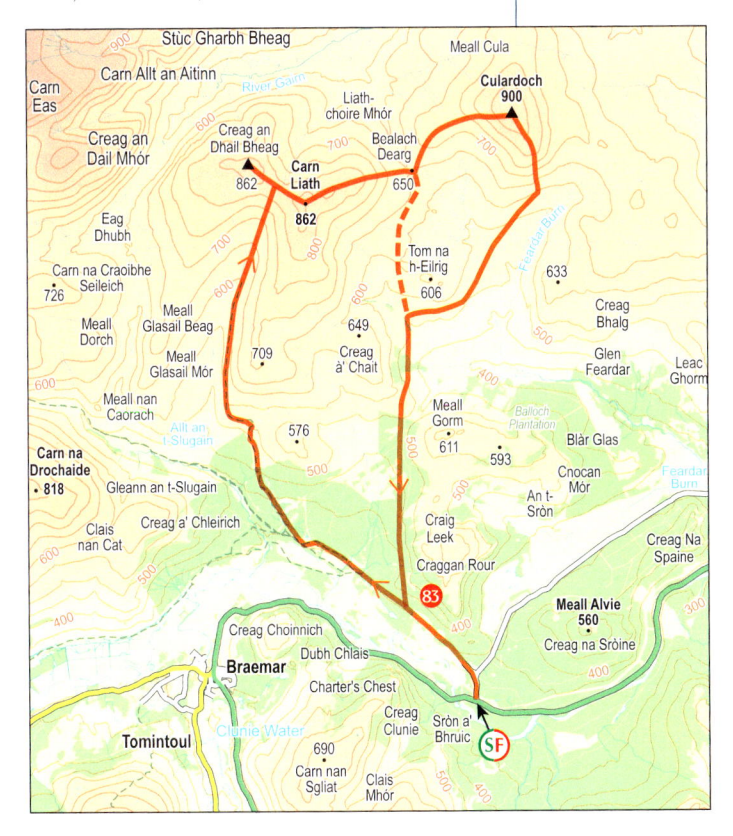

Invercauld Forest

Follow the burn and then continue climbing to the shallow saddle between the twin peaks of **Carn Liath** (828m, 16050 97860). Turn left to Creag an Dhail Bheag. This isn't the top you reach first, with a prominent cairn, but a top with a small rock outcrop further W (863m, 15740 98150). Retrace your steps and continue to the E summit. The highest point isn't the S or the E top, both of which have prominent cairns, but the middle top with a small cairn (2hr 30min, 862m, 16540 97690).

Continue over the E top and descend E over heather and boulderfields to the **Bealach Dearg** (3hr, 650m, 18040 98010). Turn left up the good track and continue until it turns sharp left (730m, 18590 98770). Keep straight on up a faint track, which becomes a path before fading away as it veers to climb the W ridge to the trig point on **Culardoch** (3hr 40min, 900m, 19350 98820).

Descend SE, veering S to reach a track (19580 97620, 585m). Turn right and continue, ignoring sidetracks, to reach the main track descending from Bealach Dearg (520m, 17840 96180). Turn left and fork left after entering the forest (495m, 17900 94600) and follow yellow markers back to the paved estate road (5hr 30min, 350m, 17570 92420). Turn left back to the car park (5hr 50min).

ROUTE 84

Conachcraig COMBINATION OF CRAGS

Start	Spittal of Glenmuick (NO 30980 85140)
Distance	13km (8 miles)
Total ascent	580m (1900ft)
Difficulty	The ascent is up a heather-covered ridge, which is hard work in places. Although paths are beginning to develop on the summit ridge, they may still be too faint to follow in mist, so navigation could be a little tricky. The descent route is easy.
Time	3hr 30min
Summit	Conachcraig (865m, 2827ft)
Map	OS Landranger 44
Access	From Braemar follow the A93 E to Crathie and then the B976 to the outskirts of Ballater where you take the minor road to Glen Muick. There is a large car park at the roadhead at the Spittal of Glenmuick.
Note	The easiest and most popular way to climb Conachcraig is to climb and descend the suggested descent route. This is probably the best option in bad weather, but won't be as interesting as the route recommended here. Lochnagar is well worth climbing and you could divert up Lochnagar from the descent route returning to the Spittal of Glenmuick via Loch Muick.

Conachcraig is an outlier to Lochnagar and only just meets the 500ft requirement for a Corbett. It is a heather-covered hill but has plenty of interest with many small outcrops of granite on the summit plateau. There are three tops and the highest is the SW top, not the middle one which is labelled Conachcraig on the OS 1:50,000 map.

Conachcraig is on the Balmoral Estate and the peaks were popular with Queen Victoria when she was staying at Balmoral Castle. The Queen wrote in her Highland Journal on 16 September 1848 of a trip to the summit of Lochnagar: 'But, alas! nothing whatever can be seen; and it was cold, and wet and cheerless. At about twenty minutes after two we set off on our way downwards, the wind blowing a hurricane, and the mist being like rain, and everything quite dark with it.'

Follow the track from the car park to Balmoral Estate Visitor Centre, which is well worth a visit. Turn right just past the visitor centre, signed to Lochnagar, cross Glen Muick and reach a T-junction (29950 85840). Turn right and fork left through the forest, continuing to a junction as you leave the wood (40min, 415m, 30540 87490). Climb SW, veering W up the heather-covered ridge to **Carn an Daimh** (617m, 29770 87060), descend a little and continue up to another knoll (735m, 29140 87140). Here a path appears, which takes you easily up to the middle top on **Conachcraig**, covered with small rock outcrops (1hr 55min, 850m, 28430 87150).

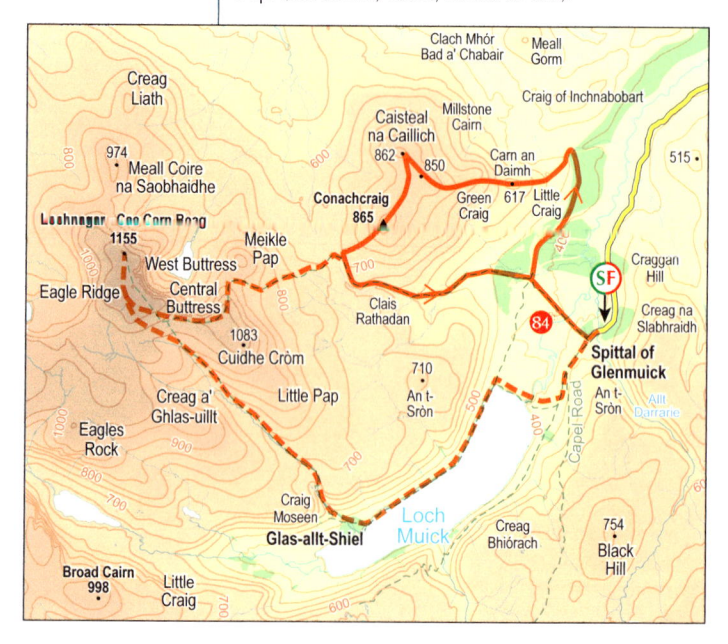

ROUTE 84 – CONACHCRAIG

Head NW to the N top, **Caisteal na Caillich**, also with many rock outcrops (862m, 28200 87450). From here a path is developing back over the middle top and SW to the SW top, which is marked by a cairn on a small rock outcrop (2hr 20min, 865m, 27990 86520).

Descend WSW down a clearer path to the saddle between Conachcraig and Lochnagar. The track joining the Spittal of Glenmuick to Balmoral Castle passes over this saddle (2hr 35min, 705m, 27390 86100). Turn left, soon passing a sharp right turn to Lochnagar, and continue down until you enter the forest. When the track veers to the right, continue straight on down an eroded path to reach the track junction in Glen Muick. Return across Glen Muick to the car park (3hr 30min).

Morven seen from Carn an Daimh

Walking the Corbetts: Vol 1

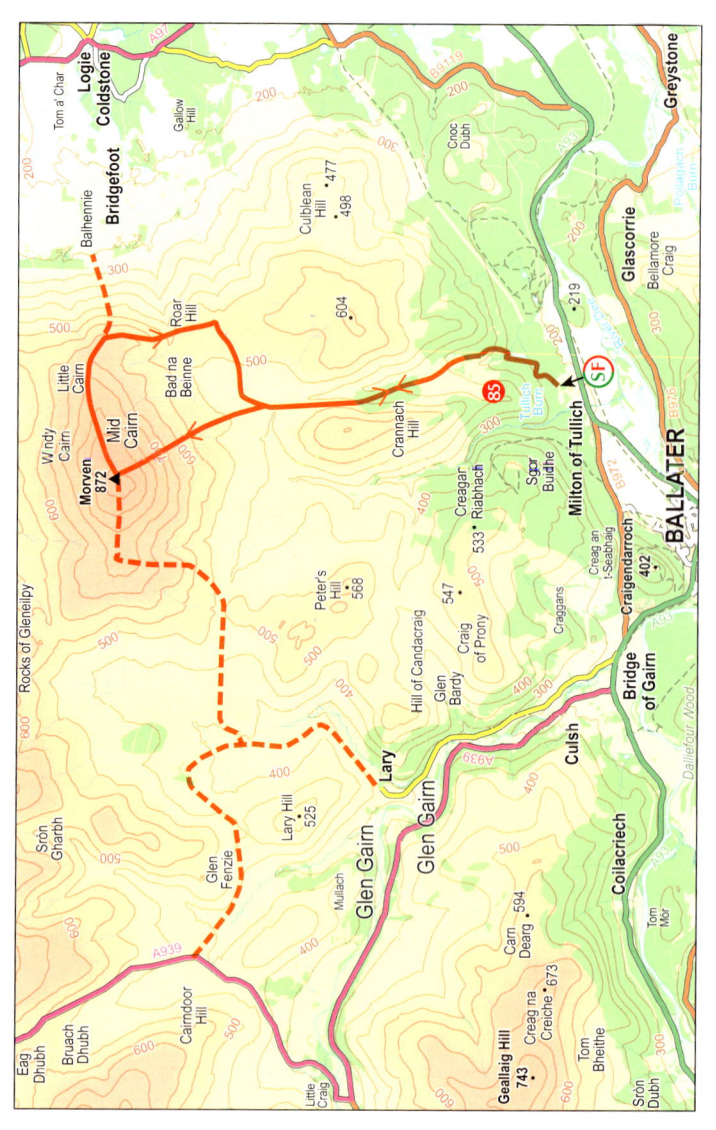

ROUTE 85
Morven BIG HILL

Start	Milton of Tullich (NO 38890 97700)
Distance	17km (11 miles)
Total ascent	740m (2400ft)
Difficulty	The ascent over steep grass slopes is hard work, but the descent is much easier. Care will be needed with navigation on descent in mist, but it is not particularly difficult.
Time	4hr 15min
Summit	Morven (872m, 2862ft)
Map	OS Landranger 37
Access	Take the A93 E from Braemar and shortcut along the B972 just before Ballater. After rejoining the A93 and crossing the Tullich Burn, take a farm track left, just before the cemetery on the right, and park on an open grassy area at the end of the track.
Note	The shortest and therefore the usual ascent is from Balhennie to the E, but the S approach is more interesting. You could also choose good routes from Lary or Glenfenzie to the W. If you could arrange transport it would be worth ascending from Tullich and descending to Lary or Glenfenzie.

Morven is an isolated hill rising above the lowlands of Cromar on the edge of the Cairngorms National Park. It gives distant views of Lochnagar and the Cairngorms as well as of the farmlands to the E. The ridges and lower slopes are heather moorland, but the S face is dominated by tussocky grass.

The **ruined church** in the cemetery at Tullich dates from about 1400, but there was a church on the site from the early days of the Celtic church, dedicated to St Nathalan who lived in the 5th century. There is a Pictish symbol stone in the churchyard dating back to the 7th century.

WALKING THE CORBETTS: VOL 1

It is reported that this deer fence has been removed.

Pass through the gate at the end of the track and turn right along a grassy track, which gradually veers left through woodland. Pass a shallow pond and the track continues, sometimes narrowing to a path, to a deer fence (370m, NO 39050 99780). ◀ Continue to a second deer fence and a high point before descending slightly to another fence (1hr, 455m, NJ 38670 01760) where the track ends. After passing through the gate you should head NNW, aiming straight for the summit of **Morven**. It is hard work through the tussocky grass, but there are sheep tracks and a vehicle track to aid progress and you eventually reach the large cairn and trig point on the summit (2hr 10min, 872m, NJ 37670 04000).

Turn right along a path alongside a ruined fence to a bouldery knoll with a cairn (725m, NJ 38940 04410). Follow the path down to a flat boggy area (2hr 35min, 600m, NJ 39360 04190). Follow the fence line, rather than the path, to a stone marker (NJ 39510 04080) and veer right to pick up a peaty track, which becomes a bulldozed track (560m, NJ 39380 03620). Follow it down to a saddle and over **Roar Hill** to a T-junction (3hr, 500m, NJ 39880 02570). Turn right, then fork right and pass through a fence to the Rashy Burn (NJ 38800 02180). Turn left along the burn until just before a stream junction (NJ 38660 01830) where you turn left back to the track end by the gate (3hr 20min, 455m, NJ 38670 01760). Follow the track back to the parking area (4hr 15min).

Approach to Morven

11 THE NORTHERN CAIRNGORMS

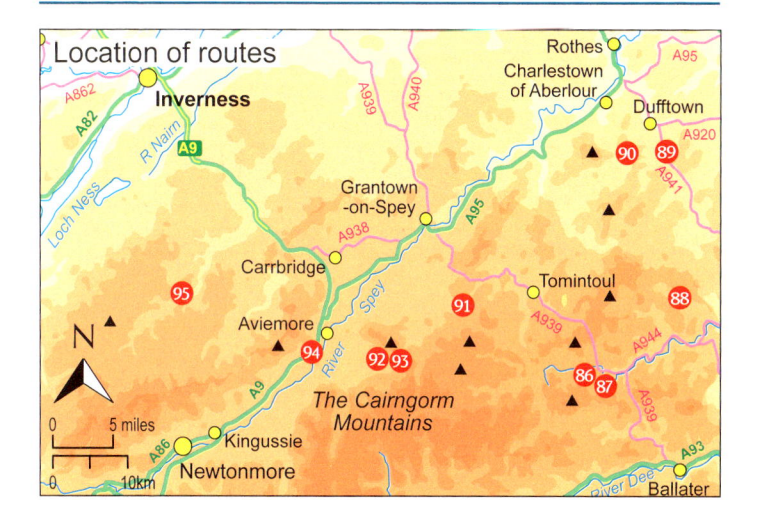

The Northern Cairngorms: Bases and facilities

Base for Routes 86–88: Tomintoul

Tomintoul is a small town planned and built in 1776 by the 4th Duke of Gordon and located on the Crown Estate of Glenlivet. At a height of 355m (1170ft) it is the highest village in the Highlands of Scotland. Tomintoul has excellent facilities for tourists, with hotels, B&Bs and a SYHA Hostel.

Tomintoul Tourist information Office, The Square, Tomintoul, AB37 9ET Tel: 01807 580 285

Tomintoul SYHA, Main St, Tomintoul, AB37 9EX Tel: 01807 580 364

Local facilities for Routes 86–88: Cock Bridge and Corgarff

The Allargue Arms Hotel at Cock Bridge is reported as being permanently closed.

There is a tearoom (9.00am–5.00pm) at Corgarff village just E of Cock Bridge.

Local facilities for Route 88: Strathdon

Strathdon has a small store.

Base for Routes 89 and 90: Dufftown

Dufftown is a small town with good facilities for tourists.

Dufftown Tourist Information Office, The Square, Dufftown, Moray
Tel: 01340 820 501 www.Dufftown.co.uk

Dufftown claims to be the malt whisky capital of Scotland and it has nine distilleries, including the Glenfiddich Distillery, which opened in 1887. www.glenfiddich.com

Local facilities for Routes 89 and 90: Tomnavoulin

Between Dufftown and Tomintoul there is a small store at Tomnavoulin. North of Tomnavoulin there is the Croft Inn (Tel: 01807 590 361 www.thecroftinn.co.uk), a tearoom and the Glenlivet Distillery with free tours (www.theglenlivet.com).

Base for Routes 91–95: Aviemore

Aviemore is the premier purpose-built mountain resort in Scotland and has excellent facilities for the walker.

Aviemore Tourist Information Centre, Grampian Road, Aviemore, PH22 1PP Tel: 08452 255 121 www.visitaviemore.com

Aviemore SYHA, 25 Grampian Road, Aviemore, PH22 1PR Tel: 01479 810 345

Local facilities for Route 91: Nethy Bridge

Nethy Bridge has a shop, two hotels and several B&Bs. Just outside Nethy Bridge on the road towards Dorbach is the Lazy Duck Hostel, which offers hostel accommodation or lightweight camping. Tel: 01479 821 642 www.lazyduck.co.uk

Local facilities for Routes 92 and 93: Coylumbridge and Glenmore

Coylumbridge (on the road to Glenmore) has a camping/caravan site.

Glenmore, to the E of Loch Morlich has a big campsite/caravan site, youth hostel, visitor centre, small store, two cafes, watersports centre, reindeer centre and Glenmore Lodge outdoor centre.

Cairngorm Lodge SYHA, Glenmore, Aviemore, PH22 1QY Tel: 01479 861 238

Glenmore Lodge National Outdoor Training Centre is a world-class centre providing courses in all forms of mountain activity as well as canoeing, mountain first aid and mountain rescue. Summer walkers who want to start experiencing the mountains in winter should consider enrolling on one of their winter mountaineering courses. Their facilities are open to non-residents and they offer accommodation on a B&B basis and self-catering chalets, as well as meals and drinks at the Lochain Bar. Tel: 01479 861 256
www.glenmorelodge.org.uk

ROUTE 86
Brown Cow Hill

Start	Corgarff Castle (NJ 25410 08930)
Distance	20km (13 miles)
Total ascent	680m (2200ft)
Difficulty	A relatively easy route, but there are some peat hags and some boggy ground. Navigation could be tricky in mist, particularly on the descent. There are many unmapped intermittent paths and tracks, which can be helpful but can also be confusing.
Time	4hr 45min
Summits	Cairn Culchavie (726m), Meikle Geal Charn (802m), Brown Cow Hill (829m, 2721ft), Carn Oighreag (704m)
Maps	OS Landranger 36 and 37
Access	From Tomintoul follow the A939 SE to Cock Bridge and after crossing the River Don turn right to Corgarff Castle where there is a large car park.
Note	It would be possible to walk or cycle to Inchmore and approach Brown Cow Hill more directly up the Meoir Veannaich burn.

WALKING THE CORBETTS: VOL 1

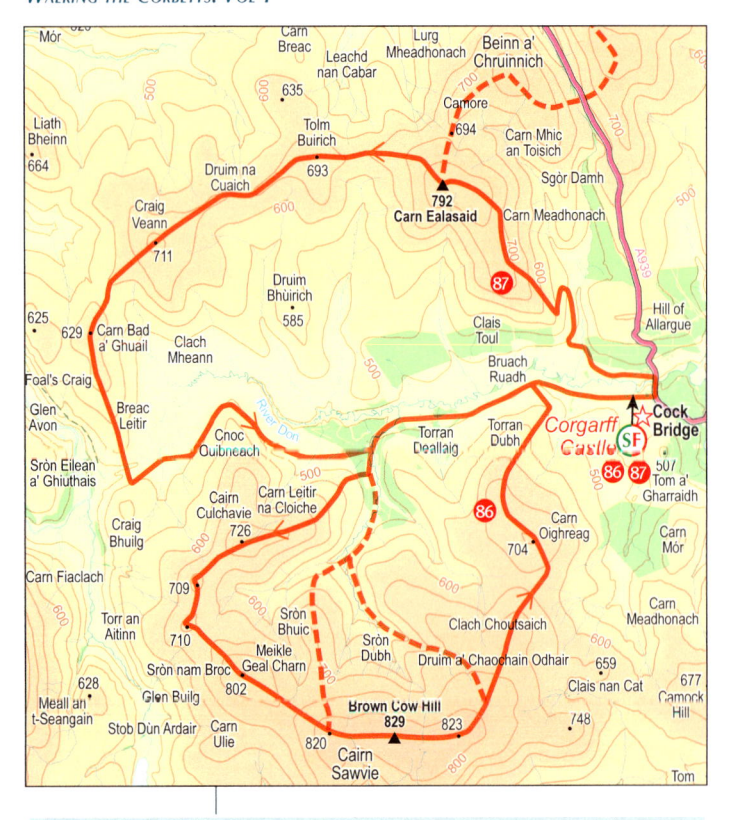

Brown Cow Hill is a rounded heather moor to the E of Ben Avon. The hill itself is of little interest, but the suggested route makes a very good walk on the horseshoe of hills surrounding the Meoir Veannaich burn, which flows into the infant River Don. The summit has three tops and the highest is the middle top, not the E top labelled as Brown Cow Hill on the OS 1:50,000 map.

Corgarff Castle was built around 1550 by John Forbes of Towie but burnt down during feuding between two clans in 1571. In 1607 the castle was

308

taken over by local bandits, who plundered the surrounding area until 1626 when it was acquired by the Earl of Mar. It was burned down during the 1689 rising and again after the defeat of the 1715 rising. The castle was captured by the Government in 1746 during the Jacobite rising and was converted into a barracks in 1748 as a base for troops in the subjugation of the Highlanders.

From the car park follow the paved estate road until it ends at Delnadamph and continue on a good track to a junction by the cottage at Inchmore (45min, 450m, 21750 08300). Turn left and 5min later turn right up a faint grass track (21750 07870). The track fades away, but its line can be easily followed to the summit plateau and unmarked summit of **Cairn Culchavie** (1hr 30min, 726m, 20020 07050).

Follow the line of an old fence left to a minor top (709m, 19430 06510) and continue left along the fence line to another minor top (710m, 19350 05960). Follow the fence line left again to the summit of **Meikle Geal Charn**. The summit, with two summit cairns, is a

Cairn Culchavie seen from the River Don

boulderfield which appears white from the quartzite rocks (2hr 10min, 802m, 20050 05270). Leave the fence line and head SE to a shallow saddle with peat hags and climb to Cairn Sawvie, the W top of Brown Cow Hill, which is just a peat bog (820m, 21213 04480). Head E and pick up an old track to the cairn on the flat summit of **Brown Cow Hill** (2hr 50min, 829m, 22100 04450).

Follow the fading track E and veer right to the cairn on the E top (823m, 23000 04540). Head NNE from here, avoiding peat hags to the right and hopefully pick up a small path leading to a point just E of a saddle (645m, 24100 06380). Keep straight on to reach an old track at the beginning of the climb. Turn left up **Carn Oighreag** (704m, 24020 07050). The track fades away on the N top, but keep going and it soon reappears and takes you down to the estate road (430m, 24040 09200). Turn right back to the car park (4hr 45min).

ROUTE 87

Carn Ealasaid ELIZABETH'S CAIRN

Start	Corgarff Castle (NJ 25410 08930)
Distance	23km (14 miles)
Total ascent	680m (2200ft)
Difficulty	The ascent is straightforward. The ridge W from Carn Ealasaid is a pathless heather moor with occasional peat hags. The going is generally fairly easy, but there are some tougher sections. Navigation could be very difficult in mist.
Time	5hr 40min
Summits	Carn Ealasaid (792m, 2600ft), Tolm Buirich (693m), Craig Veann (711m)
Maps	OS Landranger 36 and 37
Access	Parking as for Route 86
Note	The majority of people who climb Carn Ealasaid descend by the ascent route, making a short and not very interesting trip. There is also a short route from the Lecht Ski Centre, climbing over Beinn a' Chruinnich, but this also has little to recommend it.

ROUTE 87 – CARN EALASAID

Carn Ealasaid is the highest point on the ridge stretching W from the Lecht road summit on the N side of the River Don. The hills are gently rounded and covered with heather moor, with small areas of peat hags. There are good views of Ben Avon if the suggested route is followed.

Black grouse numbers have declined drastically in the past century. In the Highlands this is probably due mainly to loss of habitat diversity on moorland edges, where grazing pressure and burning practices have replaced the scrub woodlands needed by these birds. You may see the black grouse in these hills; they are readily recognisable as a large black bird with white wing bars, shoulder patches and under-tail coverts as well as a lyre-shaped tail.

▶ Return to the main road and turn left to the Allargue Arms Hotel, then follow the farm track left from the hotel to a bridge over the Burn of Loinherry (20min, 420m, 24740 09710). Continue on the track and 2min later turn right up a rough track that is followed very easily to the summit cairn on **Carn Ealasaid** (1hr 35min, 792m, 22770 11760).

Head NNW down the pathless heather ridge to a saddle (639m, 21700 12110) and W to the summit of

See map in Route 86.

Carn Ealasaid seen from the River Don

Tolm Buirich (693m, 21070 12080). Head WSW to a saddle (640m, 20050 11690) and then over peat hags to the trig point on **Craig Veann** (3hr, 711m, 18870 10980). Keep straight on along an old fence line down to a saddle (585m, 18150 10190) and over the summit of **Carn Bad a' Ghuail** (629m, 17990 09860), then descend the fence line until it veers off left. At this point it is best to continue SSE down the ridge to a good track by Lagganauld Cottage (3hr 40min, 450m, 18420 08030).

Turn left and follow the track, ignoring a footpath signed to Corgarff, and pass the cottage before veering left. Keep straight on at a junction and when a track joins from the left, to reach a junction by Inchmore Cottage (4hr 35min, 445m, 21750 08290). Turn left along the track, which becomes a paved estate road at Delnadamph Cottage and is followed back to the car park (5hr 40min).

ROUTE 88

Carn Mor BIG CAIRN

Start	Torrancroy (NJ 33540 15800)
Distance	24km (15 miles)
Total ascent	830m (2700ft)
Difficulty	There are few paths once the access tracks are left behind. The going can be tough, particularly if it is wet and the peat hags are boggy. Navigation will be difficult in mist.
Time	6hr
Summits	The Socach (719m), Carn Liath (792m), Carn Mor (804m, 2639ft)
Map	OS Landranger 37
Access	From Tomintoul follow the A939 to Corgarff and the A944 to Strathdon. Turn left at the Spar shop, signed to Glenbuchat Lodge, and fork left at a sign to the Lost Gallery. There is a rough parking area on the left after about 300m by a sign for Tolduquhill Farmhouse.
Note	Carn Mor is most often climbed from the ski area at Lecht Summit. This is the shortest route but not particularly interesting.

ROUTE 88 – CARN MOR

Carn Mor is the highest point of the Ladder Hills on a broad rounded ridge stretching E from the Lecht Summit. These are heather-covered hills with plenty of peat hags.

Lost Gallery is an art gallery of Scottish and international contemporary art. It is housed in the 19th-century farmhouse at Aldachuie cottage deep in the forest of Glen Nochty. The gallery has an impressive collection of sculptures and paintings, including Scottish mountain paintings. (Open 11.00am–5.00pm, except Tuesdays) **www.lostgallery.co.uk**.

Follow the track S signed to Tolduquhill Farmhouse and turn right before the bridge over the **Water of Nochty**. Follow this track to the farmhouse, pass between the farm buildings and continue until the track ends in a field of improved pasture (35min, 390m, 30940 15090).

The Lost Gallery, Aldachuie

WALKING THE CORBETTS: VOL 1

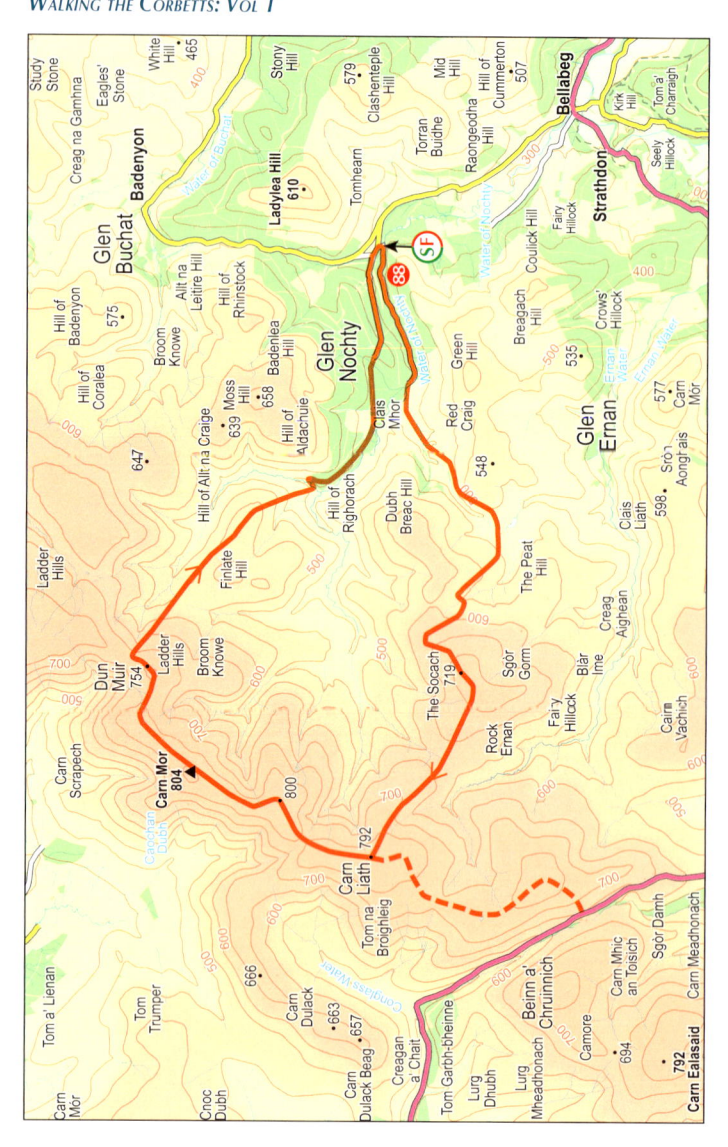

ROUTE 88 – CARN MOR

Bog on Carn Mor

Continue to the top of the field (staying left of the burn), then pass through the gate and follow the track up the Quillichen Burn. Keep straight on when a better track joins from the right and on to a junction by a wooden shelter (1hr, 445m, 29810 14010). Turn right and continue to a track junction (625m, 28450 15130), then turn left to the summit of **The Socach** (719m, 27920 14590). Continue for about 3min to a cairn (27650 14430), then head WNW down a ridge covered in peat hags to a saddle (625m, 26870 14950) and climb over more peat hags to the boggy summit of **Carn Liath** (2hr 55min, 792m, 25320 15860).

Turn right along an old fence line, and then keep straight on when the fence line veers left at a cairn. Continue to a saddle (745m, 25720 16730) and up to a small summit cairn on Monadh an t-Sluich Leith (800m, 26200 17110). A faint path leads N down to a broad saddle (770m, 26130 17510) and NNE to the trig point on the summit of **Carn Mor** (3hr 45min, 804m, 26580 18340).

Continue NE for about 15min to a flat plateau (772m, 27250 19020). Turn right (ESE) and follow the line of white posts, which are too far apart to help much in mist, across a saddle covered in peat hags to the summit of **Dun Muir**, marked by a small stone (4hr 15min, 754m, 27910 18850). Descend NE to a saddle with several cairns (735m, 28060 19150). Follow a path, sometimes unclear, to the right down to a track junction (595m, 28690 18430). Keep straight on over **Finlate Hill** until a faint track goes off right (585m, 29610 17620). Turn right down to the ruins of Duffdefiance and then turn left crossing the burn to a gate into the forest (395m, 30420 16650). Follow the track to the Lost Gallery at Aldachuie Cottage (5hr 35min, 380m, 31280 15870). After visiting the gallery continue down the track back to the car park (6hr).

ROUTE 89
Corryhabbie Hill

Start	Bridgehaugh (NJ 34020 35750)
Distance	25km (16 miles)
Total ascent	840m (2800ft)
Difficulty	Easy
Time	5hr 15min
Summit	Corryhabbie Hill (781m, 2561ft)
Maps	OS Landranger 28 and 37
Access	Take the A941 S from Dufftown. After about 5km there is an unmarked estate road on the right just before the River Fiddich. There is limited parking in the gateway, but take care not to block either of the tracks. If the gate on the estate road is locked there is a pedestrian gate in the fence a little left of the main gates. It is possible to cycle up to Glenfiddich Lodge.
Note	The shortest approach is from Ellivreid to the N, but that route has little interest. It would be possible to cycle to the head of the River Fiddich and then ascend and descend by the descent route.

ROUTE 89 – CORRYHABBIE HILL

Corryhabbie Hill is a large, rounded, heather-covered hill. The hill itself is of little interest, but the suggested route gives good views of Ben Rinnes on the ascent and then an interesting descent of the River Fiddich from its source.

Dufftown Highland Games take place on the last Saturday of July each year. Athletic events include track events, a hill race, hammer throwing, putting the shot, tug of war and tossing the caber. Highland dancing and massed pipe bands are a major component of the games. Highland Games originated many years ago, probably during Pictish times, when a Chief would organise competitions to find

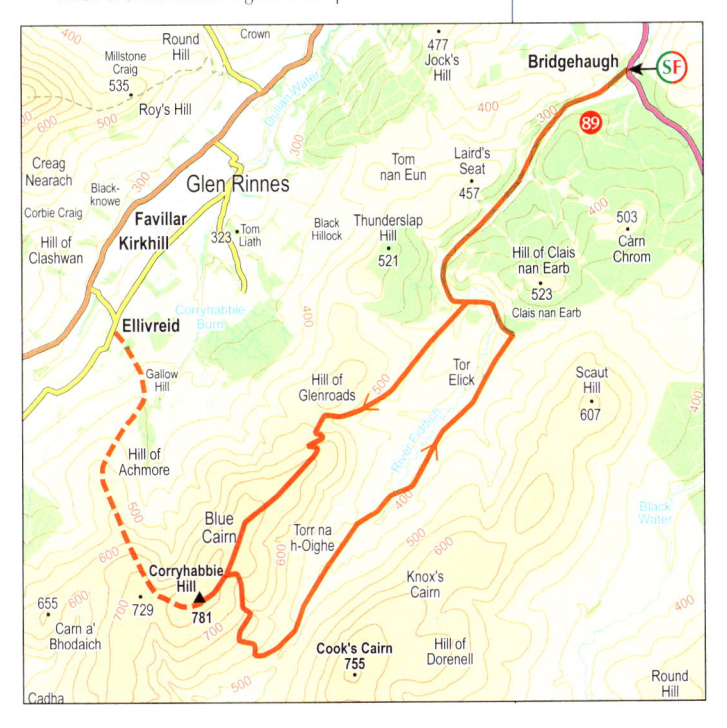

317

Ben Rinnes seen from the summit of Corrryhabbie Hill

the best bodyguard, runners to act as couriers, as well as musicians and dancers for entertainment. Nowadays Highland Games are devoted to preserving and promoting Scottish culture.

Follow the estate road to Glenfiddich Lodge, which has many dilapidated buildings. Pass two sets of buildings to a track junction with other buildings to your left (50min, 325m, 31750 32780). Turn sharp right and fork left by a wood, then follow the track to a junction on a saddle (1hr 30min, 530m, 29620 31290). Turn left up Morton's Way and continue until the main track bends left near the summit (765m, 28240 29130). Keep straight on along a fainter track to the trig point on the summit of **Corryhabbie Hill** (2hr 30min, 781m, 28100 28860).

Retrace your steps about 300m and turn right to descend SE to a track junction at the head of Glen Fiddich (3hr, 525m, 28970 28080). Turn left and follow the track down the **River Fiddich** to the main estate road (4hr 10min, 345m, 32380 32340). Turn left and return to the parking area (5hr 15min).

ROUTE 90

Ben Rinnes HEADLAND HILL

Start	Round Hill (NJ 28490 35940)
Distance	14km (9 miles)
Total ascent	650m (2100ft)
Difficulty	The ascent is easy up a well-maintained 'tourist path'. The recommended descent route can be boggy in places. Care would be needed not to lose the path when descending in mist.
Time	3hr 30min
Summit	Ben Rinnes (840m, 2755ft)
Map	OS Landranger 28
Access	From Dufftown follow the B9009 towards Tomintoul and turn right, signposted to Edinvillie. After 600m there is parking on the left at the foot of Round Hill.
Note	Most walkers descend by the ascent route, but they miss the interesting crags on the summit plateau. If you can arrange transport it would make sense to descend to the road from the N point of the featured route.

Ben Rinnes is an isolated hill that gives superb views in all directions. Its distinctive outline makes it a prominent landmark. There are interesting rock outcrops on the summit and on the summit plateau.

A feature of the Dufftown Highland Games is the **Five Tops Hill Race**. The 22.4km route, with 1570m of climb, passes over the rounded summits of Little Conval and Meikle Conval before climbing to the summit of Ben Rinnes, returning by the same route. The record time for this event is 1hr 54min for men and 2hr 21min for ladies.

Head up the good track from the car park. The track becomes a good path on the summit of **Roy's Hill** (536m, 27210 35500). Continue to the trig point on the

Walking the Corbetts: Vol 1

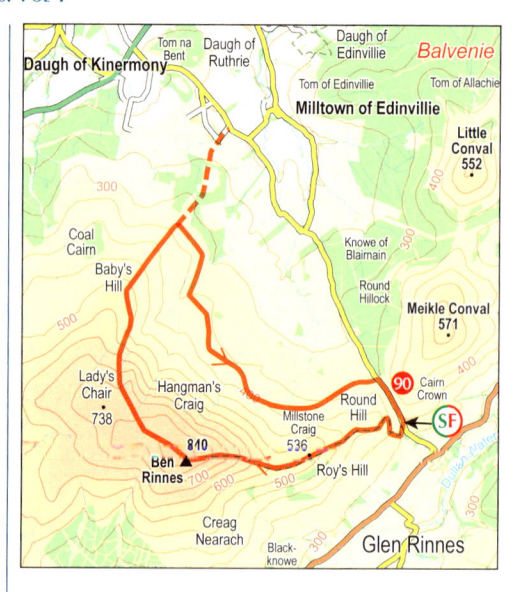

summit crags of **Ben Rinnes** (1hr 10min, 840m, 25510 35450).

Head NW to pick up an eroded track and take the right fork at a junction. The track soon deteriorates to a path, which leads to some interesting rock formations (1hr 25min, 730m, 24750 36290). Follow a small path right past other rock formations. The path veers left at the bottom crag and descends, becoming boggy and indistinct in places. When you reach a good track (505m, 24780 37740), turn right and descend to a track junction by a gate (2hr 10min, 320m, 25440 38690). Turn right and follow the track that veers uphill before crossing a burn. Keep straight on at a junction (355m, 25800 37330) and continue along the often boggy track to the road (3hr 20min, 315m, 28170 36470). Turn right back to the car park (3hr 30min).

320

Tor on Ben Rinnes

ROUTE 91
Geal Charn WHITE HILL

Start	Dorbach Lodge (NJ 07770 16810)
Distance	18km (11 miles)
Total ascent	610m (2000ft)
Difficulty	There are few useful paths once the access tracks are left behind. There are a few boggy areas and small areas of peat hag, but the going is generally good. Navigation would be difficult in mist.
Time	4hr 15min
Summit	Geal Charn (821m, 2692ft)
Map	OS Landranger 36
Access	From Aviemore follow the B970 to Nethy Bridge, turning right after the bridge, and follow the minor road to Dorbach Lodge. There is very limited parking at the roadhead. Please do not park in the turning area. There is more parking 1km before the roadhead (06940 17220).
Note	It would be possible to cycle up to the shooting hut below Carn Ruadh-bhreac and follow the recommended ascent route, returning the same way. When the Dorbach Burn is in flood it would be best to descend by the ascent route.

Walking the Corbetts: Vol 1

> The gently rounded Geal Charn is the highest point of the vast heather moorland plateau to the NE of the Cairngorm Mountains.

On the road from Aviemore to Nethy Bridge you will see signs for Loch Garten and the RSPB **Loch Garten osprey centre**, which is well worth a visit. Ospreys became extinct in the UK in 1916 due to persecution and egg collecting. In 1954 a pair returned to breed at Loch Garten and there are now about 200 pairs throughout Scotland. Watching ospreys diving into the water to catch fish, their sole diet, is one of the spectacles of the natural world. **www.rspb.org.uk/reserves/guide/l/lochgarten/index.aspx**

Follow the good estate track past Dorbach Lodge, forking right immediately after the kennels, and keep going, ignoring all sidetracks, to a wooden shooting hut (probably unlocked) on a saddle below Carn Ruadh-bhreac (1hr

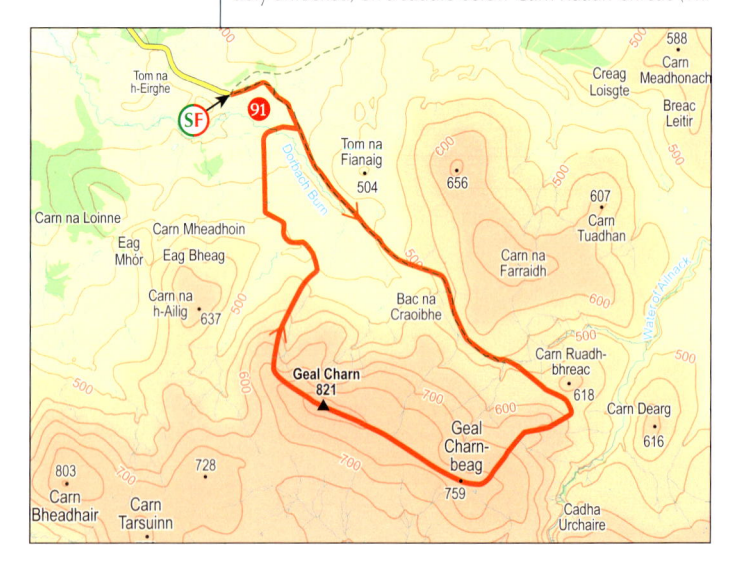

Route 91 – Geal Charn

Dorbach Lodge

30min, 575m, 12430 12740). Keep straight on along a lesser track, which gradually veers right up the NE ridge of Geal Charn-beag, past an interesting memorial and to the track end on a knoll (680m, 11800 12310). Continue SW across a small peat hag and pick up a poor track past some shooting butts and onto the pathless boggy summit plateau of **Geal Charn-beag** (759m, 11010 11690). Head WNW towards **Geal Charn**. Two fence lines appear from the left. Follow the older, intermittent post line to the quartzite cairn on the summit (2hr 45min, 821m, 09060 12690).

Continue WNW down the fence line and gradually veer right, away from the fence, following the ridge to the W of the Allt nan Gamhuinn burn down to a track (3hr 20min, 475m, 08950 14380). Turn left past a wooden shooting hut (probably unlocked) (08970 14700) and cross the Allt na h-Eirghe burn, possibly getting wet feet. Continue along the track and turn right immediately after the abandoned Upper Dell farmhouse to the **Dorbach Burn** (3hr 55min, 365m, 08330 16320). Ford the burn, probably getting wet feet. ▶ Pass a barn and continue to a junction with the main estate track (08700 16400). Turn left back to the roadhead (4hr 15min).

The ford could be dangerous when the burn is in flood.

ROUTE 92
Meall a' Bhuachaille SHEPHERD'S HILL

Start	Glenmore Lodge (NH 98780 09480)
Distance	16km (10 miles)
Total ascent	720m (2400ft)
Difficulty	The ascent by the 'tourist route' is straightforward. The mountain path along the ridge to Craiggowrie and down to the forest has a few boggy patches and is generally easy to follow.
Time	4hr 5min
Summits	Meall a' Bhuachaille (810m, 2654ft), Creagan Gorm (732m), Craiggowrie (687m)
Map	OS Landranger 36
Access	From Aviemore follow the road to Glenmore and turn left to Glenmore Lodge. There is limited roadside parking at the road end (NH 98780 09480). It may be better to park at one of several car parks at Glenmore and start by walking to Glenmore Lodge.
Note	The shortest route is the direct ascent N from Glenmore and this would be the normal 'tourist' descent route.

Meall a' Bhuachaille, a popular mountain, is the E peak on a ridge that overlooks Loch Morlich in the Glenmore Forest Park. There are good views across to the N corries of the Cairngorm Mountains.

Reindeer were re-introduced into Scotland in 1952 by Swedish reindeer herder, Mikel Utsi, and a herd of about 150 reindeer is maintained today living in the Cairngorm Mountains. The Cairngorm Reindeer Centre keeps a small group of reindeer in paddocks for visitors, and in summer organises daily guided hill visits to see the reindeer in their natural environment.

ROUTE 92 – MEALL A' BHUACHAILLE

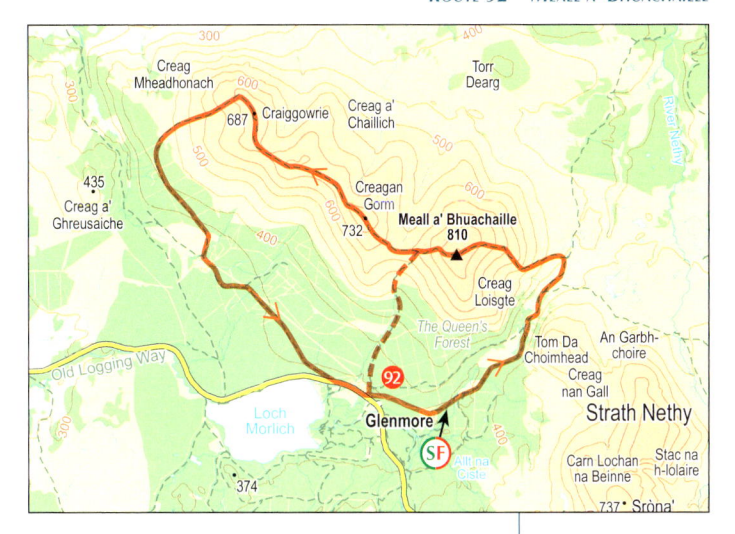

Follow the main track from the parking area at Glenmore Lodge, past An Lochan Uaine to a track junction just after leaving the forest (365m, NJ 00290 11050). Fork left, signed to Nethy Bridge, to the well-maintained Ryvoan Bothy (35min, 405m, NJ 00610 11510). Turn left up a well-engineered path to the summit cairn on **Meall a' Bhuachaille** (1hr 15min, 810m, NH 99090 11540).

Ryvoan Bothy below Meall a' Bhuachaille

Continue W to a clear path junction (650m, NH 98540 11590, 650m). The quickest way down is to descend left here, but it is recommended that you continue along the ridge down to a saddle (624m), up to the summit of **Creagan Gorm** (732m, NH 97840 12010), down to a saddle (660m), over a minor summit (711m, NH 96880 12720), down to another saddle (650m)

and on to the summit cairn on **Craiggowrie** (2hr 30min, 687m, NH 96280 13490).

Continue to a minor top then veer left down to the forest (440m, NH 95020 13120, 440m). The route to Glenmore is marked with posts with orange paint rings. Continue down to a forest road (3hr, 410m, NH 94910 12770). Turn left to a junction (340m, NH 95590 11530) where you turn left through Badaguish Outdoor Centre and left again on the far side (NH 95720 11300), forking right at the next track junction to arrive at Glenmore by the store (3hr 50min, 325m, NH 97540 09840). Turn left up the road and then left up the road to Glenmore Lodge and walk up a good footpath alongside the road back to the parking area (4hr 5min).

ROUTE 93

Creag Mhor BIG CRAG

Start	Glenmore Lodge (NH 98780 09480)
Distance	29km (18 miles)
Total ascent	910m (3000ft)
Difficulty	The ascent is easy. The descent route follows paths that are boggy, rocky or unclear in places. Care would be needed with navigation in mist.
Time	7hr 15min
Summit	Creag Mhor (895m, 2932ft)
Map	OS Landranger 36
Access	Parking as for Route 92
Note	It would be quicker, but less interesting, to return by the ascent route. The Cairngorms are best explored when backpacking and Creag Mhor might be climbed as part of a multi-day trip that included climbing some of the Munros.

Creag Mhor is a remote peak situated to the NW of the Cairngorm plateau. The shortest approach is from Glenmore Lodge and the suggested return route takes you to Loch Avon in the heart of the Cairngorms before descending the River Nethy from its source.

ROUTE 93 – CREAG MHOR

You will see **juniper bushes** as you approach Creag Mhor through the Rothiemurchus Forest. Juniper is a conifer with typical needle-like leaves, but its cones are fleshy, like berries. They take three years to ripen, turning from green to bluish-black as they do so. Juniper berries are used to give gin its distinctive flavour. You will also see bearberry, with glossy red berries; bears used to feed on these when they wandered these slopes a thousand years ago.

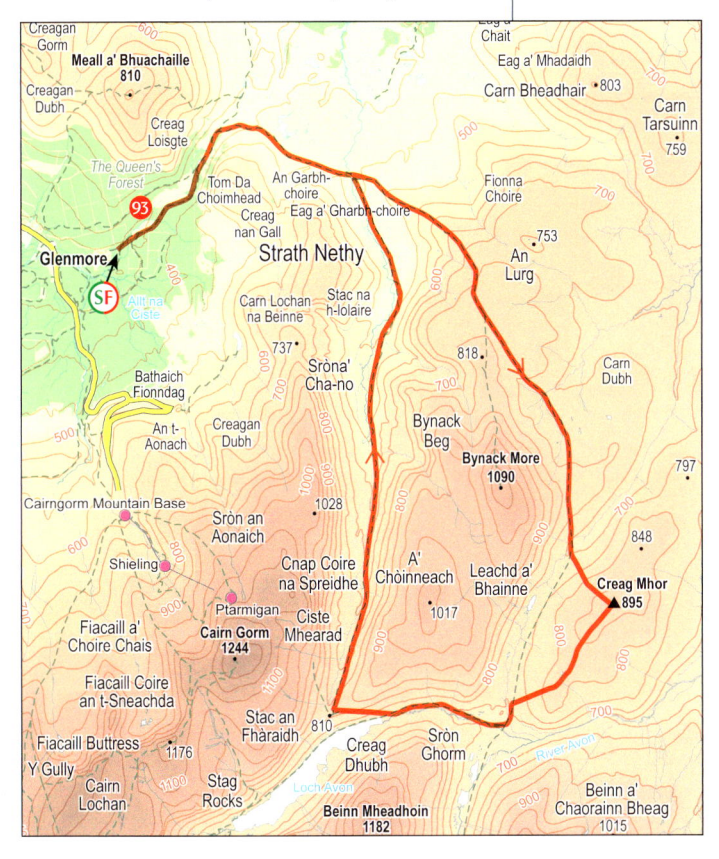

327

Loch Avon

Follow the main track from the parking area at Glenmore Lodge, past An Lochan Uaine to a track junction just after leaving the forest (365m, NJ 00290 11050). Fork right, signed to Braemar, and continue until the track ends at a bridge over the River Nethy (50min, 440m, NJ 02100 10500). Cross the bridge and continue along the footpath, almost immediately forking left. Fork left again on the N ridge of Bynack More (780m, NJ 03910 08710), descend to cross the Uisge Dubh Poll a' Choin burn (700m, NJ 04840 07560) and cross the E ridge of Bynack More before dropping down to the Glasath burn (2hr 35min, 695m, NJ 05180 05540). Head SE up heather-covered slopes to the granite tor on the summit of **Creag Mhor** (3hr 10min, 895m, NJ 05750 04770).

Head down the SW ridge of Creag Mhor, veering right when it steepens, to where the path crosses the Allt Dearg burn (3hr 40min, 695m, NJ 04240 03370). Turn left to the Fords of Avon emergency refuge (690m, NJ 04200 03180, 690m) and turn right along a boggy path to a path junction by the NE end of the dramatic **Loch Avon** (4hr 15min, 740m, NJ 02520 03300).

Fork right to a path junction on the saddle at the head of Strath Nethy glen (810m, NJ 01860 03330). Turn right and descend the narrow bouldery Strath Nethy down to the ascent path and turn left to cross **Strath Nethy** (6hr 20min). Continue back to Glenmore Lodge (7hr 15min).

ROUTE 94
Geal-charn Mor BIG WHITE CAIRN

Start	Lynwilg (NH 88140 10510)
Distance	13km (8 miles)
Total ascent	640m (2100ft)
Difficulty	Decent paths take the walker up to short heather on the summit plateau so the going is generally easy. Care would be needed with navigation on the summit plateau in mist.
Time	3hr
Summit	Geal-charn Mor (824m, 2702ft)
Map	OS Landranger 35
Access	The start is on the A9 at Lynwilg just W of Aviemore. From Aviemore head W along the B9152 and turn right, then immediately right and left to Lynwilg where there is roadside parking.
Note	The easiest route is to ascend and descend by the descent route. It would be possible to cycle up to 690m to the saddle between Geal-charn Mor and Geal-charn Beag.

Geal-charn Mor is a heather-covered plateau at the E end of the Monadhliath Mountains. There are good views across to the Cairngorm Mountains and along the Spey Valley. The trig point on the summit plateau is generally accepted as the highest point, but there is an unmarked top about 200m to the W which GPS measurements by the author suggest may be slightly higher.

While climbing Geal-charn Mor you will notice **Torr Alvie** across Loch Alvie to the SE. On the summit you will see the tall pillar of the Duke of

WALKING THE CORBETTS: VOL 1

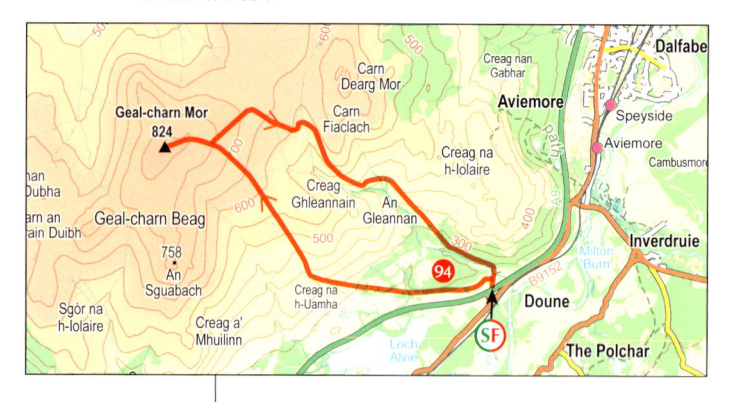

Gordon monument commemorating the last Duke of Gordon, who died in 1836. On the W top is the Waterloo Cairn, erected by the Marquis of Huntly in memory of the officers and soldiers of the Gordon Highlanders and the Royal Regiment who fell at the Battle of Waterloo in June 1815.

From the parking area, head to Lynwilg and turn left along a paved road before reaching the bridge. This soon becomes a good track. Turn left at the end of a field (87250 103250), then veer right and pass through a gate to pick up the paved road to Ballinluig. Pass between the farmhouse and the stables and onto a footpath to a gate by a deer fence (30min, 250m, 86320 10300). Pass through the gate and head uphill to the right of the burn. A small, but clear path leads easily up the hill. ◄ When the path becomes less steep and the heather becomes shorter (approx. 660m, 84800 12100) leave the path and head WNW directly to the trig point on the summit of **Geal-charn Mor** (1hr 50min, 824m, 83640 12320).

Head about 200m SW to a top (83550 12190), which may be the highest point, and return to the trig point. Follow a path, indistinct in places, that leads E then NE down to a large cairn on the saddle between Geal-charn Mor and Geal-charn Beag (2hr 10min, 700m, 84710 12900). Turn right down a good track above

The path shown forking right on the OS map isn't apparent.

330

the Allt Dubh to a track junction in the woods (305m, 87160 11300). Turn left through the gate. The track soon becomes paved as it descends to the left of the Altnacriche Activity Centre. Climb a stile at another deer fence and turn left then right over Lynwilg Bridge to the parking area (3hr).

S ridge seen from Ballinluig

ROUTE 95

Carn na Saobhaidhe CAIRN OF THE FOX LAIR

Start	Coignafearn (Old Lodge) (NH 71130 18060)
Distance	30km (19 miles)
Total ascent	770m (2500ft)
Difficulty	There is a good track to 700m after which the going is tough, with boggy terrain and peat hags. Navigation will be demanding in misty conditions.
Time	6hr 40min
Summit	Carn na Saobhaidhe (811m, 2658ft)
Map	OS Landranger 35
Access	Follow the A9 N from Aviemore. Just after the Slochd Summit turn left down the old A9 to Findhorn Bridge and follow the minor road signed to Coignafearn. There is a car park on the left at the end of the road, just before Coignafearn (Old Lodge).

Walking the Corbetts: Vol 1

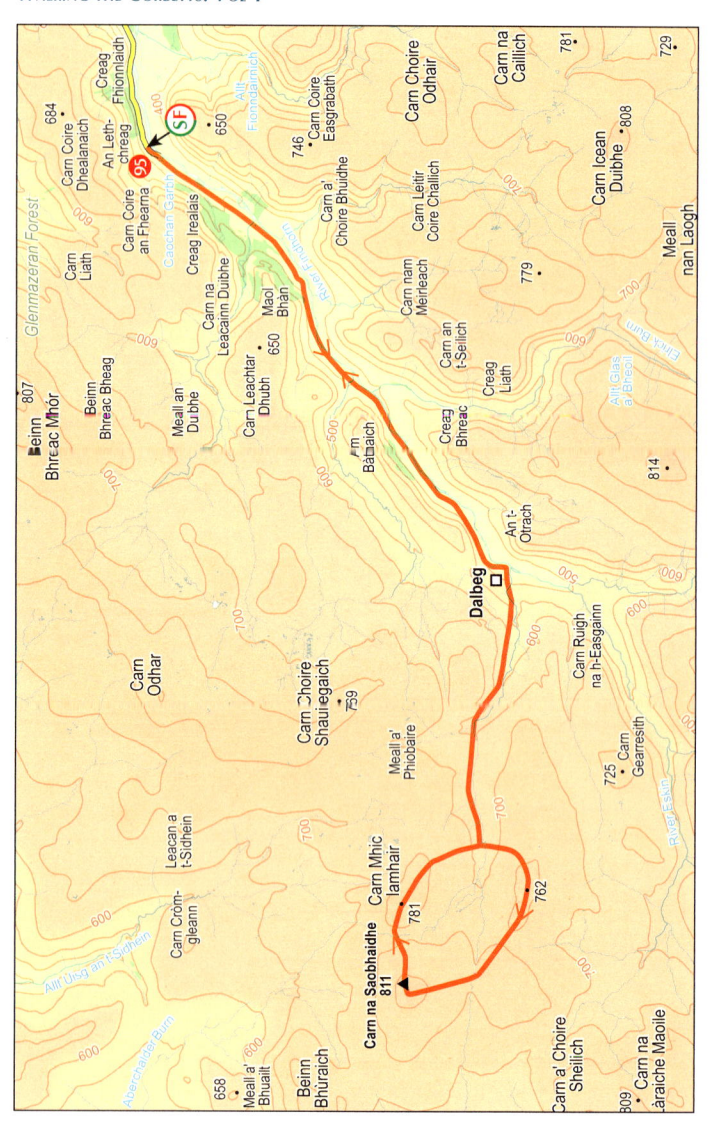

ROUTE 95 – CARN NA SAOBHAIDHE

Carn na Saobhaidhe, a large heather-covered plateau with large areas of peat hags, is the highest point in the N part of the Monadhliath Mountains. The recommended route follows the River Findhorn, which flows down one of the finest glens in the Highlands.

The Highland Council **plan** for the Monadhliath Mountains states: 'The Monadhliath Mountains comprise arguably the largest contiguous tract of accessible mountain and moorland in the Highlands. The main policy thrust of these areas should be to value their natural and semi-natural features, encourage measures which improve or reinstate their biodiversity in key habitats and to presume against intrusive developments which would detract from their intrinsic core qualities.'

The Coignafearn Estate through which Carn na Saobhaidhe is approached espouses this policy, but once you reach the summit you will see the Drumnaglass Estate has bulldozed an eyesore of a road right to the summit, with peat removed to the bedrock, leaving the track as a useless eroding mass of slurry. This estate has plans to build a wind farm initially consisting of thirty-six 110m turbines on the summit plateau.

Follow the good estate road 8km up the right bank of the **River Findhorn** past Coignafearn (Old Lodge) and Coignafearn Lodge to **Dalbeg** Cottage (1hr 35min, 480m, 65580 13170). Fork right up the right side of Allt Creagach, ignoring tracks off to right and left, to a track junction by a bridge (640m, 63510 13540). Turn left up the right bank of Allt Odhar and continue until the track ends (2hr 30min, 695m, 61990 13420). Continue up a faint grassy track that climbs the slope on the left. On reaching the ridge turn right across rough moorland with peat hags to the summit of Peak 762 (2hr 50 min, 61370 12820). Continue to a saddle (743m, 60680 13010) and then skirt round Peak 778 to another saddle with a line

River Findhorn on the descent from Carn na Saobhaidhe

of fence posts (755m, 60130 13550). Turn right along the fence line until it veers left on the summit plateau of **Carn na Saobhaidhe**. Head E to a cairn (3hr 35min, 811m, 60030 14490). ◄

Continue E on the track that runs across the plateau. This soon becomes a big bulldozed track, which is followed down to a junction. Turn right and when this track ends continue ESE to the summit of **Carn Mhic Iamhair** (3hr 55min, 781m, 61160 14530). Continue down the ridge, taking advantage of a rare bit of easy going, then veer right back to the track end and continue down to **Dalbeg** Cottage (5hr 10min). Turn left back to the car park (6hr 40min).

Whether this is actually at the highest point on the plateau is doubtful.

APPENDIX A
Alphabetical list of Corbetts

Summit	Route no	Page
Ainshval	Vol 2	
Am Bathach	Vol 2	
An Cliseam	Vol 2	
An Dun	60	227
An Stack	Vol 2	
An Ruadh-stac	Vol 2	
An Sidhean	Vol 2	
Aonach Buidhe	Vol 2	
Aonach Shasuinn	Vol 2	
Arkle	Vol 2	
Askival	Vol 2	
Auchnafree Hill	26	126
Bac an Eich	Vol 2	
Baosbheinn	Vol 2	
Beinn Airigh Charr	Vol 2	
Beinn a' Bha'ach Ard	Vol 2	
Beinn a Bhuiridh	27	131
Beinn a' Chaisgean Mor	Vol 2	
Beinn a' Chaisteil (Auch)	31	143
Beinn a' Chaisteal (Loch Vaich)	Vol 2	
Beinn a' Chlaidheimh	Vol 2	
Beinn a' Choin	18	104
Beinn a' Chrulaiste	47	189
Beinn a' Chuallaich	54	209
Beinn an Eoin	Vol 2	
Beinn an Lochain	15	94
Beinn an Oir	10	77
Beinn Bhan (Glen Loy)	Vol 2	

Summit	Route no	Page
Beinn Bhan (Applecross)	Vol 2	
Beinn Bheula	11	83
Beinn Bhreac	59	224
Beinn Bhreac-liath	29	137
Beinn Bhuidhe	Vol 2	
Beinn Chaorach	31	143
Beinn Chuirn	30	140
Beinn Damh	Vol 2	
Beinn Dearg (Glen Lyon)	38	164
Beinn Dearg (Torridon)	Vol 2	
Beinn Dearg Bheag	Vol 2	
Beinn Dearg Mor	Vol 2	
Beinn Dronaig	Vol 2	
Beinn Each	20	110
Beinn Enaiglair	Vol 2	
Beinn Iaruinn	66	246
Beinn Lair	Vol 2	
Beinn Leoid	Vol 2	
Beinn Liath Mhor a' Ghiubhais Li	Vol 2	
Beinn Loinne	Vol 2	
Beinn Luibhean	14	93
Beinn Maol Chaluim	45	184
Beinn Mheadhonach	58	221
Beinn Mhic Cedidh	Vol 2	
Beinn Mhic Chasgaig	46	187
Beinn Mhic Mhonaidh	28	134
Beinn Mholach	62	234

335

WALKING THE CORBETTS: VOL 1

Summit	Route no	Page
Beinn na Caillich	Vol 2	
Beinn na h-Eaglaise	Vol 2	
Beinn na h-Uamha	Vol 2	
Beinn nam Fuaran	31	143
Beinn nan Caorach	Vol 2	
Beinn nan Imirean	32	149
Beinn nan Oighreag	35	157
Beinn Odhar	31	143
Beinn Odhar Beag	Vol 2	
Beinn Resipol	Vol 2	
Beinn Stacach (See Stob Fear-tomhais)		
Beinn Spionnaidh	Vol 2	
Beinn Talaidh	Vol 2	
Beinn Tarsuinn	9	74
Beinn Tharsuinn	Vol 2	
Beinn Trilleachan	43	178
Beinn Udlaidh	29	137
Ben Aden	Vol 2	
Ben Arthur (See The Cobbler)		
Ben Donich	12	87
Ben Gulabin	78	284
Ben Hee	Vol 2	
Ben Ledi	19	107
Ben Loyal	Vol 2	
Ben Rinnes	90	319
Ben Tee	Vol 2	
Ben Tirran	76	278
Ben Vrackie	56	215
Ben Vuirich	57	217
Benvane	19	107
Bidean a' Chabair	Vol 2	
Binnein an Fhidhleir (See Stob Coire Creagach)		

Summit	Route no	Page
Braigh nan Uamhachan	Vol 2	
Breabag	Vol 2	
Broad Law	7	63
Brown Cow Hill	86	307
Buidhe Bheinn	Vol 2	
Cairnsmore of Carsphairn	4	55
Caisteal Abhail	9	74
Cam Chreag (Glen Lyon)	37	161
Cam Chreag (Auch)	31	143
Canisp	Vol 2	
Carn a' Choire Ghairbh	Vol 2	
Carn a' Chuillinn	69	253
Carn an Fhreiceadain	72	262
Carn Ban	Vol 2	
Carn Chuinneag	Vol 2	
Carn Dearg (Glen Roy)	67	248
Carn Dearg (S of Gleann Eachach)	68	251
Carn Dearg (N of Gleann Eachach)	68	251
Carn Dearg (See Meallan Liath Coire Mhic Dhughaill)		
Carn Dearg Mor	74	269
Carn Ealasaid	87	310
Carn Liath (See Creag an Dhail Bheag)		
Carn Mor (Lecht)	88	312
Carn Mor (Glen Dessary)	Vol 2	
Carn na Drochaide	82	292
Carn na Nathrach	Vol 2	
Carn na Saobhaidhe	95	331

336

Appendix A – Alphabetical list of Corbetts

Summit	Route no	Page
Cir Mhor	9	74
Clisham (See An Cliseam)		
Cnoc Coinnich	12	87
Conachcraig	84	299
Corryhabbie Hill	89	316
Corserine	3	52
Cranstackie	Vol 2	
Creach Bheinn (Loch Creran)	40	171
Creach Bheinn (Loch Linnhe)	Vol 2	
Creag an Dhail Bheag	83	296
Creag MacRanaich	23	118
Creag Mhor	93	326
Creag nan Gabhar	79	287
Creag Rainich	Vol 2	
Creag Uchdag	25	124
Creagan na Beinne	39	165
Cruach Innse	65	243
Culardoch	83	296
Cul Beag	Vol 2	
Cul Mor	Vol 2	
Druim nan Cnamh (See Beinn Loinne)		
Dun da Ghaoithe	Vol 2	
Faochaig	Vol 2	
Farragon Hill	55	212
Foinaven	Vol 2	
Fraoch Bheinn	Vol 2	
Fraochaidh	41	173
Fuar Bheinn	Vol 2	
Fuar Tholl	Vol 2	
Ganu Mor (See Foinaven)		
Garbh Bheinn (Loch Leven)	48	191

Summit	Route no	Page
Garbh Bheinn (Ardgour)	Vol 2	
Garbh-bheinn (Skye)	Vol 2	
Gairbeinn	70	257
Geal Charn (Cairngorms)	91	321
Geal Charn (Loch Arkaig)	Vol 2	
Geal-charn Mor	94	329
Glamaig	Vol 2	
Glas Bheinn (Kinlochleven)	50	197
Glas Bheinn (Assynt)	Vol 2	
Goatfell	8	71
Hart Fell	5	58
Leathad an Taobhain	74	269
Leum Uilleim	51	201
Little Wyvis	Vol 2	
Mam na Gualainn	49	193
Maol Creag an Loch	60	227
Meall a' Bhuachaille	92	324
Meall a' Ghiubhais	Vol 2	
Meall a' Phubuill	Vol 2	
Meall an Fhudair	17	98
Meall an t-Seallaidh	23	118
Meall Buidhe	34	154
Meall Dubh	Vol 2	
Meall Horn	Vol 2	
Meall Lighiche	42	176
Meall na Fearna	24	121
Meall na h-Aisre	71	260
Meall na h-Eilde	Vol 2	
Meall na Leitreach	61	231
Meall na Meoig (Beinn Pharlagain)	52	203
Meall nan Subh	33	153

WALKING THE CORBETTS: VOL 1

Summit	Route no	Page
Meall nam Maigheach	36	160
Meall Tairneachan	55	212
Meallach Mhor	73	265
Meallan Liath Coire Mhic Dhughaill	Vol 2	
Meallan nan Uan	Vol 2	
Merrick	1	46
Monamenach	77	281
Morrone	80	290
Morven	85	303
Mount Battock	75	275
Quinag (See Spidean Coinnich)		
Rois-Bheinn	Vol 2	
Ruadh-stac Beag	Vol 2	
Sail Gharbh (Quinag)	Vol 2	
Sail Gorm (Quinag)	Vol 2	
Sail Mhor	Vol 2	
Sgor Mor	81	292
Sgorr nan Lochan Uaine	Vol 2	
Sgorr Craobh a' Chaorainn	Vol 2	
Sgorr na Diollaid	Vol 2	
Sguman Coinntich	Vol 2	
Sgurr a' Bhac Chaolais	Vol 2	
Sgurr a' Chaorachain	Vol 2	
Sgurr a' Choire-bheithe	Vol 2	
Sgurr a' Mhuilinn	Vol 2	
Sgurr an Airgid	Vol 2	
Sgurr an Fhuaran	Vol 2	
Sgurr an Utha	Vol 2	
Sgurr Coire Choinnichean	Vol 2	

Summit	Route no	Page
Sgurr Cos na Breachd-laoigh	Vol 2	
Sgurr Dhomhnuill	Vol 2	
Sgurr Dubh	Vol 2	
Sgurr Gaorsaic	Vol 2	
Sgurr Ghiubhsachain	Vol 2	
Sgurr Innse	65	243
Sgurr Mhic Bharraich	Vol 2	
Sgurr Mhurlagain	Vol 2	
Sgurr na Ba Glaise	Vol 2	
Sgurr na Feartaig	Vol 2	
Sgurr nan Ceannaichean	Vol 2	
Sgurr nan Eugallt	Vol 2	
Shalloch on Minnoch	2	49
Spidean Coinnich (Quinag)	Vol 2	
Sron a' Choire Chnapanich	34	154
Stob a' Bhealach an Sgriodain	Vol 2	
Stob a' Choin	21	112
Stob an Aonaich Mhoir	53	207
Stob Coire a' Chearcaill	Vol 2	
Stob Coire Creagach	16	96
Stob Dubh	44	181
Stob Fear-tomhais	22	115
Streap	Vol 2	
The Brack	12	87
The Cobbler	13	90
The Fara	64	238
The Sow of Atholl	63	236
White Coomb	6	61

APPENDIX B
Useful information

Corbett and Munro information
The website www.munromagic.com is a major resource for information on the Munros, Corbetts and Grahams. It gives the pronunciation of the names of the Corbetts and also the English translation used in this guide.

At www.hills-database.co.uk Chris Crocker and Graham Jackson have created a website for those interested in statistics and statistical topics pertaining to the British hills: measurement, classification, lists and data. They have attempted to make accurate measurements of heights of mountains whose status is in doubt and have been responsible for recent demotions of Munros to Corbett status.

The Scottish Mountaineering Club is the custodian of the official lists of Corbetts www.smc.org.uk.

Access to Scottish hills
Details of the Scottish Outdoor Access Code and information on stalking can be found at www.outdooraccess-scotland.com

Hill phones for information on stalking www.outdooraccess-scotland.com/hills

Mountain weather forecasts
Mountain Weather Information Service www.mwis.org.uk

Met Office www.metoffice.gov.uk/loutdoor/mountainsafety

SportScotland Avalanche Information Service www.sais.gov.uk

Books
The Corbetts and Other Scottish Hills: Scottish Mountaineering Club Hillwalkers' Guide published by the Scottish Mountaineering Trust: more for home use than use on the hill.

Munro's Tables published by the Scottish Mountaineering Club: the 'official' listing of the Munros and Corbetts.

Climbing the Corbetts by Hamish Brown: Hamish Brown's personal experiences of climbing the Corbetts.

Climb every Mountain by Craig Caldwell: Craig's account of his epic expedition in climbing all the Munros and Corbetts in one self-propelled journey.

Map publishers
Ordnance Survey
OS produce fine maps at 1:50,000 and 1:25,000 covering the whole of Scotland in paper format and digital format for GPS devices and PCs www.ordnancesurvey.co.uk

Harvey
As well as 1:40,000 maps of the most popular areas in Scotland, Harvey have produced a Munro and Corbett Chart that shows and lists all Munros (mountains over 3000ft), Corbetts (over 2500ft), Grahams and Donalds (over 2000ft) www.harveymaps.co.uk

Other organisations
John Muir Trust is the leading wild land conservation charity in the UK, protecting 115,000 hectares of mountain, moorland, rugged coast and wooded glens across Scotland
www.jmt.org

Scottish Youth Hostel Association
Tel: 0845 293 7373
www.hostellingscotland.org.uk

Tourist information
www.visitscotland.com

The National Trust for Scotland
www.nts.org.uk

Scottish Independent Hostels
www.hostel-scotland.co.uk

The Mountain Bothies Association maintains about 100 bothies in the Highlands
www.mountainbothies.org.uk

Glenmore Lodge National Outdoor Training Centre Tel: 01479 861 256
www.glenmorelodge.org.uk

Public transport
Scotrail is the train operator in Scotland www.scotrail.co.uk

Most of the ferry services in Scotland are operated by Caledonian MacBrayne www.calmac.co.uk

Traveline Scotland has links to the bus operators in Scotland
www.travelinescotland.com

NOTES

NOTES

NOTES

NOTES

NOTES

IF YOU ENJOYED THIS GUIDEBOOK YOU MIGHT ALSO BE INTERESTED IN...

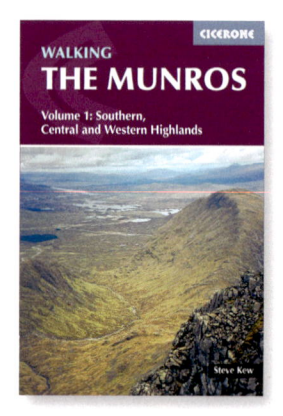

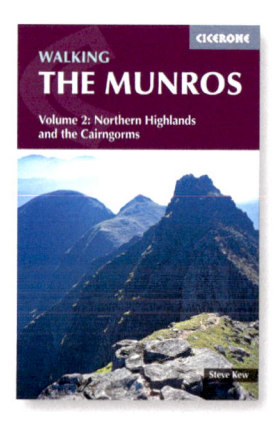

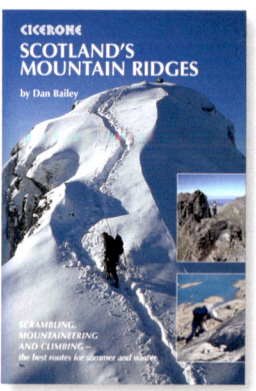

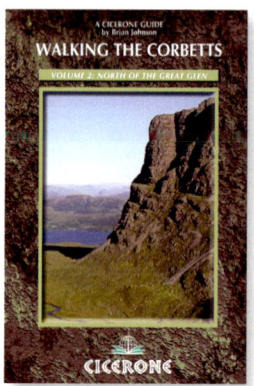

visit www.cicerone.co.uk for more detail
and our full range of guidebooks

WALKING THE CORBETTS
Volume 2: North of the Great Glen

There is a huge contrast between the generally gentle hills to the south of the Great Glen and the rugged mountains to the north of the Great Glen. To the south Munros dominate the landscape, but in the north it's mainly the Corbetts that are the major mountains.

The greatest concentration of Corbetts north of the Great Glen is along the western seaboard, where isolated rocky peaks rise steeply above the sea and inland lochs, in a wild landscape of heather and bog, dotted with sparkling lochs and lochans. There are few Munros, but there are spectacular Corbetts all the way from Ardgour to Cape Wrath. Climbing the Corbetts will also take you to the magical islands of Mull, Rum, Skye and Harris.

Walking in the US, the author has often been asked to recommend which mountain area to visit in Europe. The reply is always the same: 'The far north and west of Scotland.'

Climb the mountains south of the Great Glen first, because once you have discovered the north and the west you won't want to go anywhere else.

LISTING OF CICERONE GUIDES

SCOTLAND
Backpacker's Britain: Northern Scotland
Ben Nevis and Glen Coe
Cycling in the Hebrides
Great Mountain Days in Scotland
Mountain Biking in Southern and Central Scotland
Mountain Biking in West and North West Scotland
Not the West Highland Way Scotland
Scotland's Best Small Mountains
Scotland's Mountain Ridges
Scrambles in Lochaber
The Ayrshire and Arran Coastal Paths
The Border Country
The Borders Abbeys Way
The Cape Wrath Trail
The Great Glen Way
The Great Glen Way Map Booklet
The Hebridean Way
The Hebrides
The Isle of Mull
The Isle of Skye
The Skye Trail
The Southern Upland Way
The Speyside Way
The Speyside Way Map Booklet
The West Highland Way
Walking Highland Perthshire
Walking in Scotland's Far North
Walking in the Angus Glens
Walking in the Cairngorms
Walking in the Ochils, Campsie Fells and Lomond Hills
Walking in the Pentland Hills
Walking in the Southern Uplands
Walking in Torridon
Walking Loch Lomond and the Trossachs
Walking on Arran
Walking on Harris and Lewis
Walking on Rum and the Small Isles
Walking on the Orkney and Shetland Isles
Walking on Uist and Barra
Walking the Corbetts Vol 1 South of the Great Glen
Walking the Corbetts Vol 2 North of the Great Glen
Walking the Munros Vol 1 – Southern, Central and Western Highlands
Walking the Munros Vol 2 – Northern Highlands and the Cairngorms
West Highland Way Map Booklet
Winter Climbs Ben Nevis and Glen Coe
Winter Climbs in the Cairngorms

NORTHERN ENGLAND TRAILS
Hadrian's Wall Path
Hadrian's Wall Path Map Booklet
Pennine Way Map Booklet
The Coast to Coast Map Booklet
The Coast to Coast Walk
The Dales Way
The Dales Way Map Booklet
The Pennine Way

LAKE DISTRICT
Cycling in the Lake District
Great Mountain Days in the Lake District
Lake District Winter Climbs
Lake District: High Level and Fell Walks
Lake District: Low Level and Lake Walks
Mountain Biking in the Lake District
Outdoor Adventures with Children – Lake District
Scrambles in the Lake District – North
Scrambles in the Lake District – South
Short Walks in Lakeland Book 1: South Lakeland
Short Walks in Lakeland Book 2: North Lakeland
Short Walks in Lakeland Book 3: West Lakeland
The Cumbria Way
Tour of the Lake District
Trail and Fell Running in the Lake District

NORTH WEST ENGLAND AND THE ISLE OF MAN
Cycling the Pennine Bridleway
Cycling the Way of the Roses
Isle of Man Coastal Path
The Lancashire Cycleway
The Lune Valley and Howgills
The Ribble Way
Walking in Cumbria's Eden Valley
Walking in Lancashire
Walking in the Forest of Bowland and Pendle
Walking on the Isle of Man
Walking on the West Pennine Moors
Walks in Ribble Country
Walks in Silverdale and Arnside

NORTH EAST ENGLAND, YORKSHIRE DALES AND PENNINES
Cycling in the Yorkshire Dales
Great Mountain Days in the Pennines
Mountain Biking in the Yorkshire Dales
South Pennine Walks
St Oswald's Way and St Cuthbert's Way
The Cleveland Way and the Yorkshire Wolds Way
The Cleveland Way Map Booklet
The North York Moors
The Reivers Way
The Teesdale Way
Trail and Fell Running in the Yorkshire Dales
Walking in County Durham
Walking in Northumberland
Walking in the North Pennines
Walking in the Yorkshire Dales: North and East
Walking in the Yorkshire Dales: South and West
Walks in Dales Country
Walks in the Yorkshire Dales

WALES AND WELSH BORDERS
Cycling Lôn Las Cymru
Glyndwr's Way
Great Mountain Days in Snowdonia
Hillwalking in Shropshire
Hillwalking in Wales – Vol 1
Hillwalking in Wales – Vol 2
Mountain Walking in Snowdonia
Offa's Dyke Map Booklet
Offa's Dyke Path
Ridges of Snowdonia
Scrambles in Snowdonia
The Ascent of Snowdon
The Ceredigion and Snowdonia Coast Paths
The Pembrokeshire Coast Path
Pembrokeshire Coast Path Map Booklet
The Severn Way
The Snowdonia Way
The Wales Coast Path
The Wye Valley Walk
Walking in Carmarthenshire
Walking in Pembrokeshire
Walking in the Forest of Dean
Walking in the South Wales Valleys
Walking in the Wye Valley
Walking on the Brecon Beacons
Walking on the Gower

DERBYSHIRE, PEAK DISTRICT AND MIDLANDS

Cycling in the Peak District
Dark Peak Walks
Scrambles in the Dark Peak
Walking in Derbyshire
White Peak Walks: The Northern Dales
White Peak Walks: The Southern Dales

SOUTHERN ENGLAND

20 Classic Sportive Rides in South East England
20 Classic Sportive Rides in South West England
Cycling in the Cotswolds
Mountain Biking on the North Downs
Mountain Biking on the South Downs
North Downs Way Map Booklet
South West Coast Path Map Booklet – Vol 1: Minehead to St Ives
South West Coast Path Map Booklet – Vol 2: St Ives to Plymouth
South West Coast Path Map Booklet – Vol 3: Plymouth to Poole
Suffolk Coast and Heath Walks
The Cotswold Way
The Cotswold Way Map Booklet
The Great Stones Way
The Kennet and Avon Canal
The Lea Valley Walk
The North Downs Way
The Peddars Way and Norfolk Coast path
The Pilgrims' Way
The Ridgeway Map Booklet
The Ridgeway National Trail
The South Downs Way
The South Downs Way Map Booklet
The South West Coast Path
The Thames Path
The Thames Path Map Booklet
The Two Moors Way
Two Moors Way Map Booklet
Walking Hampshire's Test Way
Walking in Cornwall
Walking in Essex
Walking in Kent
Walking in London
Walking in Norfolk
Walking in Sussex
Walking in the Chilterns
Walking in the Cotswolds
Walking in the Isles of Scilly
Walking in the New Forest
Walking in the North Wessex Downs
Walking in the Thames Valley
Walking on Dartmoor
Walking on Guernsey
Walking on Jersey
Walking on the Isle of Wight
Walking the Jurassic Coast
Walks in the South Downs National Park

BRITISH ISLES CHALLENGES, COLLECTIONS AND ACTIVITIES

The Book of the Bivvy
The Book of the Bothy
The C2C Cycle Route
The End to End Cycle Route
The Mountains of England and Wales: Vol 1 Wales
The Mountains of England and Wales: Vol 2 England
The National Trails
The UK's County Tops
Three Peaks, Ten Tors

ALPS CROSS-BORDER ROUTES

100 Hut Walks in the Alps
Across the Eastern Alps: E5
Alpine Ski Mountaineering Vol 1 – Western Alps
Alpine Ski Mountaineering Vol 2 – Central and Eastern Alps
Chamonix to Zermatt
The Karnischer Hohenweg
The Tour of the Bernina
Tour of Mont Blanc
Tour of Monte Rosa
Tour of the Matterhorn
Trail Running – Chamonix and the Mont Blanc region
Trekking in the Alps
Trekking in the Silvretta and Rätikon Alps
Trekking Munich to Venice
Walking in the Alps

PYRENEES AND FRANCE/SPAIN CROSS-BORDER ROUTES

The GR10 Trail
The GR11 Trail
The Pyrenean Haute Route
The Pyrenees
The Way of St James – Spain
Walks and Climbs in the Pyrenees

AUSTRIA

Innsbruck Mountain Adventures
The Adlerweg
Trekking in Austria's Hohe Tauern
Trekking in the Stubai Alps
Trekking in the Zillertal Alps
Walking in Austria

SWITZERLAND

Cycle Touring in Switzerland
Switzerland's Jura Crest Trail
The Swiss Alpine Pass Route – Via Alpina Route 1
The Swiss Alps
Tour of the Jungfrau Region
Walking in the Bernese Oberland
Walking in the Valais

FRANCE AND BELGIUM

Chamonix Mountain Adventures
Cycle Touring in France
Cycling London to Paris
Cycling the Canal de la Garonne
Cycling the Canal du Midi
Écrins National Park
Mont Blanc Walks
Mountain Adventures in the Maurienne
The GR20 Corsica
The GR5 Trail
The GR5 Trail – Vosges and Jura
The Grand Traverse of the Massif Central
The Loire Cycle Route
The Moselle Cycle Route
The River Rhone Cycle Route
The Robert Louis Stevenson Trail
The Way of St James – Le Puy to the Pyrenees
Tour of the Oisans: The GR54
Tour of the Queyras
Vanoise Ski Touring
Via Ferratas of the French Alps
Walking in Corsica
Walking in Provence – East
Walking in Provence – West
Walking in the Auvergne
Walking in the Briançonnais
Walking in the Cevennes
Walking in the Dordogne
Walking in the Haute Savoie: North
Walking in the Haute Savoie: South
Walks in the Cathar Region
The GR5 Trail – Benelux and Lorraine
Walking in the Ardennes

GERMANY

Hiking and Cycling in the Black Forest
The Danube Cycleway Vol 1
The Rhine Cycle Route
The Westweg
Walking in the Bavarian Alps

ICELAND AND GREENLAND

Trekking in Greenland – The Arctic Circle Trail
Walking and Trekking in Iceland

IRELAND
The Irish Coast to Coast Walk
The Mountains of Ireland
The Wild Atlantic Way and Western Ireland

ITALY
Italy's Sibillini National Park
Shorter Walks in the Dolomites
Ski Touring and Snowshoeing in the Dolomites
The Way of St Francis
Through the Italian Alps
Trekking in the Apennines
Trekking in the Dolomites
Via Ferratas of the Italian Dolomites: Vol 1
Via Ferratas of the Italian Dolomites: Vol 2
Walking and Trekking in the Gran Paradiso
Walking in Abruzzo
Walking in Italy's Stelvio National Park
Walking in Sardinia
Walking in Sicily
Walking in the Dolomites
Walking in Tuscany
Walking in Umbria
Walking Lake Garda and Iseo
Walking on the Amalfi Coast
Walking the Italian Lakes
Walks and Treks in the Maritime Alps

SCANDINAVIA
Walking in Norway

EASTERN EUROPE AND THE BALKANS
The Danube Cycleway Vol 2
The High Tatras
The Mountains of Romania
Walking in Bulgaria's National Parks
Walking in Hungary
Mountain Biking in Slovenia
The Islands of Croatia
The Julian Alps of Slovenia
The Mountains of Montenegro
The Peaks of the Balkans Trail
The Slovenian Mountain Trail
Walking in Croatia
Walking in Slovenia: The Karavanke

SPAIN AND PORTUGAL
Coastal Walks in Andalucia
Cycle Touring in Spain
Cycling the Camino de Santiago
Mountain Walking in Mallorca
Mountain Walking in Southern Catalunya
Spain's Sendero Histórico: The GR1
The Andalucian Coast to Coast Walk
The Mountains of Nerja
The Mountains of Ronda and Grazalema
The Northern Caminos
The Sierras of Extremadura
Trekking in Mallorca
Walking and Trekking in the Sierra Nevada
Walking in Andalucia
Walking in Menorca
Walking in the Cordillera Cantabrica
Walking on Gran Canaria
Walking on La Gomera and El Hierro
Walking on La Palma
Walking on Lanzarote and Fuerteventura
Walking on Tenerife
Walking on the Costa Blanca
The Camino Portugués
Walking in Portugal
Walking in the Algarve
Walking on Madeira

GREECE, CYPRUS AND MALTA
The High Mountains of Crete
Trekking in Greece
Walking and Trekking in Zagori
Walking and Trekking on Corfu
Walking in Cyprus
Walking on Malta

INTERNATIONAL CHALLENGES, COLLECTIONS AND ACTIVITIES
Canyoning in the Alps
Europe's High Points
The Via Francigena Canterbury to Rome – Part 2

AFRICA
Mountaineering in the Moroccan High Atlas
The High Atlas
Trekking in the Atlas Mountains
Walks and Scrambles in the Moroccan Anti-Atlas
Kilimanjaro
Walking in the Drakensberg

ASIA
Trekking in Tajikistan
Japan's Kumano Kodo Pilgrimage
Walking and Trekking in the Japan Alps and Mount Fuji
Jordan – Walks, Treks, Caves, Climbs and Canyons
Treks and Climbs in Wadi Rum, Jordan
Annapurna
Everest: A Trekker's Guide
Trekking in the Himalaya
Trekking in Bhutan
Trekking in Ladakh
The Mount Kailash Trek

NORTH AMERICA
British Columbia
The John Muir Trail
The Pacific Crest Trail

SOUTH AMERICA
Aconcagua and the Southern Andes
Hiking and Biking Peru's Inca Trails
Torres del Paine

TECHNIQUES
Fastpacking
Geocaching in the UK
Indoor Climbing
Lightweight Camping
Map and Compass
Outdoor Photography
Polar Exploration
Rock Climbing
Sport Climbing
The Mountain Hut Book

MINI GUIDES
Alpine Flowers
Avalanche!
Navigation
Pocket First Aid and Wilderness Medicine
Snow

MOUNTAIN LITERATURE
8000 metres
A Walk in the Clouds
Abode of the Gods
Fifty Years of Adventure
The Pennine Way – the Path, the People, the Journey
Unjustifiable Risk?

For full information and to order books and eBooks, visit: **www.cicerone.co.uk**.

Walking – Trekking – Mountaineering – Climbing – Cycling

Over 50 years, Cicerone have built up an outstanding collection of over 300 guides, inspiring all sorts of amazing adventures.

Every guide comes from extensive exploration and research by our expert authors, all with a passion for their subjects. They are frequently praised, endorsed and used by clubs, instructors and outdoor organisations.

All our titles can now be bought as **e-books**, **ePubs** and **Kindle** files and we also have an online magazine – **Cicerone Extra** – with features to help cyclists, climbers, walkers and trekkers choose their next adventure, at home or abroad.

Our website shows any **new information** we've had in since a book was published. Please do let us know if you find anything has changed, so that we can publish the latest details. On our **website** you'll also find great ideas and lots of detailed information about what's inside every guide and you can buy **individual routes** from many of them online.

It's easy to keep in touch with what's going on at Cicerone by getting our monthly **free e-newsletter**, which is full of offers, competitions, up-to-date information and topical articles. You can subscribe on our home page and also follow us on **Facebook** and **Twitter** or dip into our **blog**.

Cicerone – the very best guides for exploring the world.

CICERONE

Juniper House, Murley Moss, Oxenholme Road, Kendal, Cumbria LA9 7RL
Tel: 015395 62069 info@cicerone.co.uk
www.cicerone.co.uk